A HEAD OF CABBAGE

A MEMOIR

BARBARA JOHNSON

BALBOA.PRESS
A DIVISION OF HAY HOUSE

Copyright © 2022 Barbara Johnson.

All rights reserved. No part of this book may be used or reproduced by any means, graphic, electronic, or mechanical, including photocopying, recording, taping or by any information storage retrieval system without the written permission of the author except in the case of brief quotations embodied in critical articles and reviews.

Balboa Press books may be ordered through booksellers or by contacting:

Balboa Press
A Division of Hay House
1663 Liberty Drive
Bloomington, IN 47403
www.balboapress.com
844-682-1282

Because of the dynamic nature of the Internet, any web addresses or links contained in this book may have changed since publication and may no longer be valid. The views expressed in this work are solely those of the author and do not necessarily reflect the views of the publisher, and the publisher hereby disclaims any responsibility for them.

This book is a work of creative nonfiction. The experiences and details written here are as the author has remembered them. Some names have been changed t o protect the privacy of many individuals.

Any people depicted in stock imagery provided by Getty Images are models, and such images are being used for illustrative purposes only.
Certain stock imagery © Getty Images.

Print information available on the last page.

Library of Congress Control Number: 2022911482
ISBN: 979-8-7652-3028-2 (sc)
ISBN: 979-8-7652-3030-5 (hc)
ISBN: 979-8-7652-3029-9 (e)

Balboa Press rev. date: 07/18/2022

CONTENTS

Chapter 1	The Psychiatrist	1
Chapter 2	Molestation	5
Chapter 3	Two Pieces of Candy	11
Chapter 4	The Blackberry Pie	15
Chapter 5	Pig and the Rooster	19
Chapter 6	Better Off Dead	23
Chapter 7	Education Ain't Shit for Black People	29
Chapter 8	Put Your Book Down	33
Chapter 9	The Ugly One of the Bunch	37
Chapter 10	Thumbtacks	41
Chapter 11	The Talk	45
Chapter 12	Fifth Grade	51
Chapter 13	Golden Sparks	55
Chapter 14	Shoes	59
Chapter 15	Father and Son	65
Chapter 16	Blanche	73
Chapter 17	We Got to Run	77
Chapter 18	Pick the Poor Robin Clean	81
Chapter 19	Live Off the Land	85
Chapter 20	God Ain't Helping	89
Chapter 21	It's Our Responsibility	95
Chapter 22	I Need Another Miracle	101
Chapter 23	The Shotgun	107
Chapter 24	This Is America	115
Chapter 25	Don't Let Nothing Stop You	119
Chapter 26	This Country Could Be Great	125
Chapter 27	You Can't Go	129
Chapter 28	You Are Not Brilliant	133
Chapter 29	No One Clapped for Me	137
Chapter 30	In Luck	141
Chapter 31	Four Dollars	143
Chapter 32	Washington, DC	149

Chapter 33	Pregnant and Aunt V	155
Chapter 34	Unhappily Married	159
Chapter 35	Southern Bell	163
Chapter 36	Troubled Water	167
Chapter 37	Your Husband Loves a Man	173
Chapter 38	My Daddy's Shoes	181
Chapter 39	A Head of Cabbage	187
Chapter 40	The Stalker	195
Chapter 41	A Time to Kill	199
Chapter 42	Mr. Sanchez	205
Chapter 43	I'm Not Afraid	209
Chapter 44	Poochie	211
Chapter 45	You Got a Car	215
Chapter 46	The Chain Gang	217
Chapter 47	Heaven or Hell	221
Chapter 48	I Wanted to Help	225
Chapter 49	Raleigh, North Carolina	229
Chapter 50	Slow Walk to Hell	233
Chapter 51	I'm Not OK	239
Chapter 52	Vengeance Is the Lord's	245
Chapter 53	No Blood	251
Chapter 54	Leviticus 7:26	257
Chapter 55	Thank You	259
Chapter 56	Shall We Dance?	263
Chapter 57	Twelve Past Midnight	267
Chapter 58	Meimei	269
Chapter 59	We Are Family	275
Chapter 60	Eeny, Meeny, Miny, Moe	281
Chapter 61	Bad News	285
Chapter 62	Confederate Flag	291
Chapter 63	Gratitude	297
Chapter 64	Make the Call	301
Chapter 65	Black People Need a Psychiatrist	305
Chapter 66	Been in Hell	315
Chapter 67	Ask a Black Man	317
Chapter 68	Made of Gold	321

Chapter 69	Hello, Marilyn	327
Chapter 70	Sit Down for the News	331
Chapter 71	It Feels like Love	335
Chapter 72	Plan a Wedding	339
Chapter 73	Cancer	343
Chapter 74	Man of God	347
Chapter 75	You're Going to Be Homeless	351
Chapter 76	Forgiveness	357

Acknowledgments 361

CHAPTER 1

THE PSYCHIATRIST

He does not even blink his silvery-gray eyes. "Mrs. Jamison, are you sure of what you are saying?" Dr. Alex asks as I sit in his brightly lit office off South Boulevard in Charlotte, North Carolina.

I reposition my body in the wolf-gray leather armchair and pull my navy-blue A-line skirt down below my knees. I look down at the glossy wooden floor full of scratches and dents.

"Yes, I'm quite sure. I'm going to kill the son of a bitch before this weekend," I blurt out.

"Who are you going to kill?" Dr. Alex stares me in the face.

I stop breathing for a moment and turn my head away. My throat is tight, and I rub it lightly while looking around the room. The interior has a beautiful dark wood ceiling and knotted paneling throughout. Several paintings and bronze wall sconces grace the walls, as do several certificates of his professional training. A three-drawer wooden filing cabinet stands flush against the north wall, and beside it are a big coffeepot and brown ceramic cups sitting on a drop-leaf walnut table. The aroma of coffee permeates the air. I'm not fond of coffee. I cough a few times before answering.

"I thought I told you. I'm going to kill my ex-boyfriend Steven Harris."

"Where?" Dr. Alex asks calmly.

"At Riverside Bowling Alley in Danville, Virginia. He bowls there every Thursday night."

Dr. Alex unbuttons his gray cardigan. His loose-fitting jeans and black tennis shoes give him the appearance of a young schoolteacher. He flips his leather pad open as he walks around the glossy mahogany desk. He swivels his gray leather chair and sits down. His long, slender fingers grab a pen from an old wooden cup sitting next to a picture of a German shepherd. He jots down a word or two; folds his fingers; and, as though we're talking about the weather, asks me, "How are you going to kill him?"

I lower my head and close my eyes for a few seconds. I try not to cry, but a few tears slide down my cheeks. It's hard for me to believe that things have come to this in a few short weeks. Now I'm in a psychiatrist's office.

I take a deep breath, wipe my face with the back of my hand, and lift my head. "I'm going to shoot him fourteen times."

"Why fourteen?" Dr. Alex asks.

My voice is just a whisper now. "That's all the bullets my pistol holds."

Dr. Alex slides a box of Kleenex toward me. I take several and dab my cheeks and eyes.

"I have to report this information to the police if you're serious," he says. "They must warn your ex-boyfriend of the danger he's in."

"Go ahead and report it. Steven should know what is headed his way," I say to Dr. Alex as cold chills spread over my body. I tilt my head away from Dr. Alex and hold my right leg to keep it from shaking.

"Why do you want to harm your ex-boyfriend?" Dr. Alex asks.

I stretch out my left arm and poke the middle with my forefinger. "Tell the authorities to put the lethal injection right here. I know that Virginia is a death-penalty state."

Dr. Alex blinks rapidly and turns the page on his pad. "Before you tell me why you want to harm your ex-boyfriend, I would like to know about your childhood. Start from your earliest memory."

I want this psychiatrist to talk me out of committing a heinous crime, and he is asking me about my childhood? I wonder if Dr. Alex is worth his fee. I roll my eyes and inhale deeply.

"My earliest memory is seeing a billy goat eat clothes off our clothesline. Mama sent me outside to get firewood for the kitchen stove. The goat frightened me, and I screamed for Daddy. I was scared that the billy goat would eat me."

"How old were you?" Dr. Alex asks in a soft tone.

"I think I was five, but my brother says we had eaten the goat before I turned five, so I must have been four."

"What did your father do?"

"Daddy laughed as I screamed, 'Help me! Daddy, help me! Don't let the billy goat get me!' My father stood there watching and laughing as I ran back inside the house." I do not tell Dr. Alex that I peed myself.

"How does this memory make you feel?" Dr. Alex asks.

A Head of Cabbage

"I feel angry and alone, afraid that something bad might happen to me and that nobody will help me or even care. Now you just made me depressed." I stand up and grab my purse from the floor.

"I would like for you to stay a bit longer." Dr. Alex glances down at his watch. "You've only been with me for seventeen minutes." He looks up at me. His piercing gray eyes hold a steady gaze. "Let's try to complete the full session. Would you like a glass of water?"

I sit back down. "OK, I'll try," I say as I watch Dr. Alex's tall frame stand and go into the kitchen. I force myself to stay calm. So far, I feel worse. I don't want to talk about my childhood. I want to talk about the present and how to feel better.

Dr. Alex returns with a glass of cold water. He sets it on the edge of the table within my reach. "Tell me more about your childhood," he says again.

I notice that Dr. Alex's pad is open, and he has a pen in his right hand. We sit quietly across from each other for a moment. Then, finally, I start to speak again, but movement catches my eye. I look through an unshaded window to my right, and a fat red cardinal is sitting on a branch of a blooming Bradford pear. I'm a little superstitious and think the bird is trying to tell me to trust Dr. Alex, although I feel stupid and ashamed in telling him about my personal life. I take the glass of water and drink it all.

"I remember working in tobacco fields from sunrise to sundown. Before I started school, I remember being cold and hungry, hot and hungry—always hungry. I remember the boyfriend of my oldest sister, Blanche, molesting me on the first day of school when I was six years old. I told Blanche what happened, and she stripped me naked and paddled my butt in front of her boyfriend. She said I was too fast. I also remember one of the landowners and his adult son. They molested me for several years. I was afraid they would make us move from their beautiful house and land if I told, and I was scared Daddy would blame me. When Daddy got mad, he would tell me I wasn't worth the salt I ate."

My palms begin to sweat, and my skin crawls with disgust as I remember the landowner's and his son's big red hands pawing over my body. I squeeze my legs tighter and become more uncomfortable, thinking about my childhood experiences. I want to scream, kick, and cuss, but most of all, I want to kill the sons of bitches for treating me like I was nothing but a filthy little bad girl unworthy of decent regard.

Dr. Alex's eyes flutter. "How do these memories make you feel now?"

I don't tell him how I feel. Instead, I say, "Like I could go insane. My parents should have done better by me."

Dr. Alex jots down more words and then runs his fingers through his sandy-colored hair. "Mrs. Jamison, I'm glad you shared your childhood memories with me."

I take in a deep breath. "Should I continue? I have not gotten to the worst part."

The look on Dr. Alex's face is one of disbelief. "Ah, no," he says as his face turns red, and he stands up. He glances at me and sighs while walking toward the door. "We will pick up where you left off next Wednesday. Then you can tell me why you wish to harm your ex-boyfriend."

I grab my purse and follow close behind him. I keep my head low, looking at the polished wooden floor, until I reach the open door. "I don't wish to harm him. I want to kill him," I say as I close the door behind me.

The grandfather clock chimes.

CHAPTER 2

MOLESTATION

I pull into Dr. Alex's driveway and park my blue 1992 Mazda 323 under a big Bradford pear tree seven days later.

At exactly 2:58, Dr. Alex opens the door to his foyer, and I slowly walk inside the modest brick house. I didn't want to come today. I came only because my best girlfriend, Jannie, threatened to tell my family of my plan to kill Steven if I didn't keep my appointment. I regret telling Jannie. I thought she would be my alibi and keep my secret, but instead, she gave me an ultimatum.

"How are you doing today, Mrs. Jamison?" Dr. Alex says, and then he steps aside as I walk by him and sit in the same soft leather chair as last week.

"I'm fine. Thank you."

He leans over his desk. "What's been on your mind this past week?"

"Nothing much," I say.

"Today I would like to get a bit more background information about your immediate family. Is that OK with you?"

"It's OK, but how is that helping me?" I ask.

"Sometimes there are unresolved situations in our lives that prevent us from becoming our best selves. Let's start with your siblings. How many brothers and sisters do you have?"

"I have eight. My oldest sister is deceased."

Dr. Alex raises his eyebrows and writes a few words on his notepad. However, he does not mention my deceased sister.

"We are five boys and four girls living." I pause.

"Continue describing your childhood to me, please," Dr. Alex says as he glances between me and his notepad.

"It was miserable. I worked in the tobacco fields before starting school. I could not go to school much, and I got my butt whipped just about every day for something. By age twelve, five different men had molested me."

Dr. Alex inhales and exhales deeply. His face shows a bit of surprise. "How does talking about this make you feel?" he asks.

I think about his question for a while. Dr. Alex remains silent as I try to find the right words to describe my feelings to a man, although a psychiatrist.

Finally, I blurt out, "It still makes me angry and ashamed. Even though I was too scared to tell my parents, I feel like they should have kept me out of harm's way. I dislike myself for not being smart enough to prevent it. I feel that something is wrong with me for that to have happened. What child is molested by that many men?" I look away as rage wells up inside. "You want to know how it makes me feel. Well, it makes me want to kill every man who hurt or molested me."

Dr. Alex sits motionless behind his desk. His face flushes red, and he keeps his slow-blinking eyes fixed on me. I realize my voice is loud and angry in the room's quietness. I slide my chair farther away from him to give myself more space.

"Dr. Alex, I'm not mad at you. I'm just tired of being mistreated. I feel as though I have been no more than garbage as far back as I can remember."

"Your feelings are real, and I want you to express them, whatever they are," Dr. Alex says, and he pushes a box of Kleenex toward me. "It is helpful to express feelings. I'm pleased that you are willing to talk about yours."

I dab perspiration from my face. I'm embarrassed, but I continue. "I was picked on a lot at school. It is called being bullied now. Unfortunately, America's corporate culture creates bullies too. Apparently, I'm supposed to be perfect, while coworkers' mistakes are overlooked. So I must keep proving myself over and over. This world is hard to live in. I don't think I can take much more."

Dr. Alex does not nod or give me any clue that he empathizes with me. Instead, he calmly says, "Tell me what you remember about your first molestation."

I wonder if I'm wasting my time by talking with this shrink. I think I should just carry out my plan and let the chips fall where they may. I stare at Dr. Alex for an extra moment and then say, "My first molestation has nothing to do with my ex-boyfriend."

"It possibly has everything to do with why you want to kill." His voice is soft but sounds confident. "Mrs. Jamison, sit back, relax, and share this memory with me."

I sit back, but I don't relax. Part of my brain tells me to drive to Virginia and blow Steven away, and another part tells me to do as this psychiatrist asks. The latter thought wins.

"I was six years old, and it was my first day of school. My five older brothers and sisters and some neighbor children walked along a wooded path to a two-room white school building. It was about two miles from our house."

Dr. Alex writes a few words down. I strain my eyes to see what they are, but they look like gibberish.

"When the school day was over, we all started walking home on the wooded path. There were a lot of us. I don't remember how many. Anyway, I fell behind and found myself separated from my brothers and sisters. They walked fast because they had to help Daddy with tobacco before night fell."

"Were you expected to help with the tobacco?"

"Yes, but they didn't wait for me. I don't know why."

I feel the familiar rage seeping up inside me. I think of myself as a little girl again, and I want to become someone else. I stop talking and look down at my lap. I'm uncomfortable with myself. I squeeze my legs together as tightly as possible.

"Go on. You're strong enough to talk about it," Dr. Alex says.

I start again. "I was scared that I would get a whipping and began to cry. Slim, my sister's boyfriend, was walking on the path too. He came to my rescue and told me he would take me home since he lived just a piece down the road. Slim took my hand, and we began to walk but in a different direction."

Dr. Alex raises his right hand and asks, "Where was your sister?"

I stop and think about Blanche, my oldest sister, for a moment. "I don't remember why, but she was not there."

"Continue, please."

"I asked Slim if we were lost, and he grinned and said no, we needed to walk a different way home because I was too little to keep up with the big children."

I cover my face with my hands. It is hard for me to discuss what happened next.

Dr. Alex slides his chair away from his desk and stands. "May I get you something to drink? A Coke or a cold glass of water?" He does not wait for me to answer. Instead, he leaves the room and returns a short while later with two cans of Coca-Cola. He sets one on a pewter coaster and slides it toward me. He pops his can and takes a sip. "Please continue."

"We walked into a small clearing. Slim piled up a bunch of fallen leaves, and then he unfastened his pants. They fell around his ankles. He stepped out of them and hung them on a tree. I knew something wasn't right, but I didn't know what. I felt scared and started to walk back the way we had come."

I don't want to tell Dr. Alex all that I remember, and I'm too ashamed to admit that I am still bothered by what happened to me as a young child. I roll my eyes toward the tall grandfather clock sitting in the corner of the room. It's 3:47. I just want to go home.

Dr. Alex takes another sip of soda and picks up his pen. "You are doing great, Mrs. Jamison. Can you go on?"

I sigh, but it sounds more like a painful groan. "Slim grabbed my arm and told me not to be afraid of him. He said he would take me home soon. Then he took off his shirt and threw it over the pile of leaves. Finally, he picked me up and laid me down on top of the pile. I told him I wanted to go home. He said I needed to rest a little longer." I pop my Coke and take a sip. "I must sound like an idiot to you," I say.

"No, not at all. You really are doing great. Please continue."

I want Dr. Alex to say something that will make me feel better, but he just takes notes.

"Slim looked like a giant. He stood over me naked. I told him I wasn't tired and wanted to go home. Slim told me to just lie there and be quiet and promised that nothing terrible was going to happen to me. He knelt over me and said he would put his 'thang' between my legs. Interpretation: Slim was going to put his penis between my legs."

"I understand the language," Dr. Alex says, and he nods for me to continue.

"The next thing I knew, my skirt was raised above my waist, and Slim was removing my homemade bloomers with one hand. His other hand was pressed against my shoulder and holding me down on the ground. Then he spread my legs apart with one of his knees and told me that my butter bean might be too small for his thang."

Dr. Alex is silent but steadily writing on his notepad. I'm glad he mostly listens.

"Slim told me to stop wiggling. Then, after a while, he got off me and told me I couldn't tell anyone, because I had been a bad girl, and Mama would beat me if she found out."

I stare at the wall for a moment. I don't want to show my face to Dr. Alex, but I manage to grab a glance at him and try to read his face.

Dr. Alex cups his chin with his hands. "It's no longer happening, Mrs. Jamison. It's the past."

I sniffle a bit before starting again. "Slim had the nerve to laugh. He told me not to worry and said it would be our secret forever."

A sound I don't recognize comes from my throat. It is of pain, disgust, and hatred for Slim and myself.

Dr. Alex shifts in his seat. "Mrs. Jamison, I know this is hard for you. But you will be fine."

I'm embarrassed, mainly because Dr. Alex is white, and I don't want him to think all black men behave like Slim. I want him to understand that. So when he lifts his head, I look directly at him and say, "Most black men don't act like Slim."

Dr. Alex leans forward. "I'm very much aware of that, and I want you to know that you are not responsible for Slim's criminal behavior." He gestures with his long, slender hand for me to continue.

"Slim got dressed and picked the leaves out of my hair. After looking me over, he stooped down to my eye level and said Mama would not whip me for being a bad little girl, because he would never tell a soul."

I pause and take several swallows of Coke. Dr. Alex waits patiently.

"When I got home and saw everyone at the old sloped-roof tobacco barn about thirty yards from our house, I relaxed. I didn't say anything. Instead, I stood in the shade and watched everyone work until Mama called me over to where she stood with an armful of tobacco leaves. I wanted to scream, 'I ain't a bad girl!' but my mouth was dry, and I couldn't say anything.

"Slim, who was helping Blanche with the stringing of tobacco leaves, turned and looked at me as his sickening grin faded from his face. Fear had crept into his molasses-brown eyes. He stopped helping Blanche and stared at Mama, fanning mosquitoes and gnats." I pause to dab my eyes.

Dr. Alex seems eager to hear what happened. "What did your mother say?" he asks.

"Mama told me I was big enough to help more on the farm and showed me how to help Blanche with the tobacco leaves."

Dr. Alex looks over at the grandfather clock and stands up. "I look forward to our next session."

CHAPTER 3

TWO PIECES OF CANDY

Once I arrive home, I take my pistol from my car and put it underneath my bed. The weekend comes and goes, and I have not made the trip to Virginia to kill Steven. I'm glad I haven't, but I feel like a coward.

When I return for my third visit at Dr. Alex's house, which serves as his office, the front door is open, so I walk in, even though I'm about seven minutes early. I don't see him, but I hear him. "She's remarkable," I hear Dr. Alex say to someone as I start to walk out the door.

"Mrs. Jamison, don't leave. I want my wife to meet you," Dr. Alex says as they enter the room.

"Nice to meet you," I say, extending my hand to a professionally dressed woman walking toward me.

His wife, a petite redhead, takes my hand and holds it for a while. "Nice to meet you too. You are a remarkable woman," she says before kissing her husband and leaving.

I'm at a loss for words and wonder if Dr. Alex has discussed me with his wife, at the country club, or maybe with men at a Friday night poker game. I don't ask, for fear he might get upset with me or have me arrested for threatening to kill Steven after he drops me as a patient. Instead, I take several deep breaths and count backward from seven to one.

"How has your week been?" Dr. Alex asks as he takes a seat behind his desk.

"It was boring. I thought a lot about my childhood," I say before scrambling in my purse to find the index cards I wrote bits of memories on.

"Well, let's get started."

"One Christmas, we all got two pieces of hard candy, an apple, and an orange in a brown paper bag. Everyone appeared gloomy and unhappy, but no one complained, except me. I asked Mama why I only got two pieces of candy, and she told me to be glad I got two pieces instead of one. Daddy heard me complaining and staggered over to where I stood. He stretched out his hand and told me to give the candy back to him since I didn't appreciate it. I threw the candy into my mouth and crunched it right in front of him. Then I moved farther away with my apple and orange."

Dr. Alex lets out a chuckle. He seems amused. I wait for him to give me the signal to continue. After a few seconds, he lifts his hand, mutes his chuckle, and nods for me to continue.

"Anyway, Daddy said that he'd just as soon see us dead as see us eat—that none of us were worth a box of salt. So Mama hurried and brought Daddy a big piece of chocolate cake. I think it was to calm him down or stop him from saying something worse. He pushed the fork aside, broke off chunks of cake with his fingers, and ate the whole piece within a few minutes. That was the first time I heard him say we were not worth very much. I stopped liking my daddy that Christmas Day when I was six years old."

"How does that memory make you feel now?" Dr. Alex asks.

"It makes me feel sad and angry that Daddy said that to us. I don't know any other way to describe the feeling."

Dr. Alex writes as I continue to talk.

"I saw Daddy cry a couple of weeks later. I didn't understand why at the time, but I do now. Early one morning, I returned from emptying the slop jar, and as I got closer to the house, I heard Daddy talking with a dressed-up white man."

Dr. Alex has a quizzical expression on his face. I take it as his not knowing what a slop jar is.

"Emptying the slop jar, because of number one and number two, was one of my chores." I pause.

"OK," Dr. Alex says, and he waves his hand for me to continue.

"The conversation between the man and Daddy made no sense to me, but Daddy sounded angry. I set the slop jar behind the brick chimney, squatted myself down out of sight, and listened. I heard Daddy ask the man to wait till he sold his tobacco crop in the fall. He appeared to be begging the man. Finally, the man told Daddy that they had found someone to take over the farm, and there was nothing anybody could do about it."

Dr. Alex's phone rings. He apologizes to me and ignores the ringing, but he glances at his watch. "What happened?" he asks.

"The man walked to his car, looking back several times at Daddy, before driving off. Later in the year, we moved to a farm that belonged to a man named Cletus Briggs. And Daddy began to sharecrop."

"Was that in a different state?"

"No, it was in the same state but in Person County, not far from our old farm in Leasburg, North Carolina. The new farmhouse had five large bedrooms, three upstairs and two downstairs. It had a screened-in back porch, and there were large trees in the center of the yard, which gave lots of shade. The interior and exterior of the house were white. It was the first house I had ever seen with a painted interior."

"Did you have any difficulties or particular trauma while living there?"

"It was not a happy time. The water well was close to the house, which was nice, though it was scary. When it rained, the water turned muddy and rose to the brim. We dipped the water out. When it didn't rain, we used a bucket that was on a wheel and pulley and let down into the well. It scared me to get water from that well."

"Why?"

"Have you ever seen a well filled with water to the very top?"

Dr. Alex shakes his head and writes on his notepad.

"I could touch the water with my hand. I was scared I might accidentally fall in and drown. And inside the house, the windows were narrow and long, near the ground. I was scared that someone would come in and get me. Anybody could have stepped right in, because the windows were always raised in the summer."

"Would you say you were scared most of the time while living at this location?"

I think about his question for a moment longer than usual while my brain scans all the scary scenes. "Yes, I was scared most of the time."

Dr. Alex jots down a few words.

"I want to talk about my mama," I say, "since she has been on my mind."

"Please do," Dr. Alex says.

"We lived probably like the pioneers did. The first summer we began to sharecrop, Mama told us that things would be tough. At night and on the weekends, she made us girls help her can and make an assortment of fruit and vegetable preserves. There is nothing better than damson preserves."

"I will take your word for it," Dr. Alex says, making a few notations.

"During the day, we worked in the tobacco fields. Mama was clever, but despite her best efforts, we were still hungry a lot of times. Sometimes we only had one meal per day—or none."

Dr. Alex continues to write and glances at me a few times.

"At suppertime, Mama always fixed Daddy's plate first. Either she or one of us girls would take Daddy's food to him in the family room or in his and Mama's bedroom. If he didn't like the meal, he would eat the food and then break the plate on the cast-iron wood stove. Sometimes he would throw the plate onto the floor to break it, depending on where he was at the time. Plate breaking became a ritual, until Mama started to give Daddy his food in a tin plate. The first time she gave him his food in the metal plate, I stopped breathing for at least a minute, waiting to see what he would do."

"What did your father do?" Dr. Alex asks, a bit amused.

"After eating, Daddy flung the tin plate across the room like a flying saucer."

Dr. Alex surprises me with a chuckle. "Perhaps the world's first Frisbee. Mrs. Jamison, you are making good progress. I look forward to next Wednesday."

CHAPTER 4

THE BLACKBERRY PIE

It's my fourth visit to see Dr. Alex. Finally, I feel more at ease in talking with him about my life, even though most of it is embarrassing. I have not told anyone in my family that I am seeing a psychiatrist. I don't try to call Steven anymore either. He stopped taking my calls after I screamed, cussed, and told him that I was coming to blow him away and that if his new girlfriend got hit with a stray bullet, I wouldn't be sorry.

I now spend more of my time thinking and writing about my childhood memories than I do about my failed romantic relationship.

"Are you ready to get started?" Dr. Alex asks as soon as I sit down in the same gray leather chair across from him in the cool, spacious room.

I nod, but I wonder if I might lose my mind. "I will talk about Mama going to work in New York. We had been sharecropping for over a year, and I was around seven years old."

Dr. Alex opens his notepad.

"One day Mama gathered us around her. She seemed excited to tell us that she was going to New York City for work to keep us from starving to death. Her sister, Aunt V, had gotten her a job working for a friendly Jewish family. Mama said that Jewish people treated colored folks better than regular white folks did—maybe because Jesus was a Jew."

I try to read the expression on Dr. Alex's face, hoping he is a Jew. But unfortunately, he gives me no indication that he is.

"Daddy was sitting at the kitchen table. He occasionally took a drink of moonshine and grunted his displeasure. Mama looked from Daddy to us. We children were kind of glad she was going to New York, because that meant we would no longer go hungry."

I take in a deep breath. Dr. Alex sits patiently with his hands folded on his desk.

"But months went by, and on most days, we were still hungry. One hot Saturday afternoon, Blanche—she is my oldest sister."

"I remember," Dr. Alex says.

"Blanche gave three of us a couple of water buckets and a hoe to go search for blackberries. The only thing we had in the house to eat was flour."

"A hoe?" Dr. Alex asks.

"Yes, in case we saw a snake or something. We found a patch of blackberries and returned with two full buckets. Blanche made a huge blackberry pie."

"How does one make a pie with just flour?"

"That's easy. You borrow a couple cups of sugar and a wad of butter from a neighbor."

"Oh." Dr. Alex looks surprised and writes more words down on his notepad. His eyes dart from left to right, and then he slowly blinks. "You all borrowed food?"

"Many times." I pause for a moment to let Dr. Alex ponder that revelation. "We all had our own personal spot at the table. On rare occasions, Daddy ate with us and sat at the head of the table. To his right, the boys sat, and to his left, the girls would sit or stand. We didn't have enough chairs for everyone to sit down, so it was first come, first served for whoever was lucky enough to get one of the four chairs."

Dr. Alex continues to jot down a few words.

"Finally, Daddy came home drunk, as usual. I stood at the kitchen window, watching him try to make it to the back door without falling. Eventually, he staggered into the kitchen. Daddy looked around the room at Blanche and me and then grabbed at a chair to steady himself. Blanche pushed the chair closer so he could reach it. He grabbed the back of the chair and dropped all his weight into the rubber-bottomed chair. It made the sound of a loud fart, and I laughed."

Dr. Alex holds up his hand, and I stop talking. "A rubber-bottomed chair?"

"Yeah, Daddy made our chairs. He used the rubber tubes from old car tires to make chair bottoms. He cut the rubber into strips and made a latticed design."

Dr. Alex smiles, but I see him shaking his head slightly just before he begins to scribble on his pad. "Amazing," he says.

"Blanche opened the door to the wood-burning stove and took out the

A Head of Cabbage

bubbling blackberry pie. The pie looked and smelled good. I could hardly wait. I had not eaten anything all day. Blanche started to fix plates of pie and set the first plate down in front of my spot at the table, to the left of Daddy. Since we never said grace, I immediately started to eat, but before the second spoonful of pie reached my mouth, Daddy slapped me hard across the face. The spoon flew across the room in an instant."

Dr. Alex sighs but does not say anything.

"Daddy said that slice of pie was his. So I slid the pie over to Daddy as tears ran down my face and pee ran down my legs."

I'm so saddened by this memory that I pause for a moment to collect myself. I want to cry for that little girl of yesteryear who felt alone, abused, and hungry. But instead, I place my hand over my mouth to ensure my silence. I tell myself that was a long time ago, and I am no longer a little girl but an adult with grown-up issues. I finally look up with open, silent lips, unable to speak.

Dr. Alex asks, his voice sounding raspy, "How old were you?"

"Seven," I say softly.

Dr. Alex rubs his forehead for a little while before turning the page on his notepad. He writes several lines before asking me to continue.

I clear my throat. "One time, Slim, Blanche's boyfriend, and Daddy got into it. Daddy came home almost drunk. Slim was with Blanche in one of the downstairs bedrooms with the door closed. Daddy busted into the room and told Slim to get his ass out of his house and not come back. Blanche walked over and stood next to Slim. I stood behind the kitchen stove, peeping into the room."

"Was your mother in the home at that time?" Dr. Alex asks.

"No," I answer, and I pause for a few seconds. I'm embarrassed to share such information about my family, but I can't think of anything good that happened.

"Would you like a glass of water?"

"No," I say, and I continue talking. "Slim and Blanche had a child together when Blanche was fourteen. I guess that was why Slim told Daddy that he had a right to visit and that no one would stop him."

Dr. Alex turns the page and writes some more. "How did you feel witnessing all of that?"

"I was scared. When Slim left, I was happy, but Daddy saw Slim coming up the hill toward our house with a rifle a short while later. Daddy grabbed his rifle and a box of bullets and went outside. I told Blanche that something was about to happen between Daddy and Slim. I was afraid I might accidentally get shot. Blanche grabbed Claudia, and we sat on the kitchen floor, peeping out the window, watching them shoot at each other. Daddy lay down behind a stack of logs at the woodpile for protection. His head would pop up, and then I would hear the ping of bullets. This went on for quite a while before they ran out of ammunition, and Daddy left in his car."

"How did you feel about your father shooting at Slim?"

"I wanted them to kill each other, so Mama would come home and get us on welfare. Our neighbors were on welfare, and they always had something to eat."

I hang my head in shame. A second or two passes before I continue.

"Having something to eat was the main reason I wanted them to kill each other. A few weeks later, Slim came back to our house with his parents, Mr. William and Mrs. Fannie McGirt. I eavesdropped behind the closed door while they talked to Daddy. A couple of days passed, and then Blanche told us she was moving out to go live with her 'husband' and her in-laws."

The grandfather clock chimes. Our time is almost up.

I sigh. "I was a child then. I didn't know any better."

"Know any better?" Dr. Alex asks, tilting his head slightly.

"No one should ever want to get on welfare."

CHAPTER 5

PIG AND THE ROOSTER

Dr. Alex raises both hands with his long, slender fingers spread open, as if he is getting ready to do benediction at church. He has a puzzled look on his face. "Your mother was in New York, and your oldest sister, Blanche, married and left home," he says before his voice falls silent. His mouth is still open as I begin to speak.

"Mildred, now the oldest girl at home, was about twelve and took charge of us while Mama continued to work in New York. Mildred's full face of freckles made her look more mature. We called her by the nickname Pig. According to Mama, when Mildred was a little girl around three, she would find a mudhole if there was any in sight of the house, and she would wallow in it, thus the nickname Pig." I pause.

"Please continue," Dr. Alex says.

"One school day during recess, I saw a boy eating a Baby Ruth candy bar. I stared at it because I was hungry and hoped the boy would offer me a piece, but he didn't. He twirled his tongue around the encased peanuts, licking the candy bar, and then told me that he knew I was hungry, but I was not going to get any of his candy. I don't remember that boy's name, but what he said has stuck with me all these years. It made me feel ashamed, as if everybody knew we were hungry and poor."

"How does that memory make you feel now?" Dr. Alex asks.

I take a minute to think about the doctor's question. I'm an adult with two children in college, a home, a 401(k), and a savings account at the local bank. Yet I feel the need to prove to the world that I'm an ordinary person who deserves respect just like everyone else. But I don't tell Dr. Alex that. Instead, I say, "I want the world to know that I'm not dirt poor or hungry anymore."

"Mrs. Jamison, you are the most resilient patient I've ever had," Dr. Alex says. "Please continue."

"Pig walked up behind that boy at school. I don't know where she came from, but she told the boy to leave me alone. The boy ran farther down the playground with his friends. Pig told me, 'That boy ain't no better than us, and he does not know whether we're hungry or not.' I knew she wanted to make me feel better, but I was so hungry that my stomach ached."

"Did you have lunch?" Dr. Alex asks.

"I don't remember if I had lunch that day or not. On most days, we didn't have lunch, even though we had to sit in the lunchroom and watch everyone else eat their hot meals or sandwiches from home."

I pause, wondering if what I am telling Dr. Alex will make him think less of black people.

"Please continue," Dr. Alex says.

"Pig got up earlier the next day and made me a fried pork biscuit for my lunch. I was too ashamed to eat the biscuit in the lunchroom; behind the coat closet seemed to be the perfect place to hide and eat the biscuit. My teacher caught me and made me eat lunch with the class in the cafeteria. After school, I told Pig that the kids in my class had made fun of my lunch. Pig told me she was going to fix it so we could have hot lunches from the cafeteria. Pig called Inez, my next-oldest sister, and me to a late-night meeting and shared her grand plan that would enable us to have hot lunches at school. Pig told me I had the most important part of the job. What she didn't tell me was that it was also the most dangerous. I was to crawl on my hands and knees into Daddy's bedroom and sneak his wallet to Pig. I knew it was wrong to take Daddy's wallet, and I protested a bit: 'Why do I have to take Daddy's wallet?'"

Dr. Alex tries to hide a rare smile, but I see it and pause until he tells me to continue. "Please continue," he says, amused.

"Inez, who was two years older and a couple of inches taller than me, explained the plot and said, 'Marilyn, you won't get caught, because you're quick, and Daddy won't catch you.' Eventually, I agreed to be the one to grab Daddy's wallet. Pig told me that when she started singing, I was to get down on my hands and knees and crawl into Daddy's room. If Daddy moved, I should lie flat on the floor and not make a sound. Then, when Daddy began to snore again, I should find his pants on the floor, take the wallet, and crawl out of his room. We did a practice run. It went well, and then, for two whole weeks, Pig sang the lyrics from a popular song—'Yeah, yeah, yeah, oh boy, I like to love 'em in the morning'—while I crawled into Daddy's room and took his wallet. I put it back the same way after Pig took out some dollar bills."

"How did taking your father's wallet make you feel?" Dr. Alex asks.

"Conflicted. I knew it was wrong to take his wallet. But for two whole weeks, we had milk for breakfast, ate a hot lunch in the school's cafeteria, and got ice cream during recess."

I snicker a bit as I recall what happened next. "But one time, while I was returning Daddy's wallet, he turned over and stopped snoring. I lay flat on the floor while Pig sang the same verse repeatedly. I waited for Daddy to start snoring again, but instead, our rooster began to crow, which usually woke up everybody in the house. I stuffed Daddy's wallet into his pants pocket as fast as I could and crawled out of his room at breakneck speed. A week later, as we sat around the wood-burning stove, studying, Daddy came home before dark. We knew that something was up, and it wasn't the sun. Pig had a stoic expression on her face. She looked at Inez and me and whispered to us, 'Ah, we don't know nothing about nothing.'"

"Was your father sober?" Dr. Alex asks.

"Maybe," I say, and I continue with my memory. "Daddy started off by telling us what a sorry brew of children he had. Then he began to cuss because someone had stolen money from him. Then, finally, he remembered someone had been in his room when he thought back. At first, he'd thought it was a field rat scurrying around, but now he knew it was one of us.

"Pig, Inez, and I made sure we didn't give ourselves away by not looking at one another. Daddy told us that if any more money went missing from his wallet, he would beat everyone in the house until our shit-ass heads caved in. I bent down and pretended to scratch my leg, but I cut my eyes upward toward Inez and Pig to see if they looked like they were going to tell on me. After all, I was the one who'd taken Daddy's wallet, and I knew what would happen to me if they indicated me. After that, I never stole any more of Daddy's money."

Dr. Alex places his pen neatly beside his pad and stands up. "Mrs. Jamison, it appears you have had some amazing experiences. I look forward to seeing you next week."

CHAPTER 6

BETTER OFF DEAD

On my fifth visit to Dr. Alex's office, I find myself madder than a rooster that can't get in the henhouse. I don't want to talk about my past anymore. Instead, I want to talk about how one of my coworkers tries to relegate me to servant status and how it's taking most of my strength to remain civil. Every month, she says or does something awful and demeaning toward me.

"How did your week go?" Dr. Alex asks before I sit down. He pops the Coke he is holding. There is a can of Coke for me too, sitting close to the edge of his desk. I let it sit unopened.

"It was not a good week for me."

"Mrs. Jamison, we can talk about this past week or your childhood," Dr. Alex says, and then he pushes his chair back from his desk and crosses his legs.

I cock my head to one side and roll my eyes upward. I have been unable to release the anger I feel toward my coworker for the past week.

"My sales manager planned a quarterly meeting and suggested that the supervisors bring a dish and make it a working lunch. So I brought lasagna to the meeting. Other coworkers brought their favorite dish, and we all helped ourselves to whatever we wanted. After everyone sat down to eat, this Neanderthal-looking coworker said to me, 'Wow, this lasagna is good. Marilyn, you can be my maid and cook.' She made me mad as hell. Every person of color has not been destined to be somebody's servant. It was so disrespectful."

Dr. Alex taps his pen on the table and says, "Interesting. Perhaps that was the Neanderthal's way of paying you a compliment." He speaks slowly, as if he wants me to consider an alternate meaning. I detect a humorous smile behind his silvery eyes. I let his statement roll over in my mind for a moment. I hold back my desire to cuss.

Finally, I say, "I don't think an insult can be a compliment. I'm sure my coworker attempted to make me feel my place in society was beneath hers. Lucky for her, I need my job; otherwise, I would have stomped the snot out of her right then and there." Beads of perspiration started to run down my face and underarms. I massage my temples with both hands as I relive the moment. "Yes," I say, nodding to myself and looking down at the plank floor, "I regret not whipping her ass."

"But why attack your coworker?" Dr. Alex asks, turning the page on his pad.

"To make her respect me."

"Most violence occurs because people are unable to clearly articulate their point of view, or they simply attempt to force their will upon another," Dr. Alex says.

I flip open the lid on my Coke, take a sip, and look across the room for a few seconds. I don't want Dr. Alex to read my thoughts by the expression on my face. Something in the back of my mind tells me not to waste more time talking about work conditions and subtle racism, which Dr. Alex probably has no experience with.

"Well, I'm sure you're right about that," I say. "I'd better start on my childhood." I take a swallow of Coke and heave.

Dr. Alex scribbles down a few words.

"In the summer of 1958, I thought Daddy was going to kill all of us. He came home drunk. And after playing with his dogs, he called all of us children together in the living room."

Dr. Alex keeps his gaze on me as I talk. I keep thinking I must appear to be an angry forty-three-year-old woman to him, wanting to fight and to kill. The thought of him calling BellSouth's security crosses my mind, and if he does, I know things will quickly get worse for me. I pause, clear my throat, and stare into his eyes for a second or two.

"Dr. Alex, are you going to call my employer and tell them about me?"

"Mrs. Jamison, everything we discuss is completely confidential," he says. "Completely confidential," he repeats.

My anxiety lessens, so I start talking about my childhood again.

"I walked from my bedroom down the winding stairs as slowly as I could. Daddy stood near the kitchen table with his shotgun in his hands. His eyes were blazed red. He told us to line up, with the oldest in the front. I didn't have the nerve to ask him why. The fear was overpowering, akin to a nightmare. The long, narrow windows were raised, and something in my gut told me to jump out and run away. But I didn't move. I was too scared."

"What were the other children doing?" Dr. Alex asks.

"They were all lined up, as instructed. Daddy told us he would kill everyone. Between his hiccups and nods, he mumbled some reason why we all would be better off dead. Daddy reached into the back of his denim overalls. *This is the end*, I thought. This was how we all would die. It turned out to be a jar of whiskey."

"Do you know why your father was homicidal?" Dr. Alex asks, and he leans forward as if he wants to capture my emotional state. He jots a few words down, keeping the pen upright on the notepad.

"Daddy said that we ate too much and that we would be better off dead. Then he ranted and raved about how terrible white men were, how they still treated colored people, and how they stole the colored man's future. He said that things would never get better for us colored folks. I think it was because we'd had to move off Mr. Briggs's land, and Daddy thought the landowner had cheated him."

Dr. Alex lets out a big sigh and then looks down at his desk. "I can empathize with your father," he says. "Life is tough for many people. I understand it can be particularly harsh for southern black men. What happened next?"

"I heard heavy footsteps. Mr. Pete Lee, one of Daddy's drinking buddies, walked into the house, looking like he'd been fishing in a mudhole. His tall rubber boots were muddy, splitting at the side seams, and all of his clothes were too big. His red plaid shirt was filthy and tucked into his sagging pants. Mr. Pete Lee was a short, stocky man with big hands and feet, brown eyes, and skin as black as a raven. His hair, beard, and eyebrows were mostly gray. I was afraid of him."

"Why were you afraid of your father's friend?"

"I'll tell you in a minute," I say, and I continue to talk about Mr. Pete. "Daddy's friend looked around the room and saw Daddy with the shotgun and us children lined up like little soldiers. 'Poochie,' he said, 'you're a damn fool. Send these chillums to bed. I don't want them staring me in the face while I take a drink of whiskey.'"

"Did your father have a lot of friends?" Dr. Alex asks.

I ponder the question before answering Dr. Alex, even though I know the answer. Finally, I say, "Daddy had a few, mostly women, but Mr. Pete was one of his male friends. Mr. Pete Lee grabbed the mason jar of whiskey out of Daddy's hand and turned it up, and then he told us to scat because Daddy was crazy. Still, we wouldn't leave the room without Daddy's permission.

"Mr. Pete Lee raised the mason jar to his lips again, taking a big gulp this time. He flapped his lips as he sucked in air through his mouth. Evidently, the moonshine was too strong and burned his throat. Under ordinary circumstances, I would have laughed—his voice sounded quite feminine when he talked. Then, suddenly, Mr. Pete Lee stomped his feet several times at us. We all scattered to different parts of the house. I didn't want Mr. Pete Lee looking for me when I went to bed, and I didn't want to be an easy kill in case Daddy changed his mind, so I sat near the top of the staircase, watching them."

"Why would your father's friend look for you?" Dr. Alex asks.

"To molest me like he did when I was five years old," I say in a soft whisper. I look down at my lap, hoping to conceal how dirty I feel when thinking of Mr. Pete Lee. I must have an unpleasant expression on my face, because Dr. Alex's voice sounds concerned.

"Mrs. Jamison, are you OK?" he asks.

"I'm fine," I say angrily and much too loudly. When I look up at Dr. Alex, he seems shaken.

"Well," Dr. Alex says, "would you like to continue, or would you rather take a break?"

I continue without answering the doctor's question. "Daddy told Mr. Pete Lee that his children were about as intelligent as a bucket of water, and not one of us was worth the salt we ate. He said we may as well be dead. Then Mr. Pete Lee told Daddy to give him the gun because there wouldn't be any shooting that night. Finally, when I got sleepy, I hid and slept in a closet underneath the stairwell and covered myself with a pile of homemade quilts.

"A few weeks later, Mama returned home after working in New York. She had a large box of clothes for us. Some were new, and some were hand-me-downs from her sister-in-law, Aunt Minnie, who was married to Mama's brother, Uncle William, but most of the clothes were from Mrs. Meredith, the Jewish woman Mama had worked for."

"Had your family moved to another location?" Dr. Alex asks.

"No. We moved about a month later," I answer. I then continue with my memory. "The first weekend after Mama's return, she and Daddy got into a fight. Mama had on a gorgeous black jacket with a white fur collar that Mrs. Meredith had given her. She looked beautiful, with soft curls framing her made-up face. Mama and I were in the kitchen, near the stove. I sat on the floor between her legs as she braided my hair, when Daddy came home. We could tell by how he walked up the steps that he was lit.

"Daddy stumbled into the kitchen. We had already eaten supper, and Mama had left Daddy a plate of food in the warmer atop the wood-burning stove. Daddy appeared unhappy about something when he saw Mama in the pretty jacket. When he opened the stove's door and saw the small portion of food, Daddy became belligerent and told Mama that he had a mind to knock her eyes out."

Dr. Alex scribbles a few words on his notepad. He does not say anything to me. I pause for just a second to see if I need to answer a question. Instead, Dr. Alex continues to write. I resume telling the memory.

"Mama didn't respond. Actually, she ignored Daddy, until he swung his right fist. Mama ducked, jumped up, and grabbed a small cast-iron frying pan sitting on the stove. She hit Daddy on the head. Blood started to trickle slowly down the side of Daddy's head and neck. Daddy swung again and again, until his fist contacted the back door. The forceful blow cracked the wooden panel, and Daddy's knuckles began to bleed. Daddy managed to grab Mama's neck and started to choke her. While blood trickled down his hand, he asked Mama to go get his shotgun so he could blow her head off."

After placing my hand on my right leg to stop it from shaking, I tell Dr. Alex I feel guilty for not helping Mama fend off Daddy.

Dr. Alex makes copious notes on his pad before telling me I should not have guilt, because I was a young child, and then he asks if Mama gave Daddy his shotgun.

"Mama told Daddy if he turned her loose, she would bring him his shotgun, which she always hid on the weekend. Daddy fell for the ruse and let go of Mama's neck. Mama ran out the back door. She returned about two hours later with two big deputy sheriffs. They handcuffed Daddy and took him away. I remember Daddy looking back at Mama as if she had betrayed him, and then the sheriffs escorted him out the back door. He looked pitiful in handcuffs. I was angry at the deputy sheriffs for hauling Daddy away."

"Why were you angry?" Dr. Alex asks.

"I don't exactly know why I was angry. Maybe because seeing two big white men with pistols on their side carrying Daddy away in handcuffs was more frightening than he and Mama fighting."

"What happened with your father?"

"Daddy returned home from jail the next day. He seemed remorseful, but Mama started to carry a pistol."

CHAPTER 7

EDUCATION AIN'T SHIT FOR BLACK PEOPLE

If Mama and my siblings had known I was in a psychiatrist's office exposing vile, ugly, and shameful things about my family and me, they would have been disappointed in me, even angry. But there is one thing I know: I have not been arrested for murder yet, and I'm able to sleep better at night without using drugs or alcohol.

"Would you like to hear a good memory?" I ask Dr. Alex on my next visit.

"Tell me whatever is on your mind," he says.

"When it stormed, we got a reprieve from working in the fields and would go to school. Once the rain was over, we planted tobacco seedlings with a peg made from a small tree limb. The peg was about eight inches long, with a smooth, pointed tip that effortlessly penetrated the soft, wet soil. One person would drop the tobacco seedlings onto the soaked row. The second person, with the peg, stooped down, made a hole, inserted the small tobacco plant, and then closed it up with the tip of the peg.

"We repeated this process until nightfall or until the work was complete. Then, one day in early May, it started to rain, which meant we didn't have to work in the fields and could go to school. We grabbed our jackets and plastic rain covers and then headed for the bus stop about two miles from our house. We had to cross over a makeshift bridge made from untreated wood slabs. Before we reached the bridge, we saw the rising muddy water overflowing. The thick, heavy planks across the bridge wobbled as the roaring water rose near the top. We walked across as carefully as possible while water splashed up between the cracks into our shoes.

"That afternoon, when the school bus arrived at our stop, the sky was clear and blue. The rain had stopped, but there was an ominous silence as we walked home. The Burtons children, our closest neighbors, were with us, but they didn't have to cross the bridge. After walking together for about thirty minutes, we waved goodbye and continued home. As expected, not one plank or slab of wood was there for us to cross to the other side of the creek. We couldn't tell where the bank began or ended. Finally, we all stopped while my two oldest brothers, Lenny and Edward, looked for the narrowest part of the creek.

"Lenny walked up and down the overflowed creek with a long tree branch, poking the ground in front of him. Finally, he found a narrow spot for us to cross. But we had to run, get up speed, and jump across. Lenny went first and landed safely across the creek."

"Where were your parents? Didn't they know of the danger?" Dr. Alex asks.

I shake my head. "I don't know where they were, but everyone jumped across the creek, except me. I tried to jump across about three times. Each time, I slipped and fell into the muddy water. I started to cry because I thought my siblings would leave me on the other side, and I wouldn't be able to get home.

"Finally, my brother Edward jumped back across, stooped down, and told me to get on his back. I closed my eyes and wrapped my arms and legs tightly around him. I wondered for a few seconds whether Edward and I would land on the other side of the bank or hit the middle of the creek and drown. I bounced up and down on Edward's back for a minute or two before we became airborne. When I opened my eyes after Edward pried my hands from around his neck, I found myself lying in the muddy water on the other side of the creek, looking like a little swamp monster."

"Really? Is Edward your favorite brother?" Dr. Alex asks, his eyes signaling approval of Edward.

I want to answer, "Yes, he is," but I can't. I still remember all the beatings Edward gave me. Most of them were unprovoked. I still get angry at Mama and Daddy for not protecting me from many years of abuse from my brothers.

Finally, I say, "No, Edward is not. I don't have a favorite brother, but Edward was a hero when I needed one on that particular day, and I will always be grateful to him for that. And that's my good memory. Edward saved me from drowning."

I pause for a moment as flashes of my past briefly float inside my head.

I find myself wanting to tell everything about me, present and past—all that I remember. Yet I don't want to talk about my ex-boyfriend, even though he is the original reason for my therapy. I feel ashamed that I ever felt the need to harm Steven. At first, I thought he was just an unfaithful person being a man without morals or honor and void of good character—a person who didn't consider how his actions and behaviors would impact the feelings of those who loved him. After a few weeks of therapy, I realize I need to focus on myself. I accept the fact that my ex-boyfriend Steven is simply an ordinary man who didn't live up to the illusions of what I thought he should have been to me. I now realize there is no need to blame him for our failed relationship. It did not survive. I decide to apologize to Steven for my bad behavior. I don't tell Dr. Alex that. Instead, I continue to talk about my early childhood.

"On the last day of school, I was lucky enough to be present. Students who passed to the next level screamed for joy, and students who were held back cried. I sat quietly at my desk, anticipating my name being called to go up front and receive my final report card. The teacher always called our names alphabetically. But that day, she called my surname, Abbott, last instead of first. I took that as a bad sign."

Dr. Alex writes a few words on his notepad while I continue to tell him about my childhood.

"'Marilyn Abbott, you just missed too many days,' the teacher said softly, using my full name, as she handed me my report card. I took the yellow folded piece of paper and opened it. Across the top, she had written the word *repeat* in big black letters. I didn't cry right away because I didn't want anyone to know I had failed second grade. But when I got home, I began to cry. I told Mama that my teacher said I had missed too many school days.

"Daddy heard me crying and complaining to Mama. He strolled into the room. His cold, surly eyes glared at me. He said, 'Shut up that shit-ass noise befo' I give yo' ass somethin' to cry about. Shit on that schoolhouse. Education ain't shit for black folks.'"

"Wow!" Dr. Alex says, apparently shocked. "I can't imagine a modern-day parent saying such things to his or her child. Your father's words were horrible, but it is reasonable to think that your father may have been a desperate man trying to navigate his own life's circumstances, as difficult as they were. Lesser men would not have survived the harshness of the South during those times, but it is the past."

Dr. Alex runs his fingers through his hair and then laces his fingers, leans over his desk, and says, "I think you have a problem with trust that stems back to your childhood. We learn our basic human nature from our childhood. Once you learn to trust, you will meet new friends, perhaps a husband, but you must relearn how to trust, specifically trustworthy men."

While Dr. Alex talks about trust, I wonder if I can relearn how to trust men, when every man who has been in my life has caused me pain.

That afternoon, when I return home, I find my old, faded composition journals that hold many memories of my childhood and youth. I spend the next week reading and remembering my past and how I ended up in therapy. Many emotions are evoked: sadness, anger, fear, hatred, and some happiness. Even though I cannot share all the disturbing details of my past with Dr. Alex, I rehash them in my mind.

CHAPTER 8

PUT YOUR BOOK DOWN

Lenny and Edward had gotten tired of begging Daddy to allow them to go to school. They both had been held back several times. Finally, they quit in the middle of the school year. I was terrified because my teacher constantly told us to study and stay in school to have a better life than our parents had. It bothered me that neither Mama nor Daddy seemed concerned about my brothers' decision to quit.

Lenny and Edward worked the farm full-time every day, while Daddy, on most days, left in the morning and returned after the work was completed. I never knew where Daddy went when he was missing. I didn't think Mama knew either.

Daddy came home one Monday evening earlier than usual and surprised us. He set a big cardboard box down on one of our rubber-bottomed chairs.

"Look at what I got us," Daddy said, his eyes beaming with excitement, as he cut the heavy packaging. "I got us our very own TV." He grinned with pride and plugged the TV into the electrical wall socket.

"Well, Jesus, we got us a TV," Mama said, and she rushed to touch it.

"Hold up a minute," Daddy said in his commanding voice, waving his hands to stop us from stampeding toward it. "I need to teach y'all how to work this thing."

He showed Mama how to turn it on and change the channels. He fidgeted with the rabbit ears awhile, and soon we saw pictures of cowboys in a gunfight.

I liked having a television, but now we had one fewer chair to sit in.

Daddy still often drank whiskey and was primarily absent during the day. He enjoyed watching western shows, such as *The Rifleman*, *Laramie*, *Cheyenne*, *Sue King*, *The Roy Rogers Show*, and *The Lone Ranger* at night, but *Tarzan* was his favorite. Sometimes, when he was lit, he tried to emulate Tarzan's hollering.

The Rifleman was my favorite. One day I told my brother Ronald Jr. that I was leaving home to find Rifleman. I wanted him to be my daddy. Ronald Jr. laughed and said I was dumb, because Rifleman was a make-believe character like comic book heroes. It took me several weeks to get over that disappointment, and it left me hating Rifleman.

On one rainy Saturday evening, while playing dominoes with Mama, we heard Daddy's black-and-red Pontiac spinning, trying to climb the long, wet, hilly driveway. We stopped our game and went to the window to watch. We laughed as the car slid backward, and Daddy tried again and again to get it up the slippery hill. Finally, Mama sent us out into the rain to help. Ronald Jr., Inez, and I got behind the car and pushed. The vehicle spun from side to side as Daddy kept turning the steering wheel one way and then the other. Finally, when the vehicle veered to the right, we moved to the left. Sweat and rain ran down our faces as red mud splattered all over us from the smoking, spinning tires.

"Y'all push harder!" Daddy yelled out the window, but the car careened out of his control.

"Get out of the way!" twelve-year-old Ronald Jr. hollered, jumping away from the car. "Let it roll into the ditch."

Inez jumped out of the way too, but I didn't move. Luckily, the car missed me as it rolled downhill and slid into the ditch.

Ronald Jr. came to where I stood. "What's wrong with you, Marilyn?" he asked as he grabbed and shook me. "Don't you know you is too little to push a car up a hill when the ground is wet and slippery? I know you is only eight years old, but you got to be thinking how to get out of the way if the car starts to roll back."

Half scared out of my wits, all I could do was nod and look toward the ditch. Daddy sat in the car, dazed, as water gushed underneath the car like roaring rapids.

"I'll go get him," Ronald Jr. said, and he started down the slippery hill to help Daddy out of the car.

After I found my voice a little while later, I hollered to Ronald Jr., "Weren't you trying to push the car up the hill?"

My brother stopped and looked back at me. "I was tryin' to keep y'all from gettin' killed—that's what I was tryin' to do." Ronald Jr. dragged out his words. "Daddy don't know any better 'cause he's drunk, and Mama is gonna do what Daddy tells her to do because he's the man."

Ronald Jr. helped Daddy out of the car, and they started to walk up the hill. Unfortunately, they both slipped and fell down several times before reaching the house. Mama cleaned Daddy up and gave him a bowl of pintos and corn bread.

We continued going to school hungry and without lunch or money while sharecropping on Mr. Boss A's land. But school was my sanctuary, hungry or not. I would rather have been there than any other place.

One night, after supper, Daddy saw me reading while I sat on our old, broken, sagging sofa. He grimaced. "You may as well put that shit-ass book down, 'cause you ain't goin' to that schoolhouse tomorrow."

I pretended not to hear him and kept reading. Then, finally, Daddy walked over to where I sat. He looked down at me, and I flinched, afraid he might slap me.

"Gal, I said put that shit-ass book down. Don't you hear me?"

Without looking up at him, I closed my book, made my way to an empty room in the house, and continued studying. Inez, who was ten, followed behind. She placed her hands on her slim hips like Mama did when she had something important to say. Inez took in a deep breath.

"Marilyn, you know we can't go to school tomorrow. Why is you still studying?" she asked, her voice soft and matter-of-fact. I thought she was afraid Daddy was going to punish me.

I felt her honey-brown eyes looking down on me. I turned the page of my book and looked up. "I like reading, and when I do go back to school, I want to be ready in case the teacher gives us a pop quiz."

"Well," Inez said, "it's your hide." She shrugged and walked out of the room.

It rained the next day, and we went to school. Late in the evening, just before dark, we heard Daddy's black-and-red Pontiac spinning as he attempted again to climb the steep, slippery driveway. I felt sick, thinking we might have to push the car up the hill. I looked over at Ronald Jr. He grabbed his jacket off the nail on the back door and motioned for us to get our jackets and follow him.

As I pushed the back end of the car, I thought of how fast I could jump out of the way if the vehicle started to slide backward. I didn't push as hard as my siblings because I remembered what had happened the first time we tried to get the car up the hill.

Daddy stuck his head out the window and yelled, "Y'all ain't pushing hard enough! Lord Jesus, y'all can push harder than that. Maylyn, is you pushing?"

Somehow, we managed to get the car up the hill and into the driveway. Once inside the house, Daddy reached into his pocket and gave everyone a few coins, except me. He told me that I had not tried hard enough. I felt slighted and angry.

CHAPTER 9

THE UGLY ONE OF THE BUNCH

The following day, Mama sent me over to Mr. Boss A's wife, Mrs. Mattie, to help pick green beans in her garden. She was a tall, willowy woman with long, kinky reddish hair in two long braids that rested on her bosoms.

She met me in front of her beautiful white house, wearing a pleated pink dress that hung below her knees. Mrs. Mattie looked startled when she first saw me, but she didn't say anything. Finally, she smiled and started toward the back of her house, and I followed. I was startled too, because her skin was so light. I thought she was a white woman.

A big tin tub sat at the end of several rows of green beans. I thought it was going to be backbreaking work, and Mrs. Mattie might pay me a little something, but I didn't want to help her fill that big tub. Mrs. Mattie stared at me for a moment and then shook her head. I stared back without speaking, waiting for instructions.

"What in God's name happened to your face, child?" Mrs. Mattie asked, and then she stooped down to pluck greens beans off the heavy-leaning vines.

I didn't respond to her question. I was not sure what she meant. I didn't realize that anything had happened to my face. I started to pick green beans, but her question stuck in the back of my mind.

Mrs. Mattie dropped several handfuls of beans into the tin tub and dragged it down the row. Then, after a while, she spoke again.

"It's a crying shame for your face to look like that. Course, I don't know what anybody can do about it." She dabbed sweat from her forehead with a white cloth she pulled from her apron's pocket. Then she asked, "How come your hair is sticking out? Are you trying to grow horns like my cows?"

I continued to pick the beans off the bushy green vines in silence. I couldn't figure out what I had done that made Mrs. Mattie talk to me in such a way. I knew not to talk back to an adult. But I wanted to. The hot sun blared down upon us, and the sweat from my face ran into my eyes, causing them to burn. Gnats and mosquitoes swarmed around and bit. My top braids had unraveled and were stuck up because I attempted to keep flying insects away from my head. I tried to smooth my hair down, but it did not work.

I felt Mrs. Mattie's disapproving eyes rolling over me. I picked the beans as fast as I could. I wanted to get away from her. After several minutes, I looked up and saw her watching me. She had a grimace on her face.

She said, "I suppose you're the ugly child of the bunch." She then stooped down once more and resumed picking beans.

Mrs. Mattie's comment caught me off guard and left me wondering what *ugly* looked like. I had never been called ugly before, nor had I heard the term referring to a person.

I didn't say a word because I didn't know what to say to our landowner's wife. I looked into the tub. It was almost filled to the brim. I picked more beans as fast as I could. I wanted to get away from Mrs. Mattie before I became sassy and ended up getting a beating from Mama or Daddy.

The sweltering afternoon sun glared, and the little shade near her garden had been taken over by a large gaggle of geese. When Mrs. Mattie stood up from picking beans, one hand was across her forehead to shield her eyes from the blazing sun. I peeped up and thought to myself, *I sure hope she goes blind.*

Mrs. Mattie stretched her back, wiped her face, and giggled. "So you are deaf and dumb too?"

I remained silent. Glancing at a few good-sized rocks lying outside the last row, I thought of clobbering Mrs. Mattie with them, but I changed my mind. I didn't want to create any problems for Mama and Daddy, especially since we had moved to this farm less than a year ago. So instead, I bit my lower lip and continued to softly chew on it.

Finally, Mrs. Mattie said, "The tub is full." She gave me a shiny fifty-cent piece. I put it in my skirt pocket. Then, after we carried the tub to her back porch, I left running.

A Head of Cabbage

I saw Mama sitting in the back of the house, snapping her own bucket of green beans.

"Mama, what's wrong with my face?" I blurted out, but I didn't mention that Mrs. Mattie had said I was ugly.

Mama looked up at me, briefly closed her eyes, and sighed as if releasing a heavy burden. "Can't you see?" she asked, dropping a handful of beans into her lap.

I ran inside the house and returned a short while later with a small piece of a broken mirror. I looked at my face and then at Mama's face. Hers was smooth, even-toned, and flawless. I looked at my face again, and for the first time, I noticed the difference.

"What happened to me?" I screamed.

Mama twisted her lips from side to side before speaking. She held her head down and fidgeted with a handful of green beans.

Mama said, "When you was just a baby, yo' face broke out in bumps—not yo' whole face, just the right side that's messed up." She snapped a few beans and dropped them into the bucket. Then she looked up at me and said, "I kind of picked at the bumps and tried to make them go away, but they got worse. They turned into big sores full of pus. I took you to the doctor, but them white doctors wouldn't see you, and the colored doctors didn't help much either—said they thought you was allergic to cow's milk. How was I supposed to feed you?" Mama's eyes appeared to say, *Sorry.*

Mama looked as if she were about to cry. I went inside the house and stayed in the room I shared with Inez and Mildred until I was called to eat dinner.

That evening, around the supper table, I took a long look at all my siblings' faces. Theirs were flawless like Mama's. Mildred had tiny brownish freckles, but her skin was smooth. As they ate dinner and engaged in pleasant chatter, I almost choked, thinking about my face: uneven; discolored; and full of large, deep pox holes.

That day, at age eight, was the day I began to hate myself, the ugly child of the bunch.

CHAPTER 10

THUMBTACKS

In 1961, Daddy returned home late one evening after selling tobacco in Danville, Virginia. He was driving a new green 1962 Chevrolet truck. He and my brothers beamed with pride. After supper, Daddy told us we were moving up the road. I was ecstatic to move off Mr. and Mrs. Boss A's land.

The new farm was still in Leasburg, North Carolina, about three miles south of Mr. Boss A's farm. Daddy and my brothers packed our furniture onto Daddy's new truck and moved us in a couple of hours.

The new farm and house were more substantial. The house had three porches, six huge rooms, and two staircases. One set led to the boys' space away from Mama and Daddy's bedroom, and the other led to the girls' space off the hallway entrance. Each bedroom was large enough for us to have two full-size beds and a dresser. The entire interior was a pale blue, except for the dining room, which was a royal blue.

About seventy-five feet from the house was a vast orchard of fruit trees. The water well was on the right side of the house, about ten feet from the side porch. It had a heavy wooden cover to prevent leaves or rodents from falling into it.

The den was sunken, with a fireplace in the back of the room. Four large windows the length of the left wall faced south. On the right side of the den was an entryway to the kitchen and pantry.

The house had five exits, and each one led to a porch. The most extended side porch stored firewood for heating and cooking. Daddy used the back porch to store his tools. The wide front porch, which was the length of the house, was where we sat on the weekends. Beyond the house were a covered woodshed, a chicken coop, a cowshed, horse stables, and a barbed-wire pasture.

The second day after we moved in, our new landowner, Mr. William Lea, drove up in a dark blue truck. He was a big man. His hands looked to be the size of newborn babies. He was tall and muscular, with a full head of slick white hair. He asked Daddy short and to-the-point questions as he looked us over approvingly.

"How old is this one? How old is the oldest boy again?"

Daddy, much leaner and younger, looked proud as he answered the questions.

Mr. William Lea said, "Yeah, you got a fine-looking bunch."

Daddy grinned as he ruffled up the curly hair of William Winston, the youngest child. Then Daddy flashed a sober grin and said, "Yeah, I got me a nice crowd to work the fields for us all right."

Mr. William turned his gaze toward Mama, who was standing in the front door. "Is she your wife?" he asked.

"Yes, sir, she's all mine," Daddy said, still grinning, apparently proud of Mama's appearance.

A small bluish-gray lizard ran across the root of the tree where we were standing. It caught everyone's attention. Mr. William Lea stomped the life out of the small reptile and said, "Ronald, your wife is a good-looking woman."

Spring came, and the farmwork was as hard and long as ever. Finally, Daddy broke his old cycle and started to go to the fields in the early mornings with us. He still went missing two to three days a week, and we still missed many days of school. Ronald Jr. and I were the only two children who got visibly upset when we couldn't go. Mildred, Inez, and Levi didn't complain.

Ronald Jr. and I stopped asking Daddy if we could go to school. Instead, we just got up earlier, quietly left the house, and sneaked to catch the bus. Daddy always sent Mama to school to bring us back, but the teachers had already marked us present before Mama arrived. Sometimes the teachers told us which chapters to study for the next few days.

At eleven years old, in the fifth grade, school was no longer a haven for me, because some of my classmates had started to bully and tease me. One day during lunch period, one of my classmates, Jean, told me that looking at my face took away her appetite. So I avoided her as much as possible. I put her in the same category as Mrs. Mattie, but some boys at school were much worse.

One boy called me Frankenstein's bride when he saw me. He and

A Head of Cabbage

his mean friends would laugh as if it were a clever joke. Finally, I asked someone who Frankenstein was. When I found out he was a hideous monster, I wanted to line my tormentors up and shoot them with Daddy's rifle for making fun of me.

Another day in class, one of the mean boys pointed a finger toward me and said, "She must be part leopard, y'all. Look at the spots on her face."

Several of the students turned and stared at me. I was so embarrassed that I just looked down at my desk. I didn't know what to say to any of them. All I could think of was shooting that boy—to make him stop teasing me. So I began to think of ways to get one of Daddy's rifles onto the school bus without anyone's knowledge.

"Marilyn, the class is just curious," the teacher said. "Come up here, and tell us what happened to your face."

The shame and anger I felt about the teasing were overwhelming. I remained seated. My mind raced with thoughts of how to stop the humiliation. Shoot the boys? Fight each time someone said something unkind to me? I didn't know what to do.

"Marilyn, come on up, and tell the class what happened to you," the teacher said again in a slow, whiny voice.

Reluctantly, I walked up front to the teacher's desk. Feeling awkward and embarrassed, I looked over at my teacher. She smiled and nodded. I wanted to shoot her too, for going along with the mean boys.

I said, "My mama told me I was allergic to something when I was a baby, and it caused sores to break out on my face." I rushed back to my seat and laid my head down on the desk. The explanation seemed to please my teacher, but it left me feeling like I was not a person. I cried until it was time to catch the bus home.

I didn't tell Mama or Daddy about what had happened at school. I feared they might keep me home. Although I had to endure cruel teasing, I always wanted to go to school.

I didn't take Daddy's rifle the next day, but I sneaked two thumbtacks off my teacher's desk. I placed them on the seat of the boy who'd said I must be part leopard. He jumped up, screaming and rubbing his butt. I pretended to be reading and took delight in knowing he felt some pain inflicted by me. I remained quiet and tried to look innocent as he told the teacher that someone had put thumbtacks on his seat. The teacher tried to find out who had done it by asking several students sitting next to him.

I didn't think she suspected me. At least she never asked me about the incident.

Several weeks after school closed for the summer, we all sat on the front porch one Saturday afternoon, resting from working in tobacco.

Daddy stood up and lit a cigarette. After a few puffs, he came over closer to where I sat. He stared at my face for a few seconds and then said, "Gal, I had a conversation with Mr. Fuller early this mornin'. You know 'im—he lives up yonder behind Mr. William's house. He said I needed to keep you out of the sun and do somethin' 'bout yo' face."

Instinctively, I covered the scars with my right hand, but I felt hopeful that Daddy would do something. "Is you gonna take me to a doctor?" I asked, removing my hand and tilting my face toward him.

Daddy bent down and took a closer look but said nothing. Then he started to walk toward his truck, which was parked in the center of the yard, under a big maple tree. I walked behind him, holding my breath. Then, finally, he turned around, looked down at me, and opened the door to his truck.

"Daddy, is you gonna take me to see a doctor?" I asked again, more forcefully.

Daddy hopped into his truck and then turned his face to look at me. "Shit naw. I ain't taking you to see no doctor. There ain't nothin' no doctor can do for yo' face. Just accept the way you look. Everybody can't be pretty."

I watched his truck take the last curve out of our long driveway and held my tears back. Then, as my eyes began to well up, I ran back inside the house, and I didn't stop until I was upstairs, where I prayed to God to create a miracle for me.

CHAPTER 11

THE TALK

The winter of 1961 was the first year we didn't go hungry. Mr. William Lea, the landowner, sometimes brought us something edible—maybe a hog's head, a pig's shoulder, or some other type of meat. One day he and his son Frank surprised us and came to our house with a truckload of furniture: a long, sturdy mahogany dining table; a long, beautiful buffet that matched the table; an upright piano; and several heavy straight-backed chairs.

Mr. William Lea wiped the sweat from his brow and looked at Mama, who came rushing out of the kitchen when she heard the commotion.

"Flora sent this furniture down here for the children. She thinks a mighty heap of them," Mr. William Lea said. "They work hard, and they're mighty respectful too."

Mama's face swelled with happiness as she glanced at the beautiful antique furniture.

"Flora went to Roxboro and got herself a brand-new dining room set just in time for Thanksgiving. She told me to give this one to Nora's children."

Mr. William Lea ran his fingers through his slick white hair as sweat rolled down the sides of his face. Mama sat in one of the chairs, obviously pleased with it, and then she jumped up and ran her short, petite fingers across the glossy table. When she saw the long-inlaid mahogany sideboard with brass pulls, Mama stopped in her tracks. Her hand went to her mouth in admiration, and I thought she would cry.

"Please tell Mrs. Flora we sure do appreciate her—and you too. We sure do." Mama's eyes were moist when she looked at me, and she was hardly able to speak. "Marilyn, go get Mr. William a glass of water," she said in a whisper.

I got the water, but before I gave it to him, I stopped for a moment to admire the furniture. We now had a long dining room table and eight beautiful chairs to match. Our dining room looked like a picture in the Sears, Roebuck, and Company catalog.

Mr. William Lea sat down in one of the chairs, and when I gave him the glass of water, his big, rough hand engulfed mine for a few seconds. I felt uncomfortable and quickly slid my hand away from his.

"Whew! Lord, that was good," he said, grinning, as he handed me the empty glass a few seconds later. He looked over at Mama and wiped his mouth with a clean handkerchief that he pulled from his shirt pocket. "Mrs. Nora, a lot of folks think I'm a white man, but I'm colored," he said, with emphasis on *colored*. "My daddy was white, though. He took my mama when she was just thirteen years old and gave her his seed."

I could tell Mama thought Mr. William was being too familiar. She gestured with her head for me to leave the room. But since she didn't ask me to go, I pretended I didn't see her head gestures and sat down in one of the new chairs to listen.

"I was told that my mama was black like a lump of coal and as pretty as God could make a woman. My daddy took one look at her and had to have her."

Mr. William looked over at me again and grinned. His gray eyes made me feel that something was not quite right, but I stayed put and listened. He lowered his head and looked sad. Then, after a short pause, he continued.

"Yes sirree, that's what happened all right. He just had to have her." His piercing eyes rolled over me again as he said, "I'm a bastard child." He shook his head and ran his fingers through his damp, clingy hair. "My poor ole mama—I was all she ever had in her whole life. They told me that the white folks wanted to raise me white, but my mama squalled so much that they gave me back to her." Mr. William stood up to leave and said, "I thank you for the water." He nodded at me and then at Mama.

As soon as Mr. William Lea and his son left, Mama turned to me. "Marilyn, there ain't no need to go blabbing everything you heard."

"But, Mama," I said, "I don't understand how Mr. William can be both white and colored at the same time. He looks like a white man to me. And how come he thanked us for giving him a glass of water?"

Mama walked toward her bedroom. She looked back at me, stopped, and said, "For one thing, he got manners, and the second thing, he can look white, but if he's got any amount of colored blood in 'im that white folks know 'bout, then he's colored."

Mama entered her bedroom. I was right behind her with another question. "How come he ain't white with colored blood instead of colored with white blood?"

"Shit, Marilyn—you ask too many questions about things we can't do nothin' about. If truth be told, there ain't but one race, which is the human race, but white folks wanted to be special and different 'cause they think they smarter and better. They scientists done divided everybody up into different groups. So everybody got to pick one race or the other. Now you know they done put the white race on top."

"Why'd they do that?" I asked.

"So one group can boss and mistreat the other group, I suppose. You do know that colored people used to be slaves here in America, don't you?"

I nodded.

A few months after Mr. William gave us the furniture, Mama got sick and believed a white-owned restauranteur had poisoned her when she dined there earlier in the day.

While grimacing in pain, Mama said, "Them shit-assed white folks didn't want to serve me. I just should've stayed hungry. They might have poisoned that hot dog I ate."

After several hours of severe pain, Daddy took Mama to Person County Hospital in Roxboro. Late in the night, he came back without Mama. We knew something was seriously wrong.

Daddy was drunk and could hardly stand. "Y'all's Mama will be all right in a day or two," he said, and then he kicked off his shoes and got into bed fully dressed.

Three days later, Daddy put on his best clothes and left. He told us he was going to get Mama. Late that afternoon, we saw dust rising on the dirt road before seeing Daddy's truck. He pulled up into the yard, got out, and opened the truck's door for Mama—something I had never seen him do before.

Mama got out with a bundle in her arms. A wide grin spread across Daddy's face. Then he helped Mama into the house and proudly exclaimed, "I got me ten chillums now!"

A few days later, Mr. William Lea came to visit. When he got ready to leave, he peeped at the baby and then winked at Daddy and nodded to me. I couldn't figure that out, and curiosity got the best of me. He and Daddy stepped into the hallway to talk. I hid behind the door and listened.

Daddy said, "Yeah, we real men. Any young buck can get a young woman pregnant, but it takes real men like us to get older women pregnant."

Mr. William Lea shook his head and laughed so hard he doubled over and wiped tears as he stepped out into the cold, windy night. Daddy stood in the open doorway proudly with his chin up, as if counting stars.

One spring day, Mama sent me to help Mrs. Flora pick green peas out of her garden. It was about a forty-five-minute walk to her house. My older siblings didn't want to be with Mrs. Flora on a Saturday evening, picking vegetables, so it was just the two of us. I liked that because it got me out of the house, and Mrs. Flora Lea was friendly to me.

After we picked an entire bushel of peas, she suggested we sit under a nearby shade tree for a little while because she felt a dizzy spell coming on. Then she poured each of us a glass of cold water from her jug.

She rubbed her temples and lowered her body down onto her three-legged stool. Then she said, "I've been aiming to talk to Nora's girls. I have noticed that you're beginning to fill out a bit."

Mrs. Flora adjusted her body on the stool and took a sip of water. I tensed up. I didn't want another talk like the one Mrs. Mattie had given me a couple of years back. I stared at the ground, wondering how fast I could jump up and run away if she started to insult me. But I took a deep breath and forced myself to show respect by listening.

She was a tall, full-figured woman, appearing to be in her early sixties. Her skin tone was odd—not black or brown but more of a bronze hue. Her facial features were pleasant—nothing too big or too small.

"Now, girls and boys are different. Boys will want to touch you in your private area, but you can't allow that." Mrs. Flora sighed. "If you do, you will end up like Mr. Fuller's daughter up there on that hill." She pointed in the direction of a small log cabin beyond her house.

I looked toward the house. Several small children played in the yard while an older man sat nearby in a white rocking chair under a persimmon tree.

"Uncle Sam is the daddy of Mr. Fuller's grandchildren. And that's a real shame." Mrs. Flora took another sip of water and said, "That's a shame and scandal."

I could see Mrs. Flora in my peripheral vision. She heaved, rubbed her temples again, and then repositioned her stool to face me. "Don't have babies without a husband and daddy for your children," she said while sweat poured down her face.

"Yes, ma'am," I said, all the while wondering how anyone could have children without a daddy and why Uncle Sam was so shameful. I thought to myself that he couldn't have been as mean as Daddy. I almost told her that and then remembered not to be sassy.

We finished picking the green peas and later went to her house, where she put some into a bucket for me to take home to Mama for letting me help her.

My mind kept going back to Uncle Sam and why Mrs. Flora did not think much of him. The question itched inside my gut. Finally, I asked, "Mrs. Flora, how come Uncle Sam is so bad?"

She stopped hulling the peas, twisted her body so she could look me directly in the face, and then said, "Child, just sit down here awhile and listen. You really don't understand, do you?"

I shook my head, afraid she was going to scold me.

"How old are you now?" Mrs. Flora pulled out a chair for me to sit.

I said, "I'm eleven."

"You sure do need a talking to." Pressing her lips together, Mrs. Flora said, "If a woman does not have a husband and daddy for her children, then her children are bastards. Uncle Sam is the United States government, and out of pity, the government feeds the children."

Mrs. Flora raised her voice and lifted her thick eyebrows high as she leaned in closer to my face. "That means the children's mama is on welfare, she will probably stay on welfare, and her bastard girls will probably get on welfare too, because they continue to let menfolk come visit and have their way. Understand now?"

I slid my chair away from her. "Yes, ma'am, I understand. I ain't never going to let a boy touch me anywhere, and I ain't never going to get on welfare."

I felt like a liar, and I was afraid she somehow knew that Slim had already touched me on my privates when I was six years old.

"Well now," Mrs. Flora said, "when you have a husband, it's OK to let him touch you. You are supposed to then, and you'll want him to." She laughed and started to hull her peas again. "Now, you get on home with these peas before it gets too late."

Mrs. Flora was still laughing when her husband, Mr. William Lea, walked in and held the screen door open as I was leaving. I thought I felt his hand brush up against my backside, but I quickly dismissed the thought. *It must have been the wind.* He looked down at the bucket of peas.

Mr. William Lea said, "Flora, put a few more peas in that bucket. Marilyn Ann is a growing child." He took my bucket and topped it off. Then he said, "That's better," and handed the bucket back to me.

I said, "Yes, sir," and left for home.

CHAPTER 12

FIFTH GRADE

My fifth-grade teacher, Mrs. Turner, was considered the meanest teacher at New Dotmond School. But she made me feel as though the world would become a wonderful place if I could get an education. She talked to the class about what we could accomplish and change if only we stayed in school.

I could tell she was not expecting much from me, though. I was mostly ignored, like the other poor students in the class. Mrs. Turner seldom looked my way or toward the students in the back of the room. I always thought we, the impoverished students in ragged clothes who always missed many days, were an embarrassment to our school. We were the sons and daughters of sharecroppers.

She focused on the better-dressed students who came to school every day and whose parents attended the monthly PTA meetings. But when Mrs. Turner talked about the need to study hard every day to do well in high school and be accepted into college, I listened.

One day Mrs. Turner told the class that Caswell County schools would eventually integrate. As a result, we would be respected more and probably learn more. She said we would have a chance at a better life than our parents had—that was, if we became educated, got a job, and saved our money.

On September 10, 1962, I made a vow to myself: I would not let anything or anyone prevent me from finishing high school and going to college.

I didn't have many friends at school. I was never considered anyone's best friend. I was a best friend only for a day whenever the more popular girls were sick and out of school. It was mostly my fault. I could not spend the night at their homes, because I could not reciprocate. We didn't have indoor plumbing, so Mama wouldn't allow overnight visits.

One evening, Daddy came home early and sober. He saw me studying and did not say anything but peeped over my shoulders. It was intriguing to see him interested in a book.

"Daddy, did you like school when you were young?" I asked, feeling safe since he was not drinking.

"It don't matter now," he said, and he turned the TV on. Then he took a seat next to me and continued to gaze into my book.

"Did you finish high school? What was it like back then in high school?" I asked, and I put my book down and waited for his answer.

"I finished the third grade," he said in a whispered tone.

"Third grade! You just finished the third grade?" I shouted. "Didn't you want to at least finish high school?"

"Why is you asking such a dumb question? Can't nothing be done about it now," Daddy said, and then he turned his attention to the TV.

"Granddaddy didn't let you go to school?" I asked.

"Shit, gal, you don't know nothin'. You need to understand that this country was built on slave labor." Daddy rolled his eyes at me. "Everybody wants somebody to work for 'im for free or for a few pennies, including yo' shit-ass granddaddy John."

I turned the page of my math book and almost panicked when I realized I didn't have any paper to do my homework. I spoke more softly. "Daddy, can I have five cents to buy some notebook paper? I don't have any more to do my schoolwork." I showed him the empty binder.

Daddy jumped out of his seat. "Shit, gal, if you got to have five cents to go to school, keep yo' ass home. Don't be asking me for money to go to school." He moved his chair away from me and closer to the TV.

I started to erase my used notebook paper to reuse it to do my homework. I looked over at Daddy. He seemed to be enjoying the program on TV, but I had a question. "Why do you call Grandpa John?"

"'Cause he ain't my blood daddy, and he didn't want to feed me. He didn't even want me around, so he worked the shit out of me for nothing." Daddy came closer and leaned into my face. "John Abbott is half near white with green eyes. Do you think I look like 'im?"

I shook my head, paying close attention to his dark skin and brown eyes. "Nope, you look better than Granddaddy," I said, and I watched Daddy's frown fade into a wide grin.

"Now, nobody else knows that but you," Daddy said, and he lit a cigarette before he resumed watching TV.

Not long after that revelation, Daddy took us to visit Grandma and

A Head of Cabbage

Granddaddy one Sunday afternoon. Grandma came to the door and welcomed us into their unpainted barn-looking house, which sat behind their landlord's much larger two-story modern white house. Grandma was petite, standing about five foot two, and had short, puffy brown hair; brown eyes; and dark brown skin.

Granddaddy remained seated in his rocking chair, sucking on hard candy and making funny noises with his tongue and teeth. He didn't speak as we walked in. Instead, he just looked up and down at all seven of us children. His green eyes made me uncomfortable, especially when he put his glasses on and looked over the rims at us.

Mama went into the kitchen to help Grandma. Daddy sat down on a scuffed-up bench and talked with Granddaddy about the tobacco crop, the garden, and how dry it was. Along with my siblings, I stood around in the family room, quietly listening and hoping to eat some of the good-smelling food.

After a short wait, Grandma called us into the kitchen to eat soup and corn bread. Granddaddy jumped up out of his rocking chair, rushed into the kitchen ahead of us, and stood over the big pot of steaming soup.

His shifty green eyes rolled over us, and then he said, "Now, I ain't trying to fill up y'all's bellies. I'm gonna give y'all just enough food to make it home."

We each got a small bowl of steaming-hot soup and a chunk of crackling corn bread. Each time I raised a spoonful of soup to my mouth, I felt guilty for eating at Granddaddy's house. Finally, Grandma sat next to Granddaddy, who was now guarding the food. He repositioned the pan of corn bread and the pot of soup so they were near him at the front of the table.

Granddaddy looked over toward me and said, "Yo' eyes so black you must have coon blood." Then he chuckled. Grandma looked embarrassed and started to talk about the garden and how dry it was to Mama. The seven of us children said nothing as we ate.

On our way home that night, my siblings and I talked about how stingy Granddaddy was. But I didn't want to break Daddy's trust, so I didn't tell them that Granddaddy was not our blood granddaddy, which might have been why he seemed not to like us.

CHAPTER 13

GOLDEN SPARKS

Late in October 1962, after being absent from school for several consecutive days, I returned and found my teacher completely unsympathetic. As soon as the first bell rang, she called me to the front of the class.

"Marilyn Abbott, why haven't you been to school this week?"

I explained that Daddy had made me stay home to help get our tobacco crop ready for market.

She snorted and rolled her eyes at me. "Well, I'm giving a test in two days. So I suggest you be here to take and pass my exam."

I returned to my seat, fearful that I wouldn't be present even to take the test, much less pass it. So during recess, I went to one of my classmates, Marilyn Hughes, who was without a doubt the most intelligent person in the class and probably had never missed a day of school in her life, and I asked to borrow her notes to copy and study for the test. Reluctantly, she loaned me her binder of summaries on every chapter we were to review, and I promised to return them the next day.

When I got home that afternoon, the house was quiet. Daddy had gone to the tobacco market with Mr. William Lea, and Mama had gone to work her night job at the tobacco factory in Roxboro, North Carolina.

I changed out of my school clothes and cooked supper. I made buttermilk biscuits, fried some white potatoes with onions, fried porkside meat, and made brown egg gravy.

I was careful to put aside enough food for Daddy, Edward, and Lenny since they were not home.

After everyone ate supper, Inez and I cleared the table. Then I started to review Marilyn Hughes's chapter summaries. Lenny, my oldest brother, returned home and headed straight for the kitchen with a small brown paper bag in hand.

I dragged my chair closer to the blazing fireplace to keep warm when the fire began to die. Ronald Jr., Levi, William Winston, and Inez were watching TV and had stacked their books on the dining room table.

Lenny walked out of the kitchen and threw the brown paper bag to me, but I didn't catch it. Then, looking at the floor, he said, "Marilyn, fix me something else to eat. I ain't eating that cold shit on the stove. I got some hamburger meat in that bag for you to cook." He walked over closer to me and stopped just shy of my bare feet.

I said, "Lenny, I'm studying for a test. Can you ask Inez to cook you something else? She ain't studying; she's just watching TV."

"Naw, I ain't asking her, because I'm telling you," Lenny said. "Now, get yo' ass in the kitchen, and fix me some different food." His nostrils flared, and his small brown eyes stared down at me.

I continued to copy Marilyn Hughes's notes but glanced up at Lenny a few times. As I turned another page, I said as calmly as possible, "Then fix yourself something else to eat if you don't want to eat what the rest of us ate."

In an instant, Lenny snatched the binder from my lap, grabbed my arm, and jerked me out of my chair as he threw the binder into the wood-burning fireplace.

Lenny said, "I told yo' ass to fix me different food, and you gonna fix it. I'm tired of yo' hard head. I don't care if you have to study for a test. Get your ass in the kitchen, and cook for me right now."

I tried to grab the binder out of the fire, but it was no use. The flames were too high. I stood and stared in shock, watching the review notes turn gray as they crumbled on the burning logs.

"What am I going to do? You put Marilyn Hughes's review binder in the fire!" I said in a state of panic. "Lenny, how could you do that?"

Lenny pushed me toward the kitchen. "Now, fix me something to eat. I ain't eating that cold shit on the stove."

I jerked my arm loose and walked back to my seat. "I ain't cooking no more tonight. I need to study for my test, and that's what I'm gonna do." I stared him in the face and asked, "Just what do you expect me to tell Marilyn Hughes about her study binder?"

Lenny bowed closer to my face and said, "I don't give a shit about yo' test or Marilyn Hughes's study binder." Then he grabbed me again and,

A Head of Cabbage

with his calloused palm, slapped me several times hard across both sides of my face. "Now, get yo' ass in the kitchen, and fix me something hot to eat."

My face felt as if it were on fire. I saw golden sparkles dancing around my head. I began to cry and wiped my eyes with the tail of my blouse. Lenny grabbed my arms and carried me into the kitchen.

I screamed, "I need to study! I ain't cooking no more tonight!"

"So you want a real good ass whipping." Lenny pushed me down onto the floor and started kicking me all over my body.

Tears streamed down my face, and saliva ran out of the corners of my mouth. My nose started bleeding, and I could hardly see. I covered my face with my hands to block the kicks. I tightened my stomach muscles and curled up into the fetal position. I felt my throat, lips, and face swelling.

Lenny pulled me up off the hardwood floor and shoved me toward the kitchen again. I fell against the cold kitchen stove. Lenny picked up the bag of meat and yelled, "Now, start cooking!"

I screamed, "I told you I ain't cooking no more tonight! I need to study for a test, and you just burned up the papers I needed." I held on to the top of the stove with one hand and wiped my eyes with the back of my other hand.

Lenny cleared his throat and said, "You is gonna do what I tell you to do, or you can keep getting yo' ass whipped."

He balled up his fist and drew it back to hit me. I braced myself against the side of the stove, closed my eyes, cringed, and waited for the impact of his punch. It didn't come.

"Naw, Lenny, you ain't gonna hit Marilyn no more. She done told you she ain't cooking no more tonight. Now, you just leave her alone." Those words came from Ronald Jr., child number five, younger and smaller than Lenny. I opened my eyes and saw him holding on to Lenny's right arm.

Lenny was caught off guard by Ronald Jr. and appeared startled. He looked over at his arm. Ronald Jr. maintained a firm grip. Lenny rubbed his thin mustache, blinked fast for a few seconds, and then said to Ronald Jr., "So you want some too?"

Ronald Jr. stared up at Lenny without letting go of his arm and said, "If you want to give me some, fine, but you ain't hitting Marilyn no more."

Lenny tried to free his arm. Ronald Jr. lifted his face high as he strained himself to hold back Lenny's arm. Then I saw the poker iron on the fireplace hearth. I ran and grabbed it with the intent of helping Ronald Jr. beat Lenny. But I just stood next to them, crying and holding the poker firmly in my hand.

"OK. I ain't gonna hit her no more," Lenny said. "Now, let me go, damn it."

Ronald Jr. released his arm. Then Lenny heated the food that was already cooked and ate his supper.

I went upstairs without saying a word to anyone. I was grateful to Ronald Jr. for stopping Lenny, but I didn't know what to say, so I said nothing. Eventually, I stopped crying, but I was too angry to sleep or pray. I lay awake until the wee hours of the morning, thinking about what I would say to Marilyn Hughes about her notes I couldn't return.

The next day at school, I was too ashamed to tell her what had happened to her study binder, so I tried to avoid her. But ultimately, just before lunch, she came over to me.

"Marilyn, I need my review notes so I can study some more," she said with her hand extended, expecting to receive her binder.

Inside, I cringed because I knew I was about to lie. With a straight face, I said, "Marilyn, I did ask to borrow your study binder and you said you would loan it to me, but you never actually gave it to me."

Marilyn Hughes did not argue with me. Instead, she rolled her eyes toward the ceiling and then walked into the cafeteria. I was not sure if she was questioning herself or me about her notes or if she was wondering why I had two swollen eyes and a busted lip.

I never asked to borrow any review notes again.

CHAPTER 14

SHOES

In the spring of 1963, New Dotmond, my new school in Milton, North Carolina, prepared for the annual May Day Festival. It was an all-day outside event held on the first Friday in May. Some local farmers brought animals for the children to see and pet. I had no interest in seeing the farm animals, since they reminded me of farmwork. There were all kinds of goodies for purchase: cotton candy, popcorn, ice cream, cookies, and soda pop. I looked forward to spending the twenty-five cents I had saved.

The best part of May Day was the wrapping of the flagpole. Five boys and five girls alternately went around the flagpole winding red, white, and blue ribbons attached to the top of the pole. When wholly wrapped, the flagpole was symmetrically red, white, and blue, representing the American flag.

On the third Friday in April, Mrs. Johnson, my sixth-grade teacher, told us that her class had been honored to wrap the flagpole this year, and she had to choose five boys and five girls to represent the school. She walked up one aisle and down the other, speaking and looking everyone over.

Finally, she said, "If I select you, you have to abide by the rules and wear the proper costume. You have the weekend to ask your parents whether you can participate. You will need black shoes, a navy-blue skirt or pants, and a white shirt or blouse, and the girls will need white socks."

On Monday at school, while Mrs. Johnson made her final selection of students to wrap the flagpole at the May Day Festival, I began to pray.

Dear God, I want to wrap the flagpole this year. Please make Mrs. Johnson select me. I have never been chosen and will be too big next year. When I opened my eyes, Mrs. Johnson was looking at me.

"Marilyn Abbott, would you like to wrap the flagpole this year?"

I jumped up. "Yes, ma'am."

"Come up here, and stand beside Joel. I need to match up your height," she said.

Slowly, I walked to the front of the room and joined the other nine students, and I continued my silent prayer: *God, please don't let me be too tall.*

Mrs. Johnson appeared pleased with her selection of students and told me I was the perfect height. As she reminded us of our costume requirements, I looked down at my old, scuffed-up black-and-white oxfords, the only shoes I had.

"You may take your seats, except you, Marilyn," Mrs. Johnson said, placing a hand on my left shoulder.

I started to panic and rushed a silent prayer: *God, please don't let her change her mind. I really want to wrap the flagpole this year.*

Mrs. Johnson was a large woman with big bosoms, tiny feet, and small hands. Thick, curly black hair framed her round dark face like a baby doll's. We students, on occasion, watched and waited, expecting her big bosoms to topple her over, but she never fell. Sometimes the boys in the class called her the Milky Way behind her back. Mrs. Johnson carried a long leather strap across her broad shoulders that she used to pop anyone who acted up in class or the hallways.

"Marilyn, do you have black shoes and a blue skirt?" she asked as she looked down at my feet.

"Yes, ma'am, I do," I lied.

When I got home that afternoon, I excitedly told Mama I would help wrap the flagpole for the May Day Festival.

"I need new black shoes and a navy-blue skirt."

I lost my excitement when I saw Mama frown. "Child," she said, "we can't buy you any new shoes or a skirt. We just don't have the money."

I knew Daddy had the last word in our family, so I decided to wait up for him. He arrived late that night, just in time to see the ending of *Wagon Train* on TV.

"Guess what," I said excitedly. "I got picked to wrap the flagpole at school for May Day this year."

"Well, ain't that something," Daddy said, taking a seat in the den.

I ran into the kitchen and got his supper. "My teacher said I only need a pair of black shoes and a navy-blue skirt to wrap the flagpole."

A Head of Cabbage

Daddy looked up at me. "Gal, if you got to have new stuff, you better not wrap that flagpole. I don't have any money to buy you anything. Shit, everybody need new shoes."

I went to bed and prayed: *God, please help Daddy and Mama get me some new black shoes and a navy-blue skirt. Amen.*

I repeated that prayer each night before I crawled into bed between my sisters Mildred and Inez. I rehearsed wrapping the flagpole with my classmates every day because I fully expected God to help me get what I needed.

When the final week of practice came, Mrs. Johnson told us to bring our costumes to school and leave them there for dress rehearsal.

When I got home that Monday afternoon, I laid out my white socks and white blouse and prayed a more urgent prayer: *Dear God, I have been asking you to tell Mama and Daddy to buy me new black shoes and a navy-blue skirt for almost two weeks now, and you ain't done it. You're supposed to be able to do everything. But, God, we only have four days left before May Day. So please tell Daddy to get them for me. Amen.*

I lied to Mrs. Johnson on Monday and Tuesday and told her I'd forgotten to bring my costume.

Tuesday evening, my older brother Edward brought a date home. She was pretty and petite and had on a navy-blue outfit. I followed them into the living room. Edward gestured for me to leave, but I wouldn't. I kept staring at the navy-blue skirt. Finally, Edward excused himself and then returned a few minutes later with Mama, who made me leave the room, but by then, I had discussed my costume problem with his date.

Later that night, Edward returned home with a brown paper bag in his hand. "Marilyn, Shirley said to give this to you."

The navy-blue skirt was in the bag. It fit perfectly. I got down on my knees and prayed: *Thank you so much for the blue skirt, God, but what about my new shoes? I need them before Friday. Please make Daddy get them for me. Amen.*

On Wednesday, Mrs. Johnson was upset with me. "Marilyn Abbott, where is your outfit?" she asked with a scowl on her face. "Once and for all, do you have your full costume?"

"Yes, ma'am, I have everything," I said. "My mama has to fix the zipper on my skirt, but she told me to tell you not to worry. It will be ready on Friday."

Mrs. Johnson looked down at my feet, paused, and then said, "Do you even have black shoes to wear on Friday?"

"Oh, my daddy is getting me new shoes today," I said.

That evening, when the school bus stopped in front of our house, I saw Daddy chopping wood under the woodshed.

"Daddy," I said, taking a big gulp of air, "I really need a pair of new black shoes. Please get them for me. I don't want anything for Christmas, and I won't ask for a penny for the rest of this year."

"Gal, I got me ten chillums, and nine of 'em need shoes," Daddy said as he let the ax come down hard on a log, splitting it in the center. "It will take a miracle to get you some new shoes, so just stay home on May Day."

I started to cry. "Well, I ain't got to have new shoes. I just want to go to school," I said, and I ran inside the house.

I didn't stop crying until I was upstairs on my knees, praying. *God, did you hear my daddy? He said for me to stay home on May Day. I can't stay home. My teacher is depending on me! What am I gonna do? God, please help me get new black shoes.* I prayed until Mama called me down for supper.

On Thursday, when I went to school without my costume, Mrs. Johnson was panicky. "Marilyn Abbott, where is your costume?" she screamed as sweat ran down both sides of her fat face, and her voice cracked with anger. She walked to the back of the room, where I sat. Her big brown eyes glared down at me.

I sat in my seat and willed myself to stay calm and lie yet again, "Mrs. Johnson, my daddy is getting me new shoes today."

Later in the day, we practiced our skip around the flagpole, and I grew more embarrassed and afraid. All the other students had black shoes, and my twisted, scuffed-up black-and-white oxfords stood out like the white belly of an Adélie penguin.

When I got home in the evening, I thoroughly washed my oxfords. After they dried, I took the dishrag, got soot from the kitchen stovepipe, and dyed the white parts black. Then I set the shoes upstairs beside my navy-blue skirt, white socks, and white blouse. They looked horrible, but they were almost black.

I crawled into bed, disappointed in God, but I began to pray. *Dear*

A Head of Cabbage

God, I don't believe in you anymore. I don't believe that Moses parted the Red Sea. I don't believe that Lazarus was raised from the dead, and I don't believe Shadrach, Meshach, and Abednego were in a fiery furnace. If you can't help me to get a pair of shoes, how could you do all that other stuff? I just don't believe in you anymore. God, just in case you really are real, please get me a pair of new black shoes. I need them in the morning before I go to school. Amen for the last time.

I tossed and turned in bed, unable to sleep. I thought of how embarrassed I would be in the morning when trying to pass off my soot-dyed ugly oxfords as black shoes.

Before I dozed off, I saw car lights pull into our driveway. I got out of bed and peeped through the window.

A tall, slender white man pulled a bulging sack from the backseat of his car. He threw the pack onto our porch and then got back into his car and drove off.

A little while later, I heard murmuring from Mama. I went and stood at the top of the stairs.

"Ronald, I think somebody dumped something on the porch," Mama said. "Didn't you hear that thud?" I heard fear in her voice.

"Nora, I'm trying to watch *King Kong* on this here television. Give me a minute, please," Daddy said, sounding irritated.

I felt compelled to see what was going on. I started down the stairs and saw Mama and Daddy standing near the front door in the hallway.

"Ronald, you need to go see what that man threw onto our porch. It might be trouble," Mama said, sounding worried.

"See? There you go again," Daddy said. "You want me to look for trouble, when I want to look at King Kong." Daddy was trying to be clever, but he seemed somewhat frightened. I stood several steps up the staircase and became afraid too as I watched and listened to them.

"White folks ain't got no business throwing stuff at us," Mama said as Daddy dragged the sack into the hallway.

"Well, Nora, ain't nothing bit me yet," Daddy said as he lifted the sack and dumped the contents onto the floor. "It was probably Mr. Briggs, giving us his chillums' old clothes." He looked up at Mama and grinned teasingly. "You gonna invite him for supper?"

"Shit, what do you think?" Mama snapped.

Girls' clothing fell into a pile, and on top was a pair of black patent-leather shoes. I strolled down the steps, staring, afraid they would be too small.

Daddy reached down and picked up the shoes. He appeared in disbelief as he cut the price tag off with his pocketknife and handed the shoes to me. He did not speak. His eyes met mine, and I saw tears welling up in his. Daddy turned his face away from me and quickly walked back into the family room. I slipped the shoes on, ran upstairs, and knelt beside my bed. I didn't say a word to anyone; I could not speak, nor could I pray. I was overwhelmed with joy.

On Friday, the next day, Mrs. Johnson saw me in my costume for the first time as I walked down the long hallway. She rushed toward me with outstretched arms. There was a big smile on her glistening, pudgy face.

"Child, just come here!" she said. "Marilyn Abbott, you look beautiful—just beautiful—in your costume." She kissed me on the forehead and escorted me by the hand to where the other children were all dressed in white and blue, waiting to wrap the flagpole.

CHAPTER 15

FATHER AND SON

A few weeks after school closed for the summer, Mama selected me to stay home from the tobacco fields to have dinner and supper ready when they returned in the early afternoon and the evening. Although I was only eleven, my duties were clear and straightforward: I had to make sure there was something ready to eat at 1:00 p.m. and 7:00 p.m. and have hot water for handwashing.

For dinner, I usually got vegetables from the garden. Sometimes I had to dig white potatoes or pick turnip greens, kale, tomatoes, squash, green beans, or sweet peas. I searched around the horse stables for poke salad to cook when vegetables were scarce. About twice a week, I would kill, pluck, and fry or boil a chicken or fix some other type of meat, such as rabbit, squirrel, raccoon, or deer meat Mama had put up from Daddy's hunting.

One day I was at home, getting dinner ready, when I saw the landowner, Mr. William Lea, in our dining room. He was bent over and panting for breath. I hadn't heard him knock, and since we never locked the doors in the daytime, he had just walked in.

He stood up as straight as a fishing rod when he saw me. Mr. William Lea said, "Child, you sure are blooming just like a wildflower. It won't be long before that cherry will be ripe for plucking. Now, when you're ready, I want to be the one to pluck it for you."

Not sure what he meant, I ignored his comments, but I felt they were not good for me.

"Mama and Daddy have gone to the fields," I said, and I walked back into the kitchen and started washing and peeling white potatoes for dinner. He followed me into the kitchen.

"I've got a brand-new hundred-dollar bill just waiting for you," he said, exaggerating the word *new*. "You could tell your mama and daddy that you found it."

I didn't respond because I knew better than to take money from men.

Mr. William Lea grabbed me from behind and started to rub his hands across my small budding breasts. Then he turned me around to face him. His piercing gray eyes seemed to look right through me. I glanced up at him and then cast my eyes down. I didn't want him to think I would accept his money.

"Mr. William, please stop," I managed to say in a nervous whisper.

He grinned and grabbed me by the arms, holding them tightly. I thought of his wife, Mrs. Flora, and her advice about not letting boys touch me. I wondered if she had any idea how her husband behaved toward young girls when she was not around. I stared down at the bare planked floor, afraid of her husband, our landowner, for whom Daddy sharecropped.

"You're going to be something to behold when you fill out a little bit more," he said, and then he walked out the side door toward the tobacco barn.

I didn't tell anyone about Mr. William Lea. I didn't know how to start such a conversation, and I didn't want Mama punishing me for being too fast.

About a week later, I saw Mr. William Lea walking toward our house again. I hoped he would go straight to the tobacco barn, where everyone gathered when they first returned from the fields. I shoved several small logs into the stove to heat a pot of water that I would later use to pluck a chicken for dinner. When I started to knead the dough for biscuits and an apple pie, I heard the side screen door open and close.

"Hey, child, everyone gone to the fields?" he asked, looking around the room.

"Yes, sir, everybody is at the fields," I said nervously.

Mr. William Lea walked over near the kitchen window, a few feet from where I stood. He unzipped his pants and took out his big, erect pink penis.

"Child, come over here, and rub Jumbo a little while for me."

I didn't move. I stared out the open kitchen door, wishing Mama would come home. I tried to send my thoughts to her, but of course, she did not hear them.

"This thing will turn blue and fall off if you don't rub it for me right

A Head of Cabbage

now," Mr. William Lea said, and after a few seconds, he came over to me, took my hand full of flour and dough, and put it on his penis.

I was scared that his penis would fall off. What could I say to my family when they returned home for dinner and saw Mr. William's penis lying on the kitchen floor? I didn't want that to happen.

Mr. William Lea said, "Just move your hand up and down real slow-like. Don't be scared. I ain't going to hurt you—no sirree. I wouldn't ever hurt you."

After what seemed like hours, my hand got tired, his penis was not turning blue, and I stopped rubbing Jumbo.

"You're doing a fine job, child, but don't stop rubbing Jumbo. He is going to be just fine in a minute or two." Then, finally, he said, "Whew, Lord," and told me that the colored part of him had given him a big dick.

I felt awful, like I was doing something terrible. If Mama found out about it, she would surely beat the stuffing out of me. Eager to finish dinner, I asked if Jumbo was all right.

"Almost," he said. "Just rub Jumbo a little bit longer and faster. They tell me my white papa took one look at my mother and had to have it. He just went and took it."

I had heard him tell Mama that same story earlier. I didn't say anything as I continued to rub his penis as fast as possible.

Then Mr. William said, "It was nothing to cry over, though. White men have to have some colored stuff every now and then. It's been happening ever since." He moaned louder. "Whew, Lord!"

After a few more seconds, he grabbed the top part of the stove with one hand and hollered, "Whew, Lord! Whew, Lord!" Then he asked me, "Child, do you know what just happened to me?"

I shook my head.

Mr. William Lea released me and then used the bottom part of the kitchen curtains to wipe off his genitals. "I just had what you call a *climax*. Dumb folks call it *coming*—but it's a climax. Yes sirree, Lord, that was some climax all right."

The pot of water on the stove began to boil over. I went to the stove, lifted the pot of scalding water, and set it near the front eye, away from the hottest part of the stove, to prevent overflow. I thought of throwing the hot water onto Mr. William Lea.

He asked, "Child, what are you going to do with that pot of boiling water?" He seemed to have read my thoughts and appeared to be a little shaken up as he tucked in his shirt.

I thought he would make us move from his beautiful house and land if I scalded him with the hot water. And who would believe me if I told what Mr. William Lea had done? I did not want to get punished for causing trouble. I quickly dismissed the thought.

I said, "I've got to kill a chicken and cook it for dinner before everybody gets back from the fields." Then I shoved more small logs into the side of the stove to keep the temperature constant.

Mr. William Lea went out the back door, and within a few minutes, he returned with a headless chicken. He handed the chicken to me, and without saying another word or looking at me, he left, walking in the direction of the tobacco barn. I had once thought Mr. William was a good man. Now I didn't know what to think or how I was supposed to feel around him.

Around one o'clock, everyone came in from the fields for dinner. I had a bucket of warm water and a small square of homemade lye soap sitting on an oblong wooden table near the kitchen window so everyone could wash his or her hands. Daddy washed his hands first and grabbed the kitchen curtains to dry them before I could stop him.

I screamed, "Wait a minute, Daddy! Don't use the curtains! I'll get a towel for you." I ran to a basket of unfolded linens in the hallway. I was too late. Daddy let go of the kitchen curtains just as I hung the towel on the nearby hook.

"Shit, gal," Daddy said, "that'll teach you to have a towel ready when we need one." Daddy walked into the dining room and sat at the table.

I was afraid to tell Mama the truth about the dirty curtains, but I wanted Daddy to rewash his hands.

"Mama, Daddy needs to wash his hands again. I don't think he should've used curtains to dry his hands; they're real dirty."

Mama shrugged and said, "You know to keep a clean towel on that hook so we can dry our hands. Ain't no need to complain about yo' daddy. You just have to wash the curtains."

I said nothing more about the curtains. Instead, I took a big bowl of gravy into the dining room.

A Head of Cabbage

"Gal, put another plate on the table. Mr. William is gonna eat dinner with us," Daddy said proudly.

I found another plate. It was cracked, chipped, and discolored. I put the faded plate at my spot on the table and put the unchipped plate where I thought Mr. William Lea would sit, near Daddy.

Mr. William Lea looked around the table at everyone as he filled his plate with fried chicken, a forkful of turnip greens, some mashed potatoes, and gravy. Then he moved down the table and sat next to me. He bit into the golden fried quarter of a chicken breast and looked toward Daddy.

"Yes sirree, Marilyn Ann sure is going to make some man a fine wife one day. Just look at these fat biscuits. Pass me one, please."

Daddy was pleased to hear such comments about me from Mr. William Lea. "Now, that's for sho'," Daddy said. "Nobody can beat my Maylyn making biscuits."

Mr. William Lea nodded and placed his left hand on my knee under the table. I got up and went into the kitchen to check on the apple pie in the oven. As I lifted the pie, I remembered I'd forgotten to add sugar. I motioned for Mama to come into the kitchen and told her the pie was not sweet. She tasted it.

"Oh, we'll just fix it right up. Give me two cups of sugar." Mama mixed butter, sugar, and cinnamon with some hot water; poured the mixture under the pie's crust; and set the pie back in the oven. She said, "That pie will be just fine, and no one will ever know what went on in this kitchen today." She giggled and gave me a nod.

I thought to myself, *No, they won't know.*

Several weeks went by without a visit from the landowner. I thought his fondling of me must have been over, and I didn't have to worry anymore about him, when I heard the front door screech open. I tensed up, thinking it was Mr. William Lea. I peeped around the kitchen door and saw his taller and much thinner son Frank coming in the front door.

Frank saw me peeping and said, "Boy, that was a long walk down here." Then he sat down in one of the dining room chairs.

I was relieved it was not his daddy, and for a moment, I almost told him how his daddy had been behaving toward me. But instead, I went back into the kitchen to check on the food. Frank followed me.

"You sure can cook for someone so young," he said as he took a piece of fried green tomato and popped it into his mouth.

I didn't pay him much attention. I wanted to make sure the food was on the table and ready to eat when everyone came in from the fields. Just as I set a pot of pinto beans in the middle of the table, Frank stepped behind me. He unzipped his pants and exposed his enormous penis. I looked at it in horror and shame. I wanted to scream and run out of the house, but I didn't because I saw Mama and Daddy coming back from the tobacco fields. They were about thirty yards from the porch, so I felt safe.

Frank said, "I just want you to rub it up and down a little bit for me," while pulling me back into the kitchen.

We stood in the middle of the kitchen floor, watching Mama, Daddy, and my siblings as they walked closer to the house. Frank rubbed his penis on my backside and massaged my small breasts.

I was scared that someone would see us and blame me for causing trouble. I didn't know what to do. I felt I would be in a pickle no matter what I did. Finally, I begged Frank to please go into the dining room and leave me alone. He said he would in a minute. I remained silent; tense; and, for a while, too scared to breathe. Then I heard Mama and Daddy talking, and so did Frank. Only then did he zip up his pants, and he calmly walked outside onto the porch just as Mama started up the steps. Sweat rolled down the sides of Frank's face.

He said, "Mrs. Nora, it sure is hot out today. Had I known it was this hot outside, I would have driven down here, but I needed that walk. Papa doesn't feel well, so I came to see if y'all needed anything." He pushed the screen door open for Mama.

Daddy was right behind Mama and wiped sweat with his shirttail. He spoke up. "Naw, we is all right for now," Daddy said, and he sidestepped Frank, went into the kitchen, and washed his hands.

Frank did not eat with us. Instead, he sat and watched *As the World Turns* while the rest of us ate dinner. While I ate, all I could think of was how to keep Mr. William Lea and his son from molesting me.

After my third encounter with Frank, I told Mama I didn't want to stay home and cook anymore. I preferred farmwork.

"Why do you want to work in the hot sun? Yo' face is messed up as it is," Mama said. "You is a stupid child, wanting to do field work."

A Head of Cabbage

I did feel stupid, but I didn't tell her the real reason. Instead, I held my head down, fearing my face might reveal the truth to her.

I said, "I'm tired of chopping wood, killing chickens, picking string beans, and digging potatoes. I want to learn how to pick and string tobacco like everyone else." I looked up at Mama and waited for her to hurl more insults.

Mama grunted. "I ain't never heard tell of anybody wanting to do field work. Go on and fix a jug of iced water. You is getting ready to see what real work is like." She threw her head back, put on her straw hat, and then said, "Huh, digging potatoes—that ain't no work."

Inez began to stay home to cook for everyone. Even though I was afraid Mr. William Lea and his son Frank might try to molest her, I remained silent because Al Jr., Mr. William Lea's grandson, was sweet on Inez. I felt that gave her an edge over their wayward behavior.

CHAPTER 16

BLANCHE

One hot Sunday night, Mr. James Raymond Smith brought my siblings Mildred, Inez, and Ronald Jr. and me home from the little Holiness Church we attended in Leasburg, North Carolina. Mama and Daddy seldom went to church, so Mr. James Raymond Smith was kind enough to pick us up and return us home.

We knew something was wrong as soon as Mr. James Raymond Smith pulled into our driveway. Our oldest sister's car was parked where Daddy's truck should have been. Usually, Blanche would have been home on a Sunday night, preparing for Monday's workday. She and her husband, Slim, also sharecropped.

When we walked into Mama's bedroom, which served as the family room, Blanche was sitting on Mama's bed with her face twisted to one side in a downward tilt, as though she had had a stroke. I went over and sat on the opposite side and saw two teeth protruding through her jaw. Her left eye was bruised and swollen shut. Blanche's children were asleep on our old, sunken sofa in the back of the room.

Mama came into the room with a wash pan of cold water and set it on the floor beside the bed. She took a good look at Blanche's bruised and swollen face and grimaced in anger.

"You married a dumb, mean-assed man. You need to leave Slim before he kills you," Mama said as she patted Blanche's eye with the wet cloth.

Blanche shrugged. "Mama, Slim is just jealous of me. He thinks I'm fooling around on him."

"And why does he think that?" Mama snapped. "I know how I raised you."

Blanche looked up at Mama. "He's the one fooling around, but I told him that if he hits me again, I am going to leave him for good."

Mama said, "Shit, when is that—after he kills you?" She gently dabbed ointment onto Blanche's bruises.

Just as the TV news went off, Slim knocked on the front door. Blanche looked scared and stayed close to Mama. Mama jerked the door open and grabbed Slim by his shirt collar, pulling him inside.

"Boy, don't you know there ain't a place on a female's body that's fit for a man to hit?" Mama's eyes rolled up and down over Slim, who stood still with his big hands in his pants pockets. He attempted to speak.

"Mrs. Nora, Blanche—"

Mama interrupted. "Mrs. Nora my ass! The next time you want to hit my child, you bring her home to me, and then you can get on 'bout yo' business. Just bring her where you got her from." Mama's lips quivered, and her forehead creased into a full frown before she said, "Do you hear me, boy?"

Slim flinched, nodded, and then said, "Mrs. Nora, Blanche made me beat her. She has another man. That ain't right. She is my wife."

Blanche stood silently behind Mama.

Mama said, "I don't care if she has another man, a dog, or a frog. You don't beat up on females, no matter what. You can leave her, or she can leave you, but menfolk don't go round beating up females."

Mama released Slim's collar and turned to Blanche. "Shit, Blanche, this boy is too stupid to understand that a man ain't supposed to hit a woman. Slim, you go back home. Blanche and the chillums is going to stay with us awhile." Then Mama shoved Slim out the front door.

"But she is my wife," Slim repeated as he walked off the porch, got into his friend's car, and left.

I cooked for fourteen people on the weekends after Blanche and her children moved home, and I didn't like it. So after I cooked, I lay down to rest. All of us couldn't eat at the same time, because we didn't have enough plates.

Whoever got to the table first ate first. After that, others ate what was left. Sometimes Mama took food off a person's plate if he or she took too much, and she put it back in the pot for those who ate last. Edward, the oldest child at home since Lenny went to New York, always wrapped his arms around his entire plate to prevent Mama from taking food off.

Blanche cooked dinner and supper for everyone for several weeks while the rest of us worked in the fields. Frank, the landowner's son, came to see if we needed anything almost every day. I felt his concern was just a ruse

A Head of Cabbage

to get close to Blanche. But Blanche seemed to be happy with him there. I always wondered if he had his way with her.

One night, just after sundown, Blanche's husband, Slim, returned to our house. Daddy, Edward, and Mildred were not home. He walked into the house and started looking around.

"Where is Blanche?" he asked, and I pointed upward. Slim walked upstairs to where Blanche and their children were.

Mama came running out of the kitchen, peeped through her bedroom window, and saw Slim's friend's car parked in the driveway. "Where is the scoundrel?" she asked.

I pointed upward again. Mama was about to have a fit. She mumbled as she headed for the stairs but stopped in the hallway and yelled.

"Slim, come down here—right now! You ain't got no right to be in my girls' room. Come on down here right now!" Mama paced the floor while she waited.

Slim hollered back, "I got a right to be where my wife is!"

"You is one ignorant scoundrel! What man is stupid enough to go into the girls' room. Ain't yo' daddy taught you manners? Don't you know anything 'bout respecting females? Menfolk is supposed to stay out of the females' room. And I ain't having it in my house. Now, you come on down here, and Blanche can come on down with you if she wants to."

After a few minutes, Slim and Blanche came down the stairs with their three children and left in their old white Chevrolet.

The next evening, Frank, the landowner's son, visited to see if we needed anything. I noticed him looking around the room. I sat close to Mama and watched Daddy as he wrapped the silver lining from a pack of cigarettes around the blown TV tube. Then Daddy reinserted the tube into the back of the TV, and it started working.

Daddy grinned. "Everybody don't know how to do that."

Frank walked over to the TV and inspected it. "You figured out how to get the picture back? I thought you would have to buy a new TV once the tube was shot."

Daddy said, "See? Everybody knows something." He then left in his truck just as *Tarzan* was going off.

Frank turned to Mama. "Where are Blanche and her children?"

Mama answered without taking her eyes off the TV. "She went back to her dumbass husband."

Frank seemed disappointed and said, "I can't believe she did that. Why did she do that?"

Mama threw up her hands in frustration and said, "I don't know why. I guess Slim done knocked out all of her senses."

CHAPTER 17

WE GOT TO RUN

One weekday afternoon late in August 1963, just before school started, Mildred and I were returning home from Mrs. Flora's. Mama had sent us to get some butter from her. We were about a mile from home, when we saw a black Chevrolet truck blaring down the narrow gravel road. It came to a skidding halt a few yards in front of us. Dust and gravel flew high into the air, and a flock of birds took flight from the nearby pine trees.

We both tensed up as we watched a tall, thin man jump out of his truck. He ran to the right, to an old, dilapidated tobacco barn surrounded by lots of trees and a variety of tall, thick drying weeds. Wild plum trees loaded with ripe fruit entwined with honeysuckle vines. Their sweet aroma permeated the air like a splash of gardenia water.

Mildred looked toward the man. Her nostrils flared out like those of a frightened animal. She increased her pace, and I did the same. Mildred looked over at me but didn't speak right away.

I looked at the man standing in front of the falling, lopsided barn as he fumbled with the front of his pants.

At first, the man yelled vulgarities at us, and then he politely said, "Hey, you girls, y'all come down here with me for a few minutes."

I looked at the man and then at Mildred, and I said, "That white man is gonna pee in front of us."

"He don't want to pee, Marilyn," Mildred said nervously.

She glanced at the man again and gasped, raising a hand to her mouth. Then, in a rushed, authoritative voice, she said, "Don't look at him; look straight ahead." But I turned my head and looked anyway.

Both Mildred and I saw the stranger as he stepped out of his pants. "He's naked!" I shrieked.

"Marilyn, I told you not to look at that man. Don't look at him anymore." As Mildred admonished me, the man started to hurl vulgarities at us again.

"Hey, come down here, and give me some pussy right now!" the man yelled. "You hear me? Come down here right now."

"Dog foot it!" Mildred said, using words Daddy and Mama used when things were not going their way. "You'd better do what I say, and I mean it. We got to run!" She grabbed my hand, and we started running toward our house. "Don't let go of my hand, no matter what," Mildred said as we picked up the pace.

I looked back after a few minutes and saw the man fully clothed, running toward his truck. "He's going to run over us," I said to Mildred as my twelve-year-old legs began feeling like lead.

Mildred scolded me. "Didn't I tell you not to look at that man? Don't look at him again. Just run with me."

I heard the roar of the truck's engine. I felt as if we were running in slow motion. My chest and rib cage ached and burned as if an explosion had occurred. My stomach was in knots as I gulped in as much air as I could. But I could feel my legs slowing down.

Between gasping breaths, Mildred said, "He has to go up the road to turn his truck around. That will give us a chance to get home. We will make it!"

Small pieces of gravel had gotten in my shoes, and I stopped running.

"Wait," I said to Mildred as I tried to dislodge the pebbles.

She jerked me along and said, "I've got rocks in my shoes too, but we can't stop!"

"Please, can't we rest for just a minute? I asked, panting for breath. I barely had any strength left.

Mildred sucked in air with every word. "We can't rest, Marilyn. He will get us if we do!" Then, finally, she spotted the top of our nearest neighbors' house through the tall pines about fifty yards away. We continued to run before collapsing onto the bank of Colemans' front yard just as the black truck sped by.

We had not seen the man up close, but we knew he was white, tall, and thin.

We told the neighbors what had happened, and after we rested for a short while, we continued home. We found Mama, Daddy, Edward, and Frank sitting on our front porch. Mildred told what had happened.

"A white man in a black truck with Virginia license plates tried to get

A Head of Cabbage

us. We had to run fast to get away from him. We made it to the Colemans' yard just in time before he drove past us."

Without saying a word, Edward and Frank eased inside the house. A short while later, they returned with two rifles.

"Mrs. Nora"—Frank spoke to Mama but looked at Mildred and me—"we're going to find that cracker and teach him a lesson."

They headed toward Frank's blue-and-white Chevrolet convertible. Edward looked back and yelled, "That's right! We gonna teach that white man some manners."

I sat on the porch and didn't say anything, but I wondered who would teach Frank and his daddy a lesson for molesting me. I thought it was a good time to tell Mama and Daddy about them, but I didn't. I was still scared that Mama would blame me and afraid we would move.

Daddy stood up and walked over to Frank and Edward. He got between them and put his arms across their shoulders. He shook his head and said, "Naw, y'all wait a minute 'fore y'all do somethin' that will make things worse. The law ain't gonna do nothin' 'cause the man is white. And if y'all do somethin', then the law is coming for y'all. So the best thing to do is nothin'. This way, everybody in the neighborhood won't know 'bout it, and everybody stays alive."

Mama nodded in agreement with Daddy. Frank nodded too, but he placed his rifle on the backseat. Edward did the same and jumped into the front passenger side. They told Daddy they were going for a bit of a ride.

Sometime before midnight, as we sat in the family room, watching TV, a car door slammed, and Edward walked in.

"We ain't seen no white man in a black Chevrolet truck," he said scornfully as he set both rifles in a corner in the back of the room.

Edward came near me. "Marilyn, is you sure that truck was black?"

I nodded and then, as usual, got up to give him my seat. Edward looked at Mildred.

"It was a black truck, and the man was white," Mildred said while watching television.

"That man shook his thang up and down at us," I said, and I watched everyone in the room become silent and turn his or her head toward me in apparent shock. No one said a word, and I knew I had said too much.

Edward stared at me with beady dark eyes. "And I suppose you stood right there and watched this white man shake his thang. Marilyn, you're in the sixth grade. You should know better. Did y'all enjoy looking at this white man's thang?"

Mildred and I both shook our heads.

Edward looked over at Mildred. "Y'all best stay away from white people, especially the white men. When you see 'em, get away from 'em fast, because they're mean people, and the law won't do nothing with them when they do bad stuff." He poked a finger at our faces. "Do y'all hear me?"

I looked at Mildred and waited for a clue from her. She looked at Mama. Mama nodded, Mildred nodded, and then I nodded.

On Sunday, the next day, no one mentioned the incident, but I felt ashamed, as though Mildred and I had done something wrong. After Sunday night supper, Daddy slammed his tin plate up and down on the cast-iron heater over and over. Mama eased it out of his hand and massaged his back for a little while. Finally, she gave us the eye, and we left the room.

"The girls is OK," I heard Mama say, and when I looked back at Daddy, he was turning up a jar of moonshine.

CHAPTER 18

PICK THE POOR ROBIN CLEAN

Mr. William Lea came down to visit on November 23, 1963, the day after President John F. Kennedy's assassination. He and Mama sat in front of our small black-and-white TV, talking about President Kennedy's assassination as though they were personal friends.

"Well, the nation sure has been set back a piece. Poor colored folks won't get an even break for another hundred years now," Mr. William Lea said, and Mama nodded.

Daddy came home later that evening, imitating the sound of Tarzan's bellowing voice. He staggered up onto the porch, and Mama helped him inside the house. I brought Daddy's food on his tin plate. He ate while listening to the news about the assassination.

Daddy swallowed hard and said, "Well, he done picked the president's robin clean."

Mr. William Lea looked confused, turned toward Mama, and asked, "What does he mean?"

"He means they done killed the president," Mama said.

After a few more minutes of listening to the news, Mr. William Lea got his hat to leave. Daddy set his empty plate on the floor beside his chair.

"It wasn't nobody but Mr. Hoover," Daddy said. "He's gonna pick some mo' robins clean 'fore it's all over. Y'all will see."

"Hoover?" Mr. William Lea stopped in his tracks, looked back, and rubbed his overgrown brow. "Well, Hoover is the most powerful man in the world."

Daddy started to sing after Mr. William left: "Pick the poor robin clean. They picked his head. They picked his feet. They would've picked his ass, but it ain't fit to eat."

Mama repeated the lyrics slowly. "Pick the poor robin clean."

I thought she would start to cry at any moment. I didn't want to see that, so I ran upstairs and began to pray. *Dear God, please let poor colored folks get an even break, and don't let the Hoover man pick any more robins clean. Amen.*

Twelve months after President Kennedy's assassination, we were still sharecropping and living on Mr. William Lea's land, except for Mildred, who had quit school and gotten married.

Each time a sibling quit school, I got scared that the same thing would happen to me. When I went to Sunday school and church, I prayed and asked God to help me finish high school. That was the main reason I went to church—so God would help me with my needs. I had faith that God loved me and could do what no one else could do. I fully believed God had sent someone to give me the exact pair of shoes I needed for the May Day Festival when Daddy couldn't get them for me. So when I got scared about anything, I would pray fervently until my fears subsided.

The first Sunday in November 1964 was harrowing. As I got dressed for Sunday school and church, I saw the sheriff's car pull into our driveway. I knew that meant trouble, and that scared me. But as I started down the steps, I thought of Mrs. Flora telling me once that the smile of a child could brighten the worst day. So I forced myself to smile as I walked into Mama and Daddy's bedroom, which served as the family room because it had a sofa and TV.

Mama looked as though she had been crying. She stood near the door and dabbed her eyes with the palm of her hand while Daddy buttoned his best shirt. The big white sheriff stood near the warm cast-iron heater with his brown hat in hand. I made sure Mama saw my smile.

"Marilyn, I don't want to see any teeth this morning, and here you come, grinning like the Cheshire Cat. Yo' brother Edward is down in Duke Hospital, all broken up. We don't know if he's dead or alive. The sheriff here just told us they think his neck is broken." Mama dabbed her eyes twice more and said, "Now, take that silly grin off yo' face."

Mama and all my siblings had heard me wish death on Edward many times after he beat me for some reason. Now I felt guilty and afraid that he might die or was already dead. I didn't want to see Mama cry, so I looked her in the face and said, "Edward is gonna be OK, Mama. He ain't gonna die."

A Head of Cabbage

"Do you know of anybody living with a broken neck?" Mama snapped.

I recoiled into the hallway and said nothing more as I watched Mama, Daddy, and the sheriff walk out the front door. After that, I didn't go to church. I mostly stayed upstairs and prayed for Edward.

After two months, Edward came home wholly paralyzed on his left side. His body from his head to the lower part of his abdomen was in a cast. He looked like a mummy lying in bed with only his eyes, nostrils, ears, and mouth exposed.

Frank came daily to visit Edward. He even apologized to Mama for Edward's accident.

"Mrs. Nora, I'm so sorry I didn't take Edward with me that night. The one time we decided not to double-date, Edward got caught up with a group of youngsters and got himself all broken up."

Frank shook his head and then began to rub his temples as though he had a headache. Edward waved from the bed with his right hand.

"Ah man, at least I'm still alive, but I thought I was dead. I could hear, but I couldn't move or speak. The sheriff kicked me and said I was dead. I was trying to say something, but I couldn't."

I stood in the back of the room, quietly observing but mostly afraid Edward would say something mean to me if I got too close to him.

Mama saw me and said, "Don't you have somethin' to say to yo' brother? You is standing over there like a deaf-mute."

I walked over to Edward's bed and stared at him, but neither of us spoke. Edward smiled at me, and I thought that meant he forgave me. Mama gestured with her hands for me to say something.

I said, "You'll be all right. You will walk again."

Edward stopped smiling and closed his eyes as if he didn't believe me. But Mama smiled, which made me feel that she approved of my words to Edward.

While Edward was convalescing, his girlfriend, Molly, came weekly to visit, and then her visits became further apart. Finally, one Saturday morning, she brought a baby with her, and Edward beamed with joy for a few minutes. He held the baby proudly and announced the baby was his son.

But that same afternoon, Edward was deeply depressed. He repeatedly complained that he was crippled and couldn't take care of his child.

He sounded so pitiful that I tried to bargain with God: *God, if you allow Edward to be healed and walk again, I won't ever do anything to anger my brother again, and I will follow the Ten Commandments.*

After several months of intensive physical therapy, Edward began to walk again with a cane, and Mama told me I should smile more often, but I couldn't. I didn't want her to think I grinned like the Cheshire Cat.

CHAPTER 19

LIVE OFF THE LAND

It was October 1966. I was fifteen and in a state of panic because I would have to stay out of school even more. Mama broke the news to me as if it were no big deal.

"Yo' sister Inez is gonna get married to that Farrington boy today," she said before looking into the dresser mirror to apply bright red lipstick to her lips. Mama turned her head from side to side, deliberately making her upturned hair bounce. "Marilyn, you can close yo' mouth and take that shit-assed frown off yo' face. You look better when you smile."

I knew Inez's share of the housework and field work would shift to me.

"Mama, Inez is only seventeen—why are you letting her get married? She ain't finished high school yet."

"She's getting married because she thinks she's grown and ready for her own family. That's why."

I stood at the window and watched them leave. I felt jealous and abandoned. Blanche, Mildred, and Inez had gotten away from Daddy's drunkenness and field work. I had not.

In late November, we moved again to a farm that belonged to Mr. William Lea's older son, LaFayette Lea. This farm, located in Blanch, North Carolina, was in another small, rural farming community. It was about twelve miles from Leasburg and about ten miles south of Danville, Virginia. It had a post office, a general store, and several churches.

The day we moved in, I was pleasantly surprised. The house was the most beautiful one we had ever lived in. It had two stories, with double front doors, a winding staircase, seven large rooms, and six fireplaces. The windows in each room had white wooden plantation blinds, except for the living room, which had pink ones.

There were two porches. One in the rear wrapped around the back and the side. The other one ran the entire length of the house, and a large white swing hung down from the ceiling. The house had five exit doors.

We could go out one exit and reenter the house in thirty seconds through another entrance, which I thought was amusing, until I found out why. Mama said there were four back doors for former slaves. They were never allowed to enter through the front door.

The day after we moved in, Daddy got around to telling us that we had a few more acres of tobacco to plant. Indeed, Daddy had gone mad, taking on more acreage without Lenny, Edward, Mildred, or Inez to help. I thought of all the field work I would have to do and felt tired.

One good thing about our move was that Ronald Jr. now had a tractor to help break and cultivate the land. However, Ronald Jr. seldom went to school and was becoming more frustrated. I was afraid he would quit school and leave home.

Early one day in May, Ronald Jr. and I sneaked off to school during tobacco-planting time, leaving Mama, Levi, and William Winston to help Daddy in the fields. After my first class, I heard Ronald Jr.'s and my names over the intercom. I knew Daddy had sent Mama to bring us back home.

Once we were in the truck, Mama said, "Y'all know yo' daddy needed you to help in the fields today. What was y'all thinking, sneaking off to school? This better be the last time you sneak to that schoolhouse, making me come up here and get you. You had yo' daddy thinkin' y'all was in the field, working, and here y'all are in school."

Ronald Jr. remained quiet, but I said, "We just want to finish high school. We don't want to work on a farm when we get grown." I coughed a few times from Mama's puffs of smoke and then said, "We need an education."

Mama rolled her eyes at me. "Y'all got to do what yo' daddy tells you to do. He can't raise this 'bacco crop all by himself."

I squirmed in my seat, wanting to say more, even though I knew I would get in trouble.

Finally, I said, "Mama, Daddy is ruining our lives. He makes us stay out of school too much. He has already caused Lenny, Edward, Mildred, and Inez to quit school because they missed too many days to pass to the next level. They ain't dumb. They just wanted to get away from farming for nothing."

I looked over at Ronald Jr. for support, but he remained silent, as if in deep thought. I was desperate for Mama to look beyond today and envision

A Head of Cabbage

a better tomorrow for us. I had to make sure my future was different from theirs. I was scared Ronald Jr. would quit school and go to New York with Lenny, leaving me, the oldest child, at home to help Daddy on the farm.

"Now, that's about all the mouth I'm gonna take from yo' ass today," Mama said when we reached home.

We stayed out of school for several days and worked in the tobacco fields. I marked an *X* in my notebook for each day absent. I read a chapter of each subject in an effort not to get behind. That type of prestudy worked pretty well for me—except when the teacher skipped several chapters and I faced an unexpected pop quiz or test when I returned to school.

One night, after supper, I sat on the floor next to Daddy, who was engrossed in *Wagon Train*. He was lit but not too drunk.

"My teacher said that things were gonna get better for colored people, and Reverend Martin Luther King Jr. was gonna see to it, but we've got to be educated."

Daddy cussed and said, "Education ain't shit for colored folks, and the only thing Reverend King is gonna do is make these mean-assed white people meaner. He ain't but one man, so don't be thinkin' 'bout things getting that much better."

Daddy coughed for a minute and then said, "You better be learning how to grow yo' own food and get some land one day, so you can always eat. Everybody thought Kennedy was gonna make things better for colored folks. You saw they picked his robin clean. The farm is where you need to be, gal. You can live off the land."

Daddy lit a homemade cigarette and gently shook his head, looking down at me. "Dr. King's ass is gonna cause a heap of trouble for himself and everybody else."

I looked over at Mama, who was hand-stitching one of her patchwork quilts. She didn't say anything, but a wry smile radiated across her face. I felt she agreed with Daddy. I began to think of Daddy as being smart, and I gave him my full attention.

"Daddy, if we raise pigs to sell, do we have to give half the profits to Mr. LaFayette?"

"Naw, my pigs, my money," he said without batting an eye.

"If we raise a few cows and chickens to sell each year, do we have to give half the profits to Mr. LaFayette?"

"My cows, my chickens, my money," he said, and he waved his fists like the fighting cowboys on TV.

I was so excited I jumped up from the floor. "Daddy," I said, "we can get rich living right here. We can live on this land for a while. There's a creek for the pigs and cows to drink water. All we need to do is fence in more of the land; get more chickens, pigs, and cows; and, once or twice a year, sell them. We can save the money—and buy our own land!"

I thought of us owning a farm again and saw Daddy's eyes beam with excitement. He scratched his belly, yawned, and then looked at me.

Daddy said, "You 'bout the smartest child I got. Is you gonna fence in the land?"

"Naw, I ain't gonna fence it in; I'm a girl," I said, disgusted with Daddy's lack of determination.

Daddy said slowly, "Shit. You should've been a boy." His jaw dropped, and the excited look on his face quickly faded. Then he said, "You sure is gonna make some man rich, though, if he can stand yo' mouth."

"Daddy, we can get rich right here," I said again. "I can help, but I can't do it all by myself." I wanted Daddy to see the dream I had of us getting on our feet.

Daddy shook his head and walked over to change the TV. "Girls get married and go with their husbands. All yo' sisters got married and left home."

I said, "I ain't getting married. I'm going to college."

Daddy turned around and looked back at me. "Yo' ass can't go to no college, Maylyn. How many times do I have to tell you that?"

Fear crept in as I thought of my six older siblings. Not one had graduated high school. Several of my cousins had finished high school, though, and that gave me hope.

I raised a finger in the air. "First, I have to finish high school." I raised a second finger. "Then God will help me go to college."

Daddy chuckled sarcastically and looked up at the ceiling. "Is God gonna pay for you to go to college?"

CHAPTER 20

GOD AIN'T HELPING

My worst fear came to pass. Ronald quit high school in the eleventh grade and was soon drafted by the army, leaving me the oldest child at home to work in the fields with Daddy.

Daddy tried to teach me how to drive the tractor about four times, when something in my gut told me not to learn menfolk's work. I thought Daddy would make me quit school if I knew how to turn over the land with the tractor and do the work that Ronald Jr. previously had done. So the last time he took me out on the tractor, I purposely drove into a grove of small pine trees. Daddy took the wheel and steered the tractor to a clearing a few feet from the trampled trees. He was angry.

"Shit, Maylyn!" he yelled. "I is trying to teach yo' ass somethin'." Daddy jumped down off the tractor and stood under a large tulip poplar tree in the shade.

I climbed down off the tractor and stood a few feet from him.

"You ain't no Miss Ann. You got to learn how to drive this here tractor, so you can take care of yo'self, so you can always eat." Daddy jerked his head around and spat on the ground. "These shit-assed white men in this world won't let you get but so far. They be sure to undermine you somehow."

I stood still and stared into Daddy's face for a few seconds before I spoke. "I'm a girl. I ain't supposed to do men's work. And I don't want to farm when I get grown. I want to finish high school and go to college."

Daddy wiped the sweat from his face. "You can't always do what you wanna do. Even the president can't do what he wants to do. You saw they picked President Kennedy's robin clean, and he was white and rich. It don't matter if you educated or not. Somethin' is wrong wit' white folks, and they gonna take it out on you."

I listened to Daddy talk. But I wanted to hit him in the mouth. I thought he spoke like a coward when he told me not to pursue my dreams from fear of white men's power to place obstacles in my path.

I looked him in his face and said, "I just have to try something different, and I need an education for that. White men may act like they got power to do anything they want to, but they ain't God. And God will help me finish high school and go to college."

"Shit! God?" Daddy rolled his eyes upward and sarcastically said, "God is gonna help? Seems like to me white men done invented God for them. You better listen to me, Maylyn." Daddy lowered his voice as he bent over and placed both hands on his knees. He appeared to be in pain and grunted a few times. Then he said, "The best we can do, gal, is stay on the land and farm, so we can raise our food."

I wanted Daddy to encourage me to go to college and be whatever my brains would allow, but he didn't understand what an education could do for his children.

"Daddy," I said, "I just want to finish high school and go to college. After that, God will do the rest. I ain't scared of white people. I don't think they are waiting to ambush all of my dreams and ambitions."

The frown on his face morphed into a grimace, and the anger I felt changed to pity. Daddy shook his head and grunted several more times after straightening up his body, but he held one arm across his gut as if still in pain. Then he pointed a finger at me.

"One of these days, yo' ass will see how white folks keep you down and poor, education or no education. You will see. They ain't gonna give yo' ass a job, and they gonna undermine you every chance they get. They do what they can to keep colored folks down on luck. All of 'em do that. You pay attention to what I say." Daddy coughed a few times and spat onto the ground but kept talking. "And if they do give yo' ass a job, you have to work three times as hard and make a whole lot less. Yo' ass gonna have to be near genius just to work with a bunch of white-ass morons."

I could hardly stand to watch Daddy talk with such a defeatist attitude.

"God will help me," I said defiantly.

"Shit. Talking 'bout God gonna help. God ain't helping. Everything ain't in them shit-assed books you always reading—and don't talk to me 'bout the Bible. The Bible don't tell you how to deal with mean-assed, uncivilized white folks. You can go round thinkin' you gonna be that and

A Head of Cabbage

do this if you want to, but you'll soon see yo' ass being blocked every way you turn. Now, I'm telling you what I know. If Jesus could crawl down from the cross, he would tell you the same thing." Daddy squeezed his stomach and grunted some more. Finally, he said, "Shit, gal, my stomach is acting up." We got back on the tractor, and I drove us home.

That night at supper, Daddy told Mama that I'd almost torn up the tractor and that I thought I was Miss Ann, and he asked her to have a talk with me. He lit two cigarettes and gave one to Mama, who took a puff and then turned toward me.

"Marilyn, the way you always crying 'bout going to school—don't you know nothin'? White folks try to make sure we colored folks don't have as good a life as they have. They have the power to control what we get out of life and what we do in life. It pleases them to see us with a bunch of chillums to work on their farms and in their houses and mills for pennies. They want all of us colored folks to be poorer than the poorest white person." Mama looked over at Daddy.

He nodded. "Now, that's right, gal," Daddy said. "You should see some of their faces when I pull up at the gas station in my brand-new truck. Boy, I tell you." He chuckled. "They sho' hate to see me coming."

I looked toward Daddy and said to myself, *That's because they know your children are hungry, and you're keeping us out of school to work on the farm while you ride around getting drunk and showing off your new truck.*

"He is right about that," Mama said. She then lowered her voice, leaned closer to Daddy, and added, "Course, not all white folks are like that, just most of 'em. When I worked for the Jews in New York—" She cut her eyes toward Daddy. "Ah, you know, they is better than regular ole white folks." She gave the cigarette one last draw and then extinguished it in her plate. "But even some of the Jews are like that. One evening, Mrs. Meredith placed a twenty-dollar bill on a dresser in her guest room. The next morning, she ran into my room way down the hall, screaming, 'Nora, Nora, I'm missing twenty dollars! Have you seen it?'"

Mama giggled, and Daddy nodded with a raised brow.

"I told her it was still where she put it, on top of that dresser. She was trying to tempt me, to see if I would become a thief for twenty dollars." Mama threw her hands up in the air. "Twenty dollars was a lot of money back then, but had I even touched it, I would have been fired. Some of 'em do set traps for you."

Daddy interjected. "I think white folks enjoy seeing colored people suffer. They do everythin' they can against you to keep you from getting ahead. Keep living, and you'll see. You can take that to the bank. It happens to all colored people, one way or another—college-educated or dumb as a bucket of water, it will happen just the same, all in good time."

I sat at the supper table and watched Mama look at Daddy admiringly as if he had just informed me of the Eleventh Commandment.

"Well," I said, "before the white folks start swarming and circling around me like a group of vultures, waiting to snatch my dreams and ambition away, I think you ought to make sure I finish high school."

Several weeks went by, and early one cool weekday morning, I saw my baby brother, William Winston, as he struggled to carry a large slop bucket to feed the hogs before we left for the tobacco field. I had just returned from feeding the chickens.

William Winston was eleven years old and small for his age, but he was proud to be responsible for feeding the hogs each day. He lugged the five-gallon slop bucket toward the hog pen.

Daddy stood at the woodpile, watching. When he saw slop being wasted on the ground, he rushed toward William Winston and yelled, "I ought to take that slop bucket and hit you upside yo' head! Maybe that will knock some sense into you. You is wasting too much on the ground." Daddy's arms flailed in the air as he looked up at the sky. "Lord, why do I have such dumb chillums? Shit, shit, shit!"

Daddy stormed back to the house in an angry fit, murmuring something I couldn't hear. I stopped next to William Winston to help him carry the slop bucket to the hog pen. I was thankful Daddy had not said anything to me, but William Winston looked scared and crestfallen. As tears ran down his face, he continued to lug the slop bucket toward the hog pen inch by inch, careful not to splash any more over the rim.

"William Winston, I'll help you carry the slop bucket," I said, empathizing with him.

"Naw, Marilyn, this is menfolk's work," William Winston said. "You go on back into the house." Then he stopped, looked back at me, and asked, "Marilyn, what did I do to deserve that kind of talk from Daddy?"

A Head of Cabbage

He had the saddest look on his face as tears rolled down his cheeks. It broke my heart to see him in such distress. I wanted to comfort William Winston, but I didn't know what to do.

"It's OK," I said. "Daddy don't know any better."

CHAPTER 21

IT'S OUR RESPONSIBILITY

On April 4, 1968, Caswell County Training School, my all-black high school, was in a painful, angry uproar because of Dr. Martin Luther King Jr.'s assassination. Teachers and students alike cried as they tried to comfort one another. Just about everyone appeared to be in shock. Some male students walked up and down the hallway, talking loudly about what they wanted to do. They spoke of revenge to make white people feel the kind of pain we felt.

Our principal, Mr. Dillard, was out of town. The assistant principal was Mrs. Greene, a petite middle-aged woman who always dressed well and frequently wore green. She cried along with us and appeared to be in a state of panic but had the presence of mind to stop us from marching in the streets. She told us that others were hoping we would march so they would have an excuse to shoot us down like rabbits.

Mrs. Greene called an assembly and quickly arranged a memorial service to be held the next day in honor of Dr. King. She asked us to write poems, essays, and songs to honor him. Most of us returned to our classrooms and worked on our part of the program.

During the memorial service the next day, Mr. Dillard returned unexpectedly. As he made his way down the aisle, touching students' shoulders and squeezing hands, he tried to console as many as he could.

Mr. Dillard, who always dressed in a suit, was of small stature, with short gray hair and wrinkled, dusty-looking dark skin. He would not have been considered handsome, but his face and demeanor exuded confidence and respect. He walked onto the stage and waved to the noisy auditorium. Everyone stood up and clapped for a few minutes. When Mr. Dillard lowered his hand, we sat down. Everyone was quiet, except for a few monitors who walked up and down the aisle, passing paper towels to students unable to control their muffled cries.

"Today, not everyone is mourning the death of this nonviolent man, and that too is a tragedy," Mr. Dillard said. "Change is coming, and I want you to be alive and ready when it takes place. Education and good behavior are the keys to change—not riotous marching in the streets. Our community needs a commitment from each of you today to become teachers, nurses, doctors, builders, lawyers, politicians, and scholars. Develop your talents, and become the best person you can be. Question this country's failure to live up to the Constitution, but do it peacefully." He paused for a moment.

I was sitting in the center of the third row, writing his words down as fast as I could to tell Daddy what Mr. Dillard said.

He continued. "Each of you should help with the solution. Revenge, hate, fear, unlawful behavior, and ignorance will not and cannot be a party to the solution."

Mr. Dillard summoned a sniffling boy from behind the curtains and said, "I just want to save you from yourselves, from harm. Dr. King's dream will live on in you and the children and grandchildren you will have someday. Cry if you must, but remember that progress will not stop. It has just begun. These classes of 1968, 1969, 1970, and so on will make history one day. I too am sad, but I am not worried about our future."

I wiped my eyes and continued to write notes on Mr. Dillard's speech, thinking that I would make history in my family if I could graduate high school.

Mr. Dillard took in a deep breath as though he were tired. Then, for a few seconds, he didn't say anything. I was afraid he would start to cry like the rest of us.

Then he exhaled and said, "I have faith that each of you will stay calm and peaceful. Go directly home, and don't cause your parents more grief. Your hearts and minds are in the right place, but strive to make this world better for your family, your community, and your country."

Someone seated a few rows behind me yelled, "This country needs to be burned down to the ground!"

I didn't turn around. I kept my eyes on Mr. Dillard. From across the aisle, someone else yelled, "Burn it! Burn this baby down!"

A Head of Cabbage

Mr. Dillard raised his left hand, and the outbursts ceased. "We must make this world a better place. It's our responsibility to show the world how barbarically some of our fellow American citizens behave. It's our responsibility to show them their error in the treatment of our people. It's our responsibility to show them how damaged a people they are to sit quietly while all kinds of atrocities happen in this land. That's how you honor the man of peace Dr. Martin Luther King Jr."

Mr. Dillard spoke slowly, as if in slow motion. "Go out into this world, and make it a better place. Do it through thought, education, and peaceful action. Make a difference."

I jotted down a few more notes. Then my friends and I huddled together and cried.

When I got home, Daddy and Mama sat mesmerized in front of our small black-and-white TV, watching riots and newscasters talking about Dr. King's assassination. Daddy appeared to be quite upset. He looked over at me as soon as I walked into the den.

"Well, Maylyn, looks like Hoover done picked another robin clean."

Daddy made it clear that he thought FBI director J. Edgar Hoover had orchestrated the deaths of President Kennedy and Reverend Martin Luther King Jr.

I said, "Yeah, Daddy, he did, but he didn't stop progress. Education is the key for us, and that's how we are going to honor Dr. King."

Daddy held his head down.

For the next several days, the TV news all over the country was full of images of burning buildings, people looting, and police officers in the streets. Every time Daddy said something about looting and rioting, I repeated Mr. Dillard's words: "Someone needs to tell them that education is the key. Become educated; don't become thieves and criminals. That's how we are to honor Dr. King."

My redheaded eleventh-grade English teacher, Miss Peony, also tried to help us vent our frustration and anger while at school. She asked us to write an essay about what black power meant to us, since that had become the talk at school.

Over the weekend, I wrote and revised my essay. Then I read it to Daddy.

"Ah, shit, gal," Daddy said. "Change it to say black power is the white man's greatest fear. They scared we're going to treat them somehow like they been treating us."

I didn't revise my essay. Instead, I washed my hair so that it would puff up in its natural state.

On Monday, when I went to English class, I was the first to give my essay to Miss Peony. She rolled her eyes at me, obviously displeased with my new Afro hairdo. I returned to my seat and sat as she began to read it. She showed her contempt for the essay every few seconds by making grunting sounds and twisting her lips to one side. Finally, she leaned forward and glared directly at me.

"When I ask you to write an essay, I want your thoughts, not thoughts written by some loudmouthed militant that you copied from some magazine."

Miss Peony dropped the paper onto her desk and jerked her head back as if my essay were poison. After a few tense seconds, she rolled her big eyes over the entire class. Miss Peony picked up the paper and started to read it a second time—this time aloud to the whole class.

"Black power is having a positive self-image. It is being a visionary to plan and execute strategies to aid in the successful outcome of black people. The mission of black power is to foster an attitude in all black people to graduate high school and college and to start businesses. It means having pride in the black race for the accomplishments we have made thus far. Power is not new. The word *black* is added to symbolize black people's struggle to be made whole citizens so that we may live our lives without fear and with justice and peace."

She paused, grunted several times, and then looked up at the class with a scowl on her face. Each time she groaned, I wanted to scream at her until she understood that we had to improve our station in life instead of waiting for white people to validate and sanction our existence and rights as human beings. I wanted to tell her that I hated her for not having pride in being black, with her hair dyed red, imitating Lucille Ball. I thought she was a sorry teacher for not valuing my thoughts and for making the class think I'd copied my essay from a magazine, when I had not.

My jaw tightened. I told myself to stay calm, or I might do something foolish and get expelled from school. I rolled my eyes at Miss Peony and then gazed over my classmates' faces. The boys appeared interested and listened intently as Miss Peony continued reading.

"People who believe in black power develop good character in their children. They are honest, fair, and courageous. Any black person who does not understand the need for black power needs a psychiatrist to help him or her deal with this hostile environment and racism. A psychiatrist can possibly help black men understand and deal with self-hatred for not being able to provide for their families and protect them from all kinds of real and imagined atrocities, past and present. Black power is part of the American dream."

Miss Peony got her red pen and made a considerable mark on my paper as she grunted for about the fifth or sixth time. She said, "Huh. Marilyn Abbott, come get your paper, and write another one. How dare you tell people they need a psychiatrist just because they're colored?"

On my way back to my seat, a couple of the boys gave me the black power sign: a raised balled fist. They said nothing, but I felt their empathy. When I sat down, I opened my paper and found a great big red *F*.

That evening, when I got home, I waited anxiously in the den for Daddy. I hoped he would be sober or, if not, at least in a good mood.

Around ten thirty, I heard Daddy's truck turn into the driveway, and shortly after that, he staggered into the house.

"Daddy, what do you think about the schools being integrated next year?" I asked as I handed him a plate of food.

"It ain't gonna make no difference for white folks, but it'll set black chillums back a piece. The white teachers ain't gonna try to teach y'all, and they gonna find a slew of reasons to rid y'all out of that shit-ass schoolhouse."

Daddy's words scared me. I frowned as I watched him bite into a piece of fried chicken. "We still have some black teachers. They'll be fair to us," I said.

"Shit, the black-ass teachers gonna be like Uncle Toms to the white kids and treat the black kids mean as hell." Daddy looked up at me and said, "They ain't gonna want to teach y'all either."

Daddy gnawed the gristle off the chicken leg and then set the plate on the floor beside him. Then, after lighting a cigarette, he looked up at me and said, "Black folks need to farm the land, so they can eat and have a place to lay their head."

CHAPTER 22

I NEED ANOTHER MIRACLE

One afternoon, Mrs. Parks, my eleventh-grade history teacher, asked me to remain in her classroom while the other students were hurrying out to catch their buses.

"Marilyn, I've noticed that you take a lot of books home from the library. Does your family have a set of encyclopedias?"

"No, ma'am," I answered timidly. Then I proudly added, "We do have a couple of Bibles."

Mrs. Parks stood up from her desk and began buttoning the pink-and-gray jacket that matched her gray skirt. She looked me up and down, and judging by the expression on her face, I knew I did not meet her standard of dress. Finally, she walked up close to me and retied the bow on my blouse.

"There. That's better," she said.

I glanced down at her shiny black pumps. Her beautifully manicured fingernails, rouge, and red lipstick sealed her look of sophistication. Mrs. Parks looked as if she could have modeled for Sears, Roebuck, and Company. She had her jet-black hair pulled back in a neat bun. I wanted Mama and myself to look like her.

Mrs. Parks said, "Marilyn, I can arrange for your family to have a set of encyclopedias and burial insurance. I will take you home this afternoon and talk with your parents. Is that all right?"

I was excited about the prospect and agreed for her to take me home.

I saw Daddy's truck in the driveway before we pulled in. I silently prayed Daddy was sober or at least not completely drunk. Mrs. Parks and I entered the foyer, meeting Mama in the middle. Mama quickly ushered us into our living room, the prettiest and cleanest room in the house. Mama was surprised but polite.

Unfortunately, I had not been able to call Mama in advance to tell her that Mrs. Parks was bringing me home. We had no telephone.

I introduced Mrs. Parks as my history teacher. Mama appeared awed by Mrs. Parks, who looked like a colored baby doll. Mama, who had on an old, faded white-and-orange checkered dress and run-over brown loafers, kept tugging at her dress pockets. That made Mrs. Parks look at Mama's dress more closely. I felt terrible for Mama.

We all sat in the living room, and Mrs. Parks started to tell Mama about the encyclopedias and life insurance she had arranged for several families in the community. Daddy must have heard Mrs. Parks, because he came and propped himself up against the doorframe. Daddy was not drunk, but he'd had a swig or two. Mrs. Parks continued to talk about the cost of everything and offered a monthly payment plan for the insurance and the set of encyclopedias.

Daddy stood up straight and said, "Shit, woman, you better git yo' bony-ass legs out of my house before I blow both of 'em off. I ain't got no money for shit-ass books. And when I die, they can throw my black ass into a gully and cover me up with some leaves. I ain't paying for no life insurance." Daddy looked over at me and asked, "Maylyn, do you got to have some shit-ass cyclepeters to go to school?"

I shook my head, too embarrassed to say anything in front of my teacher. I held my breath and silently prayed Mrs. Parks would not correct Daddy's pronunciation of the word *encyclopedias*.

I glanced over at Mama. She also looked embarrassed.

Mrs. Parks began to gather her papers. Her hands shook violently, and her silent lips twitched uncontrollably. She grabbed her briefcase and purse and ran out the front door, leaving a trail of papers on the floor. I looked at Mama and waited for her to say something. Instead, Mama remained seated and silent with her head bowed. I thought Mama was about to burst into tears.

Daddy followed Mrs. Parks outside, and I followed him. I wrapped an arm around one of the large porch posts. I watched Mrs. Parks scramble for her car keys as she glanced up at Daddy with fear written all over her face. Beads of sweat shone on her forehead, and her lips continued to twitch. I wanted to apologize for Daddy's behavior, but I was afraid to say anything that might cause Daddy to act up even more.

A Head of Cabbage

Daddy stepped down off the porch and said, "Shit, you is talking 'bout four hundred dollars, woman. You and that Ford better git on out of here."

One day in the middle of May 1968, Miss Peony, the English teacher I'd had for two consecutive years, left the class to go to the restroom. James Thomas, a popular and handsome student, was left in charge. He began to review several chapters for the final exam, as Miss Peony had directed him. The girls clamored for his attention, and I answered several of his questions, which angered a few females.

"Why doesn't she just shut up? Who does she think she is?" someone said.

I turned around and heard my cousin Ada May making the comments. I was shocked that my first cousin had turned on me.

I looked Ada May in the eye and said, "Who are you telling to shut up? You shut up."

Ada May and her siblings were popular at school. They were beautiful, bright, and well-respected students. Ada May was pretty and relatively smart, but she had the reputation of being a bully.

My cousin said, "I will shut up when you stop coming to my house begging for my clothes." Then she began to jerk her neck from side to side as the classroom of students roared with laughter.

I was humiliated and wanted to sink beneath the floor because I had on a hand-me-down outfit. However, the story about the clothes was different from the way Ada May alluded to it. My mama's sister-in-law, who lived in New York, occasionally sent gently used clothing down south for the female cousins to share. Mama had taken me to Ada May's house the previous evening to select my share of outfits. I'd chosen several pieces of clothing, but I had not begged Ada May for anything.

Anger and shame rose inside me, and to avoid further embarrassment, I decided to leave the room since the class was almost over, and Miss Peony had not returned. I didn't say another word, but I heard the students talking and laughing as I walked toward the exit.

"Marilyn sure is scared of Ada May—she's getting her ass out of here," someone said.

I thought only of graduating and going to college. I didn't want to get into any trouble at school. Just as I reached the door, I heard Ada May say, "And please, please, please keep your drunken daddy away from our house." Ada May emphasized the word *drunken*. The whole class roared with chatter and laughter again.

I couldn't contain my humiliation and rushed back to Ada May's desk. I shouted, "Don't ever talk about my daddy!"

"Well, you just keep that drunk of a daddy away from my house," Ada May said, and then she snapped her fingers in my face.

I dropped my books onto the floor, twirled around, and slapped Ada May hard across the face, surprising both her and myself.

Ada May rubbed the side of her face and said, "Oh, she wants an ass whipping for sure!"

She pushed me backward. I grabbed her, and we fell to the floor. I was on top as I punched her with my fists as hard as I could. One of her friends handed her a metal fingernail file. Ada May aimed it toward my face, but I wrestled the file from her. She kicked and hit me back blow for blow but with open hands. I thought to myself, *She fights like a girl. My brothers have taught me to fight like a boy.*

After a few minutes, I heard Miss Peony's harsh voice as she said, "I hope you both know that you're going to the principal's office. Girls fighting like boys. Get up off that floor. You're in here showing your bodies for all these young men to see. You should be ashamed. Don't you know how to act like ladies?"

My only concern was if the fight would prevent me from passing to the twelfth grade. I knew I was walking on thin ice as it was and could not afford a suspension. I had already missed nineteen days of school.

Mrs. Greene said, "So you're the one Miss Peony referred to as Cassius Clay? Well, I hear that you stood up to that Ada May girl rather good. Ada May has been a bully around here way too long."

I didn't respond to Mrs. Greene. Instead, I just stared at the wall behind her desk, which displayed pictures of different colleges.

Mrs. Greene clasped her hands and placed them across her desk. She looked me in the eye. I heard her, but I was so scared of being suspended or expelled that I couldn't speak. She noticed my glaring stare at the wall behind her desk. She got up and brought a list of colleges to me.

"So what university do you plan to attend?" she asked cheerfully.

I didn't know, but I wanted her to know that I planned to attend college. Finally, I said, "I want to go to journalism school. I want to write."

A Head of Cabbage

A surprised look came over Mrs. Greene's face, and she ran her fingers through her long brown hair. She blushed, looked down at her desk, and then said, "You need to be practical. Don't waste your time with journalism. That's a white man's profession. You need to think about teaching or social work."

I nodded and said, "Yes, ma'am."

I thought of Daddy telling me all the things I couldn't do and saying that white people would deliberately hinder my dreams for the future. I sat there for a moment, thinking that white people didn't have to do anything to hamper my goals, because black people were doing an excellent job. I wanted to believe that Mrs. Greene had given me good advice, but I was unsure. Then I remembered my elementary school teachers telling me to go to college and be whatever I wanted.

Now, in high school, I sat in the assistant principal's office, listening to her tell me I had only two options. I sighed and looked up at the clock on her wall. It was almost time for me to catch the bus. I silently prayed not to be suspended. *Dear God, I need another miracle.*

Mrs. Greene reattached the list of colleges to the bulletin board and looked down at her watch. "Well," she said, "I'll see you in school tomorrow."

CHAPTER 23

THE SHOTGUN

The conversation between Mama and Daddy about me was over in five seconds.

"She can't go, and that's final," Daddy said, rushing his words, which nullified his usual southern drawl. I stood nervously behind the old upright piano in our huge hallway, listening as perspiration ran down the sides of my face.

Daddy walked out of the bedroom and saw me. He stopped and wiped his brow with the back of his hand. "It's settled. You can't go," he said before leaving into the night in his new green 1968 Chevrolet truck.

A small lump formed in my throat as I dashed into my parents' bedroom. Mama rose slowly from her chair as if old and feeble. "I'm sorry," she said, casting her eyes down. "Farmwork comes first. You can't go to school next week. Go on to bed now; we have to get up early tomorrow morning to get started in the fields."

The next day, I got up much earlier than usual, determined to sneak to school and take my end-of-year exams. I walked down the stairs slowly, thinking I would catch the school bus at the neighbors' house a half mile up the road.

As I tiptoed down the winding stairs, they squeaked, so I stopped on every other step until I reached the bottom. I headed for the kitchen back door because it opened and closed without attracting attention. The house was dark and quiet, and I maneuvered carefully around the table and chairs.

"Where do you think you're going?" Daddy asked, popping on the kitchen light that hung from the high beamed ceiling. He stood only a foot or two from me.

Daddy usually slept late, so I'd thought I would have taken my second final exam by the time he found me missing. Trembling, I almost peed myself. I said, "Daddy, I need to go to school for three consecutive days this week to take final exams. I want to pass to the twelfth grade."

Daddy yelled, "Didn't I tell yo' ass last night that you ain't going to school this week? I don't care whether you pass to the twelfth grade or not. You got to help plant 'bacco all this week, so put yo' books down, and get ready for the fields."

My stomach started to ache. I stood still, holding my books tighter in my arms.

Mama came into the kitchen and saw me dressed for school. She looked at me with worrying eyes, frowning as she spoke. "Marilyn, you can't go against what your daddy says. He done gave the final word. You got to help plant tobacco this whole week."

Daddy balled his hands into fists and moved in a bit closer, blocking my exit.

"What are you preparing my future to be? What are you teaching me?" I asked angrily as I took several steps away from Daddy.

Daddy grimaced and looked at Mama, appearing more upset that I had mouthed back to him. He no longer looked like my handsome young father. His lips twitched, and beads of sweat formed on his lined forehead. His chest rose and fell as if he were tired and had already done a full day's work.

Mama said, "We is teaching you what we know. That's all we can teach." She reached to take the books out of my arms. Her eyes glistened with the hope that I would accept their demand.

"Mama," I said, holding the books tighter, "please talk Daddy into letting me go to school this week. I can't miss taking final exams, and they start today."

Daddy shouted, waving his fists in the air, "Didn't I already tell yo' ass that the only school you is going to see this week is that 'bacco field?"

I had already missed twenty-nine days of school. I knew I couldn't pass to the twelfth grade if I had more absences. The pit of my stomach began to burn, and the disgust I felt for my father began to balloon into hate.

I started to beg. "Please allow me to go just one day then. Please. I will explain everything to my teachers. They may be able to give me take-home exams or something. I don't want to be held back another year." I glanced toward Mama. She was silent but breathing hard and fast. I could tell

A Head of Cabbage

she was frightened and wanted me to relent. Her small brown eyes were bigger than I had ever seen, and she kept wringing and wiping her hands on her apron.

Daddy yelled, "Education ain't everything! That's all you talk about—education. Shit, I'm tired of hearing you talk about it."

I said, "Education is everything to me. You made all your children quit school to work on the farm so you could buy yourself a new truck every three years. I'm not quitting school. I'm going to graduate."

Mama held on to the bottom of her apron so tightly I thought she was going to pull it apart. Then she said, "Marilyn, shut yo' mouth."

Daddy took a step forward and said, "Don't tell no shit-ass lie on me, gal. I ain't made none of my chillums quit school, and I never taught you to be a liar." He raised one of his fists, and I cringed. Then I lowered my voice and moved farther away from him.

I wanted Daddy to see the connection between working on the farm and dropping out of school, so I said, "Daddy, you made all your children stay out of school so much that they could not pass to the next level. They quit because they were too ashamed to continue. Who wants to be seventeen years old and still in the ninth grade with classmates and teachers making fun of them?"

Daddy seemed to calm down a bit but was still adamant about planting tobacco that day. He unballed his hands. "Well, yo' ass ain't going to school this week, so get yo'self ready to go to the fields."

I was still determined to go to school and scared the bus would leave me. I appealed to Mama. "Mama, please talk to Daddy. I absolutely must go to school today. I will work from sunrise to sundown for the rest of this week. I will work all day Saturday and Sunday. Just let me go today. Please, Mama, help me to go to school this one day."

Mama squinted and said, "You heard yo' daddy."

I inhaled and cussed under my breath and then looked away. I felt I was the only person alive who had to beg to go to school. I didn't know how to make my parents understand its importance. I wanted to say that every child had a right to a good education, as one of my former teachers had said in class one day. I didn't say it, but I knew this was the last straw for me.

I exhaled and looked at Mama. "If you love me, help me. I need to go to school today. I must take final exams. It's the only way I can pass to the twelfth grade."

My stomach began to ache. I tried to quell the burning sensation by bending over and squeezing the pit of my stomach with my left hand.

Mama took a step back as though she thought I might upchuck and said, "I love all my chillums. Why is you always trying to be special? You ain't no different from the rest of 'em."

I moved maybe a foot closer to them and said, "I am going to school today, because I have to. I will not end up working on somebody's farm, being somebody's maid, getting on welfare, or becoming a criminal to survive. I don't know what I'm going to do when I'm grown, but I know what I ain't going to do! I know I ain't dropping out of school and dooming myself."

Daddy became furious and took a step closer to me. "Gal, you ain't gonna tell me what you gonna do. I said that you ain't going to that schoolhouse today. That means yo' ass ain't going. If you try to get on that shit-ass school bus, I'll take my shotgun and blow yo' head off. I said you ain't going to school today. I mean what I said." He took a step closer to me and asked, "Do you have a clue who you is talking to? I'm yo' daddy, and I tell you what you can and can't do." He turned around and looked at the shotgun hanging on the doorpost several inches above his head.

I looked up at the shotgun and trembled. I was petrified, but something in my gut said, *Start walking*. I tilted my head toward Mama and slowly started toward the door. "I will help plant tobacco when I return from school. I will work half the night, and I will work all day Saturday and Sunday in the fields but not today."

I heard the bus coming nearer to our house and knew I only had a few minutes to get to the bus stop. Blinding tears flooded my eyes and rolled down my face. I stopped walking when I reached the doorknob. I didn't touch it. I visualized my body lying on the floor, blown into tiny pieces. My stomach made rumbling noises and ached.

Daddy's red eyes appeared to want to blow me apart. His nostrils flared like those of an angry bull. Mama rushed to me just as I lifted my hand to open the door.

"Marilyn, put yo' books down. Just put yo' books down." She grabbed my arm. "Child, you can't go against yo' daddy."

A Head of Cabbage

I jerked my arm away and tried to speak. The fear I felt was so great that I thought everything was standing still. Somehow, I managed a crackling whisper.

"Mama, bury me at Hamer Baptist Church and sing 'Jesus, Keep Me Near the Cross' if Daddy kills me, because either I go to school today or I die today. It's one or the other."

Mama didn't speak another word. She went and stood behind Daddy. I opened the door and walked outside. I expected to hear a shotgun blast from behind. Bitter bile rose in my throat, and I almost choked, but I continued to walk toward the bus stop. My legs felt numb. I had to force them to move forward. The bus driver saw me walking toward the gravel road and stopped. I envisioned my head rolling down the hilly yard and wondered if I would see my own body sprawled out, gurgling and kicking, until I died. I wanted to look back to see where Daddy was, but I was too scared to stare at the barrel of a shotgun. I hesitated for a few seconds. I didn't want the children on the school bus to see me lying dead in the yard with my head blown off.

I started to pray. *God, please forgive me for all I have done that was a sin. Forgive me for disobeying Mama and Daddy right now. And, God, please take me instantly to heaven and do not let me feel any pain if Daddy kills me. Amen.*

My fear was paralyzing, but I continued to walk at a turtle's pace as salty streams of tears flooded most of my vision. I hardly noticed the students on the school bus standing and staring out the windows as I approached.

The door to the bus opened. The driver, an older male teenager, looked tense and scared himself. He seemed to be aware that I was in trouble and wanted me to get on board. I was afraid to step up, thinking it would be my last step. I stood still in front of the open door, crying.

"Come on in," the bus driver urged, gesturing frantically with one hand for me to step inside.

Somehow, I did, and the door quickly closed behind me. The bus took off, and I let out a loud wail.

Once at school, I went to all my teachers and told them that I would not return to school after that day to take final exams and that Daddy might shoot me when I returned home in the afternoon, because I'd defied him to come to school that day. My teachers were astounded by my revelation. Each one told me that I had potential and that he or she would not fail me, even if I did miss a few more days of school.

My favorite teacher, Mr. Tillman, a tall, muscular, and rugged-looking man with high cheekbones and dark features, was concerned for my safety. He asked me to sit down at his desk while the incoming students waited outside the door. He sat across from me, flipping a neatly folded white handkerchief over and over.

He said, "Marilyn, you have extraordinary courage for a teenager. And I applaud your efforts to get an education, but you should never put your educational pursuits before your safety. Going to college is worthy of sacrifice, but it won't do you any good if you're dead."

He handed me the handkerchief. I dabbed my eyes and forced back tears as I explained my defiant actions to him. Mr. Tillman sat back in his chair with a look of horror on his face.

I told him that no one in my family had ever finished high school, and it was my duty to break the family's curse because I had two brothers and a little sister at home. I had to break the curse for them.

Mr. Tillman looked sad and worried. He tapped his chin with his thumb and forefinger as if he were playing Ping-Pong, with his chin being the ball. His eyes began to tear up, and he tilted his head slightly, not wanting me to see his face, but I did. I was embarrassed for him to know the condition of my home life, but I did not want him to fail me, so I continued to explain myself.

"I would rather die than not finish high school," I said.

Mr. Tillman stood up and asked me to stay put for a few minutes while he went to talk with Mr. Dillard, the principal. He returned a few minutes later and told me that he and Mr. Dillard would take me home and have a talk with Daddy.

I became hysterical, afraid Daddy would shoot all three of us if they took me home. Eventually, they relented after I started to hyperventilate.

Later that afternoon, when I stepped off the bus, I didn't go directly home. I felt sure that Daddy would shoot as soon as he saw me. I didn't want the kids on the bus to see me get killed like a barnyard animal, sprawled out on the lawn with brains and blood oozing out of my head. So I started kicking small gravel rocks at the road to give the bus time to

A Head of Cabbage

get out of sight. I looked up at the blue sky full of cumulus clouds roaming around and changing shape.

The bus reached the dead end of the road and turned around. After a few minutes, the bus zoomed past me, leaving dust flying high in the air. Then I started toward the house, dreading every step. I gazed up at the sky again as I walked, thinking that my spirit might soon join the moving clouds.

I opened the front door and stepped inside the hallway. I placed my purse and notebook on top of our upright piano. I stood still and listened. The house was quiet, but that did not mollify my indescribable fear. I prayed and waited as my stomach knotted with pain. Finally, I bent over, holding on to the piano for support, and then I peeped into the den.

Mama eventually saw me. She came and stood a few feet in front of me and said, "Go apologize to yo' daddy. He's been sick all day because you went against him this morning. You made his ulcers act up." I knew she expected me to tell Daddy I was sorry I had gone to school, but I couldn't.

I looked up toward the ceiling and said out loud, "Thank you, God. Daddy is too sick to shoot."

Mama gasped. "What did you say?"

"I said thank God that everything is all right."

My stomach stopped hurting. I straightened my body and walked into the den to look at Daddy. He was lying on the sofa, watching TV. He looked up at me, but neither of us spoke. Mama walked in behind me.

I looked at her. "You want me to apologize? He needs to apologize to me."

Mama pointed a finger in my face. "Marilyn, you ain't gonna talk about yo' daddy like that, and you will look up to 'im. He's yo' daddy, and you will respect him, no matter what."

I had a smirk on my face and thought, *I must respect him even though he is trying to ruin my life.* Mama spoke as if she could read my thoughts.

"He is doing the best he can. You wait till you get grown with a house full of chillums to feed. Living in this white man's world ain't easy. I know yo' daddy ain't perfect. Ain't no man perfect but Jesus, and they killed him. Now, you need to apologize."

"Mama, I ain't apologizing," I said defiantly, and I ran upstairs and changed into work clothes.

We had about two acres of tobacco left to plant by the end of the week. I worked all day on Saturday, and Mama asked me not to work on Sunday. She suggested we go to church, but I wanted to appease Daddy by ensuring I completed my share of the work. Daddy seemed pleased that I chose work over the church and told Mama to let me be.

After we had completed planting our tobacco crop and the vegetable garden, Daddy was in rare form. He was sober for two days. Mama was so happy she made Daddy's favorite meal: fried chicken, gravy, turnip greens, and apple pie.

At supper, Daddy said, "Maylyn, I swear, I can't figure you out."

I looked at him and said, "Daddy, I can't figure me out either."

Daddy laughed, and everyone else at the table laughed too. After that, we were back to normal.

Mama reached into her apron pocket and gave me a long manila envelope. She looked worried as I ripped it open. I screamed when I saw the big red words scribbled across the top of my report card: "Passed to the twelfth grade."

I went upstairs and thanked God. Then I pondered. *What will next year be like when the schools integrate?*

CHAPTER 24

THIS IS AMERICA

Late one Saturday evening in June 1969, Mr. Lawrence, our white neighbor, knocked on the front door. I stood in the kitchen, trying to read the surprised expression on Daddy's face before he went out to determine the reason for Mr. Lawrence's visit. An uneasy look radiated across Daddy's and Mama's faces when two more knocks were heard. Finally, Daddy took stock of his appearance and tucked his shirt into his pants before walking outside.

Mama and I stood in front of the living room window, watching and waiting for Mr. Lawrence to leave. Finally, after several minutes, Daddy walked into the living room with a sheepish grin on his face. He stopped a few feet in front of me and rubbed his chin.

"Maylyn, Mrs. Lawrence wants to hire you. She needs someone to iron her clothes. Said she would pay you a dollar for each basket you iron."

Daddy lit two cigarettes. Mama met him halfway and took one of the cigarettes.

I was outraged at Daddy for even mentioning anything about my being a maid. The thought of ironing some white woman's clothes sickened me.

"Me? Iron her clothes?" I said. "Are you crazy? Somebody needs to find you something to drink. Tell her husband that his wife can come iron our clothes, and I will pay her a dollar a basket. The nerve of her trying to make me a servant! I ain't going to be no maid, Daddy."

Mama remained silent with a smirk on her face. Daddy rolled his eyes at me and then started to stretch.

"Well," he said, stretching his arms in several directions, "if you don't want to make a little money, it's all right wit' me."

I decided right then and there that I would do a poorer job of cleaning our house and stop ironing everybody's clothes. I didn't want Daddy to think of me as a maid or try to make me into one.

I cut my eyes over at him. "By the way," I said, "I think you should tell Mr. Lawrence to tell his wife to call Mama Mrs. Nora or Mrs. Abbott. I'm tired of her calling Mama every name in the book except the correct one. We call her Mrs. Lawrence. She needs to call Mama Mrs. Abbott."

Daddy pressed his lips together and shook his head. "Gal, I don't know what's gonna come of you."

Daddy and Mama didn't know that Levi, William Winston, and I had been discussing Mrs. Lawrence for several months, including how she didn't seem to remember Mama's name. We had agreed that the next time she called our house and asked for Nellie, Hannah, Tillie, or whatever name left her tongue, I was designated to set her straight.

Daddy and I walked into the den. The news was on, and a picture of H. Rap Brown with a big Afro graced the TV screen.

Daddy looked at me and said, "There ain't no reason for you to become a militant, Maylyn." He reached over and patted my Afro and then became silent for a few seconds, listening to the news. Then he said, "And there ain't nothing wrong with giving respect to white people."

I bit my tongue and then said, "And there ain't nothing wrong with white people giving respect to black people. It's supposed to work both ways!"

Daddy looked at me as though I had said something impossible. Then, hanging his head, he changed the TV station and finally said, "Maylyn, everythin' ain't the way it's 'posed to be."

I looked Daddy in the eye. "The next time Mrs. Lawrence calls and asks for Mama using some strange name, please pass the phone over to me. I have the guts to tell her to respect Mama. Why do they think we should be their maids and work on their farms for little or nothing? White people must be sick!"

I glanced at Mama, who sat quietly watching TV. She wouldn't get into Daddy's and my conversation, but I knew she was listening. She glanced at Daddy and me every few minutes but remained silent.

Daddy had a short coughing spell, after which he said, "That's the reason they brought us from Africa. Free labor, gal. Make them rich, and keep us dumb and poor."

"But that ain't fair," I said.

Daddy grunted and then said, "Shit, this is America. Ain't nothing fair for us. You better learn that sooner rather than later."

A Head of Cabbage

A few months went by, and one evening, as I walked through the hallway, I heard Levi on the telephone. I stopped and listened.

"Just a minute, ma'am," Levi said with a silly grin on his face. He handed the telephone to me and whispered, "Marilyn, it's Mrs. Lawrence, asking for Hattie." Levi flopped down onto the piano stool and stared at me.

I covered the mouthpiece with my hand and said to Levi, "You can go on about your business now. I've got the phone."

Levi folded his arms and said, "Shucks, I ain't leaving. You said you had the guts to tell Mrs. Lawrence to call Mama Mrs. Abbott. I want to hear your guts tell that white woman to respect Mama. Go on—tell her that no one named Hattie lives here."

I rolled my eyes at Levi and turned my backside to him. "Hello, Mrs. Lawrence. Who do you want to speak to?"

"I wish to speak with Hattie, please," she said.

Mrs. Lawrence sounded polite, as always, with her soft voice, but the undertone was that she could call any colored woman any female name, and the woman would respond without the slightest hesitation or correction.

I covered the mouthpiece with my hand again and whispered to Levi, "She's asking for Hattie."

Levi came around to face me. He nodded several times. "I know, I know." Then he raised his eyebrows and smirked, daring me to set her straight, as I'd promised to do during one of our earlier conversations. He said, "Go on, Marilyn. Tell her that no one named Hattie lives here."

My stomach churned like roaring rapids as I took in a deep breath. "Mrs. Lawrence, no one named Hattie lives here."

After I said it, my stomach felt less sick. I rolled my eyes and stuck out my tongue at Levi.

Mrs. Lawrence raised her voice an octave higher as she asked, "Is this the Abbott residence?"

"Yes, ma'am," I said, "but no Hattie lives here."

I was scared she might pay Mama a visit to tell her that I was disrespectful to her, and Mama would punish me. But my worse fear was that her husband might cause trouble for Daddy while he was driving around showing off his new Chevrolet pickup. My heart pounded fiercely as I waited for Mrs. Lawrence to respond.

"Well, just let me speak to your mother, please," she said, sounding a little annoyed with me.

I looked at the big black wall phone and then at my brother Levi. My seven-year-old baby sister, Terri, came into the hallway and started to listen as well. I didn't want them to think of me as a coward. I was the big sister and the oldest child at home. I had jumped the first hurdle, so I figured I may as well go for the second one. My voice cracked as I exhaled.

"Mrs. Lawrence, my mama should be called Mrs. Abbott, like we call you Mrs. Lawrence. We respect you. You should respect my mama."

I waited for a response. The phone was silent for a few seconds, and then I heard a click.

Levi rushed into the family room. He told Daddy that I'd told Mrs. Lawrence to call Mama Mrs. Abbott and to respect Mama. Daddy shook his head and frowned as though he disapproved, but in his eyes, I saw that he was proud of me. I felt I had redeemed Mama's dignity just a little.

"I swear, Maylyn," Daddy said, "the man who marries you will have himself somethin' if he can stand yo' mouth."

Levi turned to me and said, "Marilyn, Mrs. Lawrence won't be calling here asking for Hattie no more."

Daddy lit a brown homemade cigarette, took a long draw, and then said, "She won't be calling here again, period."

CHAPTER 25

DON'T LET NOTHING STOP YOU

Right after the Fourth of July, I started to work at night in Dan River Cotton Mill in Danville, Virginia. I got up at 5:30 a.m. and worked in the fields until 2:00 p.m. Then I went home, ate, washed up, and worked in the cotton mill from 4:00 p.m. until midnight.

One night, after standing for more than four hours at work, I decided to take a break. I joined several men and women in the center of the room. They sat on two red wooden benches while they talked and smoked. I sat down at the end of one of the benches to rest my legs. It was about eight thirty.

The supervisor, a tall red-haired man, saw me and came over to where I sat. He asked if I smoked. When I said no, the other workers laughed and looked around at one another. Not knowing what was so funny, I shrugged and remained seated.

The supervisor lit up a Winston cigarette. He blew a puff of smoke away from me. "Marilyn doesn't smoke," he said to the other workers.

They stopped laughing and talking and watched the interaction between the supervisor and me.

"Just smelling smoke makes me tired," I said nonchalantly. "I will never put a cigarette between my lips."

"Only smokers get two ten-minute smoking breaks each night," the supervisor said. "You get back to work."

I thought, *What an incredible asshole of a supervisor*, as I walked back to my twenty-seven spinning machines. I decided to take two clandestine ten-minute breaks, otherwise safely known as bathroom breaks.

I ate my sandwich while standing and working. We all did. I wore an apron with two pockets: one to keep my tools and the other for my dinner.

The airborne cotton fibers in the spinning room were thick enough to grab with one's hand. They settled on my Afro, making my hair look as if it were capped with snow. I had to fan the floating fibers away from my sandwich when I ate, and even then, I had to spit out a mouthful of cotton balls from time to time.

Later that night, it started to rain, and the humidity made the spinning machines function less than optimally. Bobbins full of cotton began to pop out of their chambers and onto the hardwood floor. I could hardly manage my workload.

Edward, my brother, worked in the doffing department, another part in the process of making cloth. He removed full spools of thread from cylinders and replaced them with empty spools as fast as possible. Finally, around ten o'clock, Edward sneaked over to me.

"Marilyn, I've got to leave. I'll let Mama know you need to be picked up at midnight." Edward left before I could protest, not that it would have done any good. He worked two jobs and had to go in earlier to his second one for some reason.

I was scared that Daddy wouldn't let Mama pick me up, or Daddy might not even be home. At midnight, I walked out of the building into a heavy downpour. I looked around but didn't see Daddy's pickup. There was a telephone booth nearby. I sat down on the concrete floor while I waited for Mama. My legs and feet ached from all the standing. I watched the third-shift workers hurry into the hot brick building as second-shift workers scurried out.

Old men and women, some stooped over with their heads white with cotton fibers, walked as fast as possible to their cars. They looked tired and haggard. Some had curled fingers and walked with a shuffle, telltale signs of many years of doffing, winding, and spinning. Some of the women's hands had black-and-blue burn marks from the hot machines, and some of the men had a couple of fingers missing because the machines had chewed them up in some unfortunate accident.

Finally, I saw Daddy's truck pull into the tall wrought-iron gate. Mama was driving, and Daddy sat on the passenger side.

Daddy got out of the truck to let me into the middle. I was a little miffed at them for being more than an hour late. After all, I had to get up at 5:30 a.m. the following day to work on the farm.

A Head of Cabbage

"This truck don't run on water, gal. You got some gas money?" Daddy asked after Mama pulled out of the iron gate.

I handed over my last five dollars without saying anything. Daddy looked at the crumpled bill before stuffing it into his shirt pocket.

"Shit, this all you got?"

"Daddy, I need to save my money for college. I don't make that much," I said before I started to cough.

"Gal, everybody can't go to college. Somebody got to be dumb," Daddy said as he blew more smoke in front of me.

I fanned the smoke and chewed on the inside of my bottom lip. I thought of our endless arguments about school and education. A mild ache surged throughout my body, and I knew I had to say something. Each time Daddy said something discouraging or hateful, I felt as though he were casting a ballooning curse over our whole family. Although the thought was reprehensible, I wished he would die before he ruined all our lives. I turned my head slightly toward Daddy before I spoke.

"You make me feel like I'm a useless person. Like I'm not supposed to want anything out of life because I'm black and a girl. Daddy, I think you're my enemy."

Daddy drew on his cigarette several more times before putting it out in the center ashtray. He shifted in his seat. "I've been trying to tell yo' ass for the longest time that you can't always do what you want to do in this world. Yo' ass is black in America. Ain't nothin' gonna come easy for you, and don't expect anything to be fair. Them shit-ass teachers done told you and everybody else to go to college. It don't mean you gonna go. Somebody got to be dumb, and if you is born poor, most likely, you gonna die poor."

Before I spoke again, I rolled my tongue around in my mouth. I knew better than to let my thoughts become words, but I opened my mouth, and they stole themselves a way out.

"Daddy, just because you're dumb doesn't mean I want to be dumb. I don't want to be anything like you. Just 'cause you're poor doesn't mean I'm gonna be poor. I'm gonna save my money."

Headlights of passing cars illuminated the inside of the truck's cab, and I saw a horrid scowl on Daddy's face. He appeared to be in shock. Then he slowly turned to face me.

"Yo' ass will walk home from the mill before I pick you up again."

Daddy stomped his feet several times on the floor of the truck—his way of signaling Mama to speed up.

When I went to work the next day, I decided not to take any bathroom breaks. I figured the only way I would make enough money to save some and give Daddy some was to make production. I resolved to provide Daddy money every week, so he would allow Mama to pick me up when Edward left early to go to his other job.

That night, trying to make production at work, I heard a loud, bloodcurdling scream coming from a man. The noisy machines couldn't drown out the man's pitiful cries.

Several workers and I ran over to see what had happened. A machinist had stuck his hand into the feeder before turning it off. Blood dripped through several towels the supervisor wrapped the man's hand in while waiting for the ambulance. The man told his supervisor that he couldn't make production with the machines turned off.

When I returned to my twenty-seven machines, some were malfunctioning, and others were completely shut down. Several white coworkers, all female, were doing my job to prevent a backlog in work. Finally, one of the ladies came over to me and said, "We have to help each other."

She showed me a few tricks to get control of the machines without shutting them down. I didn't thank the women for their help, because I feared they would later sabotage me.

Before the shift ended, someone told me that the man had lost three of his fingers. I decided to forget about making production and added working in a cotton mill to my list of things I would not do for a living after I finished high school.

Later that night, after Edward dropped me at home, I told Daddy about the incident in the mill and said that Miss Ann and her sisters had helped me with my malfunctioning machines.

"Uh-huh, you just wait a little while," Daddy said. "You'll see. They is setting yo' ass up for the kill."

Daddy waved me out of his and Mama's bedroom, and I went upstairs and prayed.

For the next several days, I waited and watched for the white women to do something awful to me. They never did.

A Head of Cabbage

We came home from the fields one Saturday evening just as Daddy pulled into the driveway. He had an older man in the truck with him.

Daddy was lit, but the other man appeared sober.

I sat down in the porch swing to rest a bit, but Mama continued into the kitchen to start supper. Daddy and the man got out of the truck. Daddy followed Mama into the kitchen. The older man sat down on the swing beside me. He looked me up and down before asking my age. Feeling uncomfortable, I blurted out, "Eighteen," and rushed into the kitchen to help Mama with supper. I looked back, and the man was right behind me.

"Maylyn, this here is my daddy—my real daddy," Daddy said proudly, placing his arm across the older man's shoulders.

The man was heavier and more muscular than Daddy. His eyes were brown with a darker brown ring around the irises. He was dressed handsomely, as though he were going to Wednesday night's Bible study. His almond-colored skin had begun to sag around the jawline and neck.

The stranger was an inch or two shorter than Daddy, but I could see the resemblance. I looked at Mama for confirmation. She nodded.

"That's his real daddy. Ronald meets his real daddy after fifty-six years," Mama said gleefully.

I fixed Daddy and my newly discovered grandfather a giant, hot buttered biscuit with a thick tomato and country ham slices. I gave each of them a mason jar of freshly brewed sassafras tea.

When Daddy left to take the man home, Mama told me the story of Daddy's parentage. Grandma Cora, Daddy's mother, had had an affair with a married man, which had resulted in Daddy's birth. That had happened before Grandma married John Abbott, the only granddaddy I knew. Mama said his name was Jefferson Lea, but he was not kin to Mr. William Lea, our former landlord.

Mr. Jefferson and Daddy began to spend a lot of time together. His wife, Mrs. Liza, who had a crisp wit, became good friends with Mama. When Daddy lost his driver's license for driving under the influence of alcohol a few months later, I became the chauffeur for Daddy and for Mr. Jefferson and his wife, who lived a mile away from us.

One day Mama sent me to take Mrs. Lea to the grocery store. When I pulled into the dirt driveway, Mrs. Lea was waiting in front of their unpainted bungalow. Short and plump, she was dressed as neatly as her husband had been on the first day I met him. Black heels made her thick, firm ankles stand out beneath her red-and-green-striped cotton skirt. I couldn't tell if her head was covered with a crown of thick, curly black hair or a human-hair wig, but it was beautiful. She looked bright and sophisticated, like a schoolteacher.

I asked Mrs. Liza if her husband was Daddy's daddy on our drive to town.

Mrs. Liza nodded and said, "He sure is, and your grandmother and I have made our peace with it. All is forgiven."

Curious, I asked another question. "Did y'all live next door to each other or something?"

"No. Your grandmother was my midwife. She came to deliver my baby and had to stay overnight. I think that was when the two of 'em got together. Later that year, Jefferson got a letter from your grandmother. I read the letter, details and all."

"How did that make you feel?" I asked, pulling into the Winn-Dixie parking lot in Yanceyville.

"Oh," Mrs. Lea said, "'bout like any woman who has a running husband." She glanced at me. "He was whorish, but I couldn't leave. So I waited for him to stay home. Most men stop being whorish when they start getting old. We just have to have patience."

"But, Mrs. Lea, why did they do that in your house?"

Mrs. Lea wiped some brown snuff juice stuck in the corners of her mouth. She placed her white lace handkerchief back in her purse as she looked at me and said, "When a woman's body is ready and a man needs a woman's touch, there is no conscience between the two. I suppose I owe your grandmother some gratitude, though. She didn't keep carrying on with my husband."

When I dropped Mrs. Lea off at her house an hour later, she gave me a dollar and said, "I hear you're trying mighty hard to finish high school. Don't let nothing stop you."

CHAPTER 26

THIS COUNTRY COULD BE GREAT

The fall of 1969 brought forced school integration to Caswell County. Bartlett Yancey High School became the only high school, and Caswell County Training School became a middle school renamed Dillard.

On the first day of school, God granted me another miracle. It rained, and I attended school and met my assigned teachers.

It didn't take me long to notice some differences between the white and black students. The white kids had money to eat in the cafeteria or brought their lunch every day. Most of them were dressed well and didn't talk loudly or hang out in the hallways before class. The most obvious observation was how they went out of their way to avoid contact with black students.

One evening, I came home from school and found two guests: a male student from Chapel Hill University and my recently discovered second granddaddy. The student, from Liberia, West Africa, was interviewing Mama and Daddy. His name was Meimei Dukuly. When he saw me, he stood up, and I stifled a laugh. His height was about five feet or less.

Meimei began to visit with us weekly, usually on a Friday afternoon. He took copious notes about living in America as a black person. Occasionally, he would ask me about my school, but mostly, he talked to the adults.

After visiting for about a month, Meimei brought Mama a small bottle of perfume. Then he surprised me by asking Mama and Daddy if he could take me out to dinner. I was eighteen and had never been in a restaurant or out on a date. I wanted to go, but I was afraid and thought Meimei might eat me. That was what the TV show *Tarzan* had led me to believe about Africans—they ate people.

Daddy nodded, but Mama frowned and blurted out, "Well, OK, but she better be back by ten o'clock."

"Well, go get dressed, dear. You heard your mother," Meimei said while a broad, pleasant smile cascaded across his square olive face.

He slid his chair closer to Daddy, and the two of them began to talk about farming and how large their vegetables grew.

When Mama and I left the room, I asked her what I was supposed to do on a date. Mama crossed her arms across her waist, stared at me for a moment, and then said, "Don't talk too much. Men have little patience for listening to women talk. Be nice, and smile sometimes."

Mama and I stood outside the door for a few minutes and listened to the men talk. "Well now," Daddy said, "in America, we know how to farm. Our watermelons grow to be the size of car tires, and our tomatoes get to be the size of cantaloupes."

Not to be outdone, Meimei said to Daddy, "In my country, the okra grows fifteen feet tall, and the yams are as big as pumpkins. The leaves of yams are tender, and they keep you looking young if you eat them."

Mama shook her head, giggling. "That African sho knows how to lie. Who ever heard of yams the size of pumpkins?"

Once we were outside, Meimei took my hand and kissed it. "Your eyes are as beautiful as Sophia Loren's, and you're tender enough to eat," he said, opening the car door for me.

I jerked my hand out of his. "Please don't eat me," I said, grimacing.

Taken aback, Meimei stopped, lifted his black-rimmed glasses, and sighed. He appeared hurt and irritated. "Africans don't eat humans. I think you have been watching too much *Tarzan*. You do know that they make the Tarzan movies right here in the United States?"

I nodded and immediately regretted the insult.

"My dear," he said, "I have a small temper, but I will do my best to control it with you." Then, after driving a few miles, Meimei pulled the car into a vacant driveway and turned to face me. "Let me try to educate you since the public schools do such a poor job of it when it comes to the continent of Africa."

His small brown eyes were wide and appeared more prominent through his glasses. He glared at me and spoke harshly, and I thought his slight temper was much larger than he realized. I felt like a child being chastised.

"The images of Africans you see are what the West wants you and the rest of the world to see. They demonize Africans to make the world think of us as savages and beasts, so as they steal our land and cleverly take our natural resources, it won't seem so horrible and humanly unjust." Meimei paused, turned his body forward, and placed both hands on the car's steering wheel. He stared straight ahead into the sunset. "Please tell me you at least understand that."

"I understand," I said, but I didn't really since this was the first time anyone had spoken to me about Africa, except when we'd talked a little about the slave trade in history class.

Meimei continued as I listened intently. "The westerners try to give us their religion to maintain their dominance. But their dominion over all the African nations will end. The white man's dominance will cease. All nations and all people will share in the wealth of this world—not just the westerners."

"That makes a lot of sense to me," I said, remembering Mama's advice not to talk too much.

"The missionaries came to teach us Christianity. They boasted of how great America is and how great God is and how his Son, Jesus, came to save the world. The first day I set foot on American soil, a fat white man, an American, said to me, 'Get out of my way, nigger,' and pushed me down onto the pavement. A nation is only as great as how its people behave, not how much wealth, how many skyscrapers, or how many bombs it has. This country could be great, though."

Meimei sounded angry and wiped a few beads of sweat from his forehead with the palm of his hand. He looked to his left, where several horses stood grazing beyond a fence. After a few seconds, he appeared to have calmed down a bit. At least the muscles in his neck had relaxed. He turned to me and took my hand.

"Do you know what is going on in Rhodesia? South Africa? Liberia? Nigeria? Do you know who Nelson Mandela is? Do you know anything about any African country?"

As he asked rapid-fire questions, all I could do was feel shame.

Meimei frowned and paused for a second. "I'm a Muslim. I will always be a Muslim. I accept Jesus as a prophet, not as God's Son or as God. God does not need a woman to create. He created everything with only his word. Do you understand?"

I shook my head and smiled. I was embarrassed. The only thing I knew for sure was that Africa was the home of my forefathers. I didn't even know the country of my ancestors.

CHAPTER 27

YOU CAN'T GO

Meimei and I had dated for several months, when he told me we needed to talk about a serious matter. He took me to his rented house in Yanceyville.

"Marilyn," he said, "I'm committed to marry a girl from my tribe back in Liberia. It is a commitment I cannot break. Our parents made this commitment when we were children. No one can change that." He turned his back to me and stared out the window.

I went and stood beside him and said, "Tell me all that is on your mind."

"As a Muslim, I'm permitted to take four wives," Meimei said, "but I will only take two. You can be my first wife. The second wife will always listen to your directions." He cleared his throat and folded his hands behind his back. "I must first finish my education, and then we can marry. I will treat you like a queen, and you will have maids to attend your every need. In addition, I will give you an allowance each month for you to do with as you please."

I thought he was crazy. Who'd ever heard of a man having two wives, except during biblical times? However, I was intrigued with the possibility of being a wife with an allowance and not doing field work again.

"How does that work?" I asked. "Will you sleep in the middle of us every night?" I rolled my eyes after I spoke.

Meimei sounded confident now. "Ah, actually, no," he said, leaning forward, "you will have your compound, she will have her compound, and I will have my compound—separate houses, so to speak."

He took my hand and held it to his chest. "I will see you almost every day. Sometimes I will be away, but mostly, I will be there with you, my virgin. Tonight I will ask your mother and father to allow you to accompany me to Pennsylvania to meet some important people in my life."

About an hour after Meimei took me home, he asked Mama if I could go to Pennsylvania with him. He told Mama he would arrange for us to have separate accommodations and would see to it that no harm came to me.

Upon hearing Meimei's request, Mama jumped up off the bed where she was sitting and rushed over to where Meimei and I stood. She inserted herself between us. "Naw, you can't take Marilyn to Pennsylvania—or to Africa. She's gonna stay right here with me! If you get her over there, there's no telling what you will do to her as soon as that mouth of hers starts to open. You're probably gonna have fifteen or more wives anyhow." Mama lit a cigarette and rolled her eyes. "I know 'bout y'all African men. All you want is a bunch of wives, and all the while, the white folks are wreaking havoc on yo' country, taking yo' land and leaving y'all living like animals and fighting each other."

Mama started to pace the floor. She glared at Meimei and blew out several more puffs of smoke. Then she looked at me. "I ain't got much education, but I know just the same. Colored folks over here in America got an excuse for being poor," she said. "Our ancestors was slaves and didn't have nothing to get started with when slavery was over. Y'all ain't got an excuse, now, do you?"

Sweat rolled down both sides of Mama's face, and she took the tail end of her apron and dabbed her face. She looked at me. "I don't know why I'm asking, but, Marilyn, do you want to go to Pennsylvania with this man?"

"Yes, ma'am, I do," I said. The farthest I had been from home was Greensboro, North Carolina. I had not even been outside the state, except for Danville, Virginia, when I worked in Dan River Cotton Mill. So I wanted to go to Pennsylvania with Meimei.

Meimei stood quietly beside Mama. His head was bowed, and he looked nervous.

"Too bad. You can't go," Mama said. "You ain't going nowhere with this man." She stomped back to her bed, sat down at the foot, and resumed watching TV.

Meimei appeared to be in a state of shock. I watched his face contort as he fumbled with his words. I had never seen him so shaken before, and I watched as he tried to remain confident and calm.

"Mrs. Abbott, I understand and have to respect your wishes," he said.

A Head of Cabbage

"If it's OK with you, I would like to say goodbye to Marilyn on the front porch. Please."

Meimei's discomfort was so visible that he appeared in physical pain. Mama didn't say anything. Instead, she pointed to the door and gestured with her head for us to go outside to the porch.

Once we were on the porch, Meimei began to speak but didn't look at me. "I'm leaving in a week," he said, staring at the ground.

I quickly apologized for Mama's insults. "I'm sorry about what Mama said in there."

Meimei took a deep breath and began to speak softly to me. "It's OK, Marilyn. Not quite what I expected, but I'm not totally surprised," he said, taking my hand into his.

Within a minute, we heard the front door open, and Mama stomped outside, pointing a finger at Meimei.

"I thought you was up to somethin', bringing presents, ice cream, and cookies here. You're such a good man." Her sarcasm was over the top. "Now you is talking about taking Marilyn with you. It'll be over my dead body. Yo' scheming didn't work." Mama went back into the house just as fast as she had come out. She slammed the door so hard that Meimei flinched.

Neither Meimei nor I responded to Mama.

Meimei pointed up toward the sky. "See that star over there? It's the North Star. When you think of me, I want you to look up at the sky for the brightest one, and there I will be. I will write to you every week, and I will send you stamps so you can write me back. You will be in college soon and old enough to make your own decisions in a few years."

He kissed me on my forehead, then right under both eyes, and then lightly on my lips. Then he let out a big sigh and pulled me closer to him. "Remember that you are mine. I leave you a virgin, and everything is intact, so when I come for you, it should still be intact. Do you understand?"

I nodded.

Meimei walked to his car. I watched him go into the dark night, looking alone and dejected. Once he got to his car, he turned around and waved until I went inside the house.

CHAPTER 28

YOU ARE NOT BRILLIANT

When I returned to school the following Monday, my social studies teacher, Mr. Moore, told me to see the guidance counselor during study hall. Afraid I had missed too many days to graduate, I quickly checked the back of my notebook. There were only twenty-one absentee stroke tallies. I felt good about that, but I was still fearful that I was about to get some bad news. I walked into the main brick building during study hall, where the guidance counselor's office was. I said my one-sentence prayer repeatedly—*God, please help me to graduate*—as I waited outside her door.

Mrs. Allman, the guidance counselor, opened the door wide and asked, "What are your plans?" She looked dismissively at me as though she were wasting her time. She shifted through a few papers on her desk and then motioned for me to sit.

I couldn't look Mrs. Allman in the face, and I couldn't answer her question, because I didn't understand it. I didn't speak. I continued to stand there like a stupid person, afraid to say anything. My head spun with unanswered questions. *Did I do something wrong? Will I even graduate? What if I miss more days of school? What does she mean by asking me what my plans are?* I was so uncomfortable that I wanted to leave her office. I turned and looked at the door behind me.

"Do I need to repeat the question, or have you not thought of your future?" Mrs. Allman asked.

"I plan to graduate," I said nervously, silently praying that I would.

I tried to remember if I had failed to record any other missed days from school. I no longer trusted my absentee tallies.

Mrs. Allman raised her voice and said, "After graduation." She shuffled a few sheets of paper in a beige folder and then stared at me.

"Oh, after graduation!" I said, and I slowly sat down in front of her desk.

I was temporarily shocked and couldn't say another word. My prayer was being answered, and my dream was being realized. I was in a state of disbelief. Several seconds passed before I was able to speak again.

"I want to go to journalism school," I said.

Mrs. Allman ran her fingers through her light brown hair. "You want to go to journalism school?"

She shook her head slowly as if surprised. I was mum and uncomfortable. I raised my head to eye level with her. Her face was flushed red. She lowered her eyes, pushed a few wayward strands of hair behind her ear, and then placed both hands on top of her desk.

Mrs. Allman sighed and then flipped open a folder with my name on it and said, "You are a colored female—and not a brilliant student, which you have to be to become a journalist. I don't want you wasting your time. Please choose a discipline that will work for you."

For the remainder of our meeting, I sat silently and nodded in agreement with every suggestion. Finally, Mrs. Allman advised me to apply to four colleges, and if my first choice didn't accept me, perhaps my second or third choice would. After ten minutes, she stood up, handed me some college brochures, and ushered me out of her office.

On my way back to class, I dropped all the pamphlets into a trash can. I felt our meeting had been simply a perfunctory one.

During study hall the next day, I went to see Miss Kittrell, my typing teacher, and discussed college with her. She told me about A&T State University in Greensboro, Johnson C. Smith in Charlotte, Central University in Durham, Winston-Salem State, and Fayetteville State, predominately black colleges in North Carolina. She gave me several booklets that I took home.

That night, when I flipped through the brochures, my dream of going to any college began to disappear. They all had application fees between fifteen and twenty dollars. I had only twelve dollars in my savings account. I thought to myself, *Daddy was right after all. I can't even apply to college with only twelve dollars.*

After supper, we all sat in the den, watching TV. I was so upset I

A Head of Cabbage

couldn't study. Finally, Daddy looked over at me. He was not drunk but had taken a swig or two.

"Maylyn, I got somethin' I need to say to you. You almost nineteen, and I ain't supposed to be taking care of you no mo'. All my girls had husbands by your age. Now, you ought to do somethin' wit yo' bushy hair. You walking round lookin' like a militant. You know yo' hair ain't good like yo' mama's." He looked over at Mama's semistraight, wavy hair. "There just ain't no need in you having yo' hair all puffed up. Menfolk ain't gonna want you looking like that."

I looked over at Mama, hoping she would come to my defense, but she said nothing.

William Winston, my baby brother, sat on the lower end of the couch, frowning as if in disbelief. He twisted in his seat and stared up at Daddy. I could tell he was itching to say something, but I waved my hand at him to remain silent. I didn't want Daddy's wrath coming down on him.

"Daddy," I said, "I've got something to say to you too. I've been earning my keep since I was five years old. I've worked on somebody's farm since before I started school."

Mama jerked her head toward me in a flash. Her eyes blinked faster than usual. I knew she wanted me to shut up, but I couldn't.

"I ain't been trying to get a husband, because I want to go to college, but I can't go now because you took my money. You made me pay to have the wheat combined and milled. You made me keep the tractor's and your truck's gas tanks full. I had to pay the telephone bill most of the time and your monthly bill at Lawrence's country store. All I got left is twelve dollars—and it costs at least fifteen dollars to send off a college application."

Daddy lowered his head and remained quiet. But every so often, Mama rolled her eyes at me and lifted a hand to her mouth, shaking her head to show me her disapproval of my rant.

But I continued. "Parents like you hinder their children's opportunities. You made me scared of everything and everybody. Why can't you help us to make something of our lives? Why don't you treat your own children better? And I ain't a militant. This here hair of mine is what God gave me." I patted my Afro all around and on top. "If God is perfect, my hair is absolutely perfect, and all hair is good."

Daddy lit a cigarette, took a draw, and coughed. "Nora, you better talk to Maylyn. She's got too much mouth."

I was so angry at Daddy that I left the room as he and Mama watched TV. On my way upstairs to my room, William Winston stopped me. He handed me one of the college brochures I hadn't seen.

He grinned and said, "Marilyn, look at this one."

Later in the week, I applied to Bennett College in Greensboro because their application fee was only ten dollars.

CHAPTER 29

NO ONE CLAPPED FOR ME

It was the first day of my final exams. God had heard my prayers. Rain was coming down in sheets, and since we didn't work during inclement weather, I could go to school.

My English teacher, Mrs. Parson, a tall, youthful-looking white woman with dark brown hair, came and stood in front of me. As usual, she was well dressed in pumps that matched her outfit—that day, everything was beige. She looked around the crowded classroom and made some notes on her clipboard. Then she looked down at me.

I cussed under my breath. "Shit!" *She is getting ready to make something happen—and it probably won't be good for me.*

Mrs. Parson made a few more notes on her clipboard and then said, "Marilyn, I need you to go to the back of the classroom and exchange seats with Willie."

I seethed with anger that she had asked me to go to the back of the classroom. My resentment grew to the point that my throat began to hurt. But I got my belongings and obliged her request, knowing she had the power to prevent me from graduating. I gave an unpleasant glance at Willie, the white male student gathering his belongings to come take my front-row seat. I thought Mrs. Parson wanted to upset me so I wouldn't concentrate and would do poorly on the final exam.

She started to pass out the test papers, and when she reached the rear of the room, near me, I stood up. My eyes twitched, and my stomach growled from hunger and fear, but I wanted to know why I had to give my seat to Willie.

"Mrs. Parson, why do I have to sit in the back of the classroom today?"

She gasped. "Oh my," she whispered. "Because I know you don't cheat. I have to put my cheaters up front near me, so I can keep an eye on them."

She touched my shoulder. "You do well without cheating, and you'll do just fine today."

At the supper table that night, I told Daddy what had happened at school. He grunted and blew over his hot cup of coffee. "Yo' ass just keep on living; you'll see the devil coming out of 'em when they start throwing up roadblocks yo' way. You always talkin' 'bout education. Shit, you need to ask yo' teacher whatever happened to our forty acres and a mule."

"I just wanted you to know that there are some good white people, and my teacher is one of them. She trusted me and said I would do well on her test without cheating."

Daddy rolled his eyes upward with a giant smirk on his face. Then, finally, he looked over at Mama as she jabbed her cigarette butt into her coffee cup, nodding in agreement.

The next day at school, I asked my black typing teacher about forty acres and a mule. Miss Kittrell was a stout young woman with long black hair and a pretty face with upturned lips. She stood up from her desk and told me she was not a history teacher. She would inform me of what she knew but said I would need to double-check with the library to ensure the information was correct.

"After slavery was abolished, former slaves were promised forty acres and a mule." As she spoke, she watched suspiciously as white students filed into her classroom.

"Oh really?" I said, thinking that Daddy's nontrusting attitude toward the government and white people was partly unfounded.

She lowered her voice. "It was supposed to be a way to compensate and help the former slaves become self-sufficient. They would be able to at least feed themselves off the land. But then President Andrew Johnson stopped the program before it was implemented."

"Why did he stop the program?" I asked in a whisper.

"I don't think anyone knows for certain, but most likely to appease the southern plantation owners. They needed the freed slaves to continue to work their farms, if not for free, then as cheap as possible."

I could hardly wait to tell Daddy what had happened to the program. Unfortunately, when I got home that afternoon, Daddy was nowhere to be found, and as it turned out, I never told him what I had learned about the unimplemented program.

A Head of Cabbage

June 3, 1970, was graduation day.

I wiped the perspiration off my forehead onto the tail of my long-sleeved white shirt as I rested in the middle of a long tobacco row I was weeding. The wooden handle of the hoe I was using had rubbed a small blister between my forefinger and thumb. It began to sting. Gnats, mosquitoes, and flies swarmed around my head, some biting and some just being a nuisance.

Mama reached the end of her tobacco row first and walked over to the shade of a giant oak tree where she had earlier put a jug of iced water.

When Daddy and I finished our rows, I stared up at the sun to gauge the time of day. I thought it must have been around two o'clock. Mama handed Daddy the jug of water. Daddy wiped his forehead with his arm and looked across the tobacco field before taking a drink.

"We need to finish Horseshoe today so we can start at the Creek on Friday." Daddy named his fields of tobacco and all the plots of land where other crops were planted. I didn't know why, and I'd never asked.

I remained silent. Mama was also quiet, but she glanced over at me and started down another row, chopping weeds and working her hoe around the tobacco plants faster than Daddy and I. Ignoring the painful blister, I began to hoe more quickly to keep up with her. She gave me a wink, and the hoeing contest was on. Unfortunately, I was no match for Mama's skill as she lengthened her distance from me.

An hour or so later, we had finished weeding two acres of tobacco, and as we walked home, I asked Mama if she would take me to my high school graduation.

"I sho plan on it," she said. "Ronald, I'm gonna need the truck for a little while this evening. I got to take Marilyn to her school's graduation."

"Graduation?" Daddy sounded surprised. He looked over at me. "She's graduating? Shit, Nora, I got somewhere to go."

Levi came rolling by with the tractor, and Daddy hopped onto the back with him. My heart was almost in my throat. I was afraid Daddy would be gone before Mama and I reached home. I prayed, *Please, God, don't let Daddy leave. I want to go to my graduation.*

It took Mama and me about thirty-five minutes to reach our house, and the truck was still in the driveway.

Later, Mama pulled in front of Bartlett Yancey Senior High School. I gathered my hat and gown and hopped out of the truck. Mama was still in her work clothes and didn't come inside with me. I wanted her to, but she waved and left.

I felt like getting down on my knees to thank God, but I saw lots of people entering the building, so I didn't kneel, but I repeatedly whispered, "Thank you, God. My family's curse has been broken."

I walked inside the school.

After forced school desegregation in Caswell County, this was the first class to graduate from Bartlett Yancey Senior High School. The hallway bustled with white and black classmates. The bleachers outside quickly filled up with parents and grandparents there to witness their children's graduation. Everywhere I looked, there were happy faces of well-dressed men and women shaking hands and congratulating one another's children.

After classmate Claude Elmore concluded his graduation speech, the principal, Mr. Plumblee, began to call each graduate's name. Parents stood up and clapped for their children. After the principal finished, we threw our caps into the air with a roar. Parents ran to their children and began to hug and kiss them. Grandparents—some stooped over and others with walking canes—beamed with pride as they shook their grandchildren's hands.

I stood there and watched everyone for a few minutes. I felt alone and sad that no one in my family had come to see me graduate from high school. No one had clapped for me, and that made me cry. Eventually, I walked outside to see if Mama had returned to take me home. She had not.

It started to rain, and I took cover inside the building, waiting and wondering if my diploma would make a difference in my life. Finally, after waiting for about thirty minutes, I started to walk home in the rain, when I saw Daddy's green truck barreling toward the school's driveway.

"I took a nap and then remembered that I had to pick you up," Mama said, and she reached over and patted me on the head, which made me feel that she was proud of me, even though she never said so. After that, I told myself not to expect things from my parents that they couldn't give.

CHAPTER 30

IN LUCK

Two weeks after I graduated, I got an acceptance letter and a thick packet of information on financial assistance from Bennett College in Greensboro, North Carolina. To my shock, it cost $4,000 a year to attend the all-girls college.

I rode to work with my brother Edward, who had gotten me a job on the third shift at Glen Raven Mills in Burlington, North Carolina. Unfortunately, even though I saved as much of my meager paycheck as possible, I had not saved enough.

For several days, I mulled over how to ask Daddy for tuition money. I didn't know if I should catch him in the morning, when he was sober, or wait until he had some happy juice.

I decided to ask, and the sooner the better. So late one Saturday night, I waited up for Daddy to return home. When he arrived, he was just about drunk and tried to mimic Tarzan's signature holler as he entered the house.

Mama seemed pleasant and watched TV while Terri fell asleep on the sofa. Levi and William Winston had gone upstairs to their bedroom. Daddy settled down on the end of the couch in a drunken stupor. Mama got him some food.

I went over to sit on the sofa beside him. "Daddy, guess what? I'm going to college in the fall." I tried not to say too much, thinking he might be more concerned about who would help him on the farm.

"Well," Daddy said. He sounded like the old deacons at church while they waited for the preacher to make his point and conclude the sermon.

"It costs about four thousand dollars a year to go to college. How much can you give me?" I held my head down, barely able to breathe, while I waited for his answer.

"Shit, gal," Daddy said, "that's close to what it costs for me to get a new truck. Forget about college. Just call it off."

I was not deterred, and a few days later, I filled out the paperwork to get a loan from the College Foundation of North Carolina while Daddy and Mama sat watching TV in their bedroom. Finally, I explained the process to them because I needed their signatures to get the loan. I promised to pay the entire loan back once I graduated.

I marked an *X* where they needed to sign and handed Daddy the ballpoint pen. Daddy took the pen and exploded.

"Shit naw! I ain't signing no papers! You got to call it off, 'cause yo' ass just ran out of luck."

I walked out of my parents' bedroom and started across the hallway to the living room, where it was quiet. I wanted to be alone, but the front door opened. I stopped in the hallway to see who it was.

William Winston, my baby brother, walked in. He was fourteen years old and had become mean and bitter. He had gotten expelled from school a month before I graduated because he got off the school bus at his friend's house one day instead of going to school. I went to the guidance counselor to see about letting him return but was told a parent had to come talk with the school's administration before he would be allowed back in school. I begged both Mama and Daddy to speak with the school's counselor and principal, but they wouldn't, so William Winston never returned to school. No truancy officer or anyone else questioned why he was not in school, even though he was not sixteen, the legal age to drop out.

William Winston looked down at the financial-aid papers I held. "What's that you got in your hand?" he asked.

"It's a loan application from the College Foundation. I need Daddy's signature, but he won't sign." I lowered my voice to a whisper. "I'm going to secretly sign Daddy's name, so I can get the loan. Don't tell anybody, OK?"

William Winston looked from left to right and followed me into the living room. "Marilyn, I believe that's against the law. It's called fraud. You shouldn't sign Daddy's name. You can get into trouble." My youngest brother stared at the papers for a few more seconds and then grabbed the documents out of my hand. "You're in luck—I'll sign Daddy's name on the loan papers for you. Don't you tell anybody."

CHAPTER 31

FOUR DOLLARS

On August 25, 1970, Mama arranged for Edward to take me to Bennett College in Greensboro. Expectedly, she did not want to come with us.

I was afraid to leave home, but I knew I must. I stood outside in the shade of the big oak tree in the front yard. I turned and took one last look at the old plantation-style farmhouse. I saw Mama standing in the living room window, peeping through the pink plantation blinds. She dabbed her eyes with the palm of her hand.

I felt guilty about leaving Mama alone to do all the housework and field work. My baby sister was only eight. I feared Mama might work herself to death. Daddy stood on the front porch, smoking a cigarette. He looked unhappy but said nothing as Edward hoisted my big trunk into the back of his car. I didn't say goodbye.

A few weeks later, I received a letter from Mama. She told me that my sister Inez and her husband were moving to Philadelphia, that Slim continued to beat up on Blanche, and that Daddy was still drinking moonshine like a camel draining a mudhole. At the bottom of the letter, she'd taped four dollars. She told me I must make it last because she could not send any more money.

How was I supposed to make four dollars last? I didn't know how I would pay for my books. I soon organized a poker game with three of my classmates in my room. It had been a long time since I'd played poker with my brothers and their friends. I didn't remember all the rules, but they didn't matter to me. I had to win regardless. So I explained the basic rules of seven-card stud: betting, raising, folding, and calling. I deliberately gave incomplete information on how the hands were ranked, and lucky for me, no one asked for clarification.

From Thomasville, North Carolina, Jessie suggested we play for fifty cents. That was a lot of money to me, but I agreed.

After several hours, we heard the intercom buzz. One of the cafeteria workers—the one we called the Chicken Lady—invited everyone to buy freshly fried chicken. I stayed in my room alone while they all went to buy chicken sandwiches and sweet potato pie. While I waited for their return, I counted the money I had won—sixteen dollars—and hid it in my top dresser drawer.

They soon returned with their fried chicken and sweet potato pie. It smelled delicious, but the smell of fried chicken could not compare to how my sixteen-dollar win made me feel.

We played my brand of poker for several nights. Again, I won every hand. Two of my wealthier friends, Linda and Jessie, eventually asked me if I accepted checks.

I kept a stern face and answered, "I will just once."

Tall, dark, and bosomy, Linda was from Whitakers, North Carolina. Without a doubt, she was a brilliant student. I was impressed by Linda's smarts and considered myself lucky to have her as a friend.

One night, Linda suggested we raise the ante to one dollar. I didn't like it, but I went along and continued my winning streak for several hands. After a short while, Linda began to tap the bottom half of her chin. She glanced at the two other girls and shook her head. Linda wrote me a check for twenty dollars. She handed it to me, but just before I took it, she snatched it back.

"Abbott," said Linda, who often called me by my last name, "how can you win all the time?" She looked me straight in my eyes.

I knew I must look directly into her eyes as well; otherwise, I would look dishonest, and my gig would be over. I needed more money to pay for my books. I pretended to be concentrating on my hand, and then I looked Linda in the face without blinking. My heart throbbed fiercely, but I willed it to slow down.

"I'm just lucky," I said, hoping to get on with the game, but the other two players became quiet and looked from Linda to me.

Linda started to laugh, but she stopped abruptly. "Abbott, Abbott, I don't believe anybody can be that lucky." She raised her eyebrows high as she handed the check over.

She usually called me by my last name, but this time, I sensed that she said my last name twice as a signal or some sort of warning to the other

A Head of Cabbage

girls—or to me. So I lost the next two small hands and then accused Linda of breaking my winning streak.

After several nights of playing my brand of poker, my four dollars had become forty-five dollars.

Linda and I were in the same math class. I soon learned that she had an aptitude for math, and I needed Linda to help me pass. After a few days, I felt so guilty about cheating my friends that I stopped playing poker.

Under the student aid program, I got a secretarial job in the English department. I worked for Miss Georgia B. Lassiter, who tried to teach me to lose my southern drawl. She said it made me sound unintelligent.

The first Friday in November, right after my last class, I caught a Greyhound bus to Danville, Virginia. Mama picked me up. She seemed excited and happy that I had come home for the weekend and was proud to be driving Daddy's brand-new green 1970 Chevrolet truck.

As she pulled the truck away from the bus station, Mama said, "It's good you came home, 'cause we gonna kill two hogs first thing tomorrow morning."

I gave a shrug. I would have stayed on campus had I known this would be a hog-killing weekend.

The following morning, while still in bed, I heard two gunshots and the squeal of pigs. It was about six o'clock and colder than usual in the house. I pulled the heavy covers up around my neck and sank farther down in the bed.

Like many times before, Mama called me downstairs to eat breakfast and get ready to help her with the fresh meat. Then she lit a cigarette and made herself a cup of black coffee.

"Hurry up and finish eating," she said. "They'll be bringing in the hog guts in a few minutes. It's best we clean them while they're still warm."

I stopped eating. The thought of cleaning and dressing hog guts took away my appetite. I got up from the table and waited for my brothers to bring the pig intestines inside.

Mama sprinkled a few dabs of Gardenia, a cheap cologne, onto two towels to mask the smell. We pinned the towels around our noses and moved into position. We stood in front of three big tin tubs of warm water. Once we dumped the intestines' contents into a five-gallon bucket, we were to wash the pig guts and rinse them twice.

When I saw Edward and Ronald Jr. coming with the first batch of guts, I felt sick. My brothers set the big metal tub down and then stood by the stove to keep warm.

After a few minutes, Ronald Jr. walked over to where Mama, my little sister Terri, and I cleaned the pig guts. He twisted his head sideways and looked directly at Edward.

"Edward, did you know that Marilyn don't eat chitlin's?" Ronald said with a tinge of mischief in his voice.

Edward looked surprised and turned to me. "You don't eat chitlin's?"

"No, I don't, and I never will eat anything that smells this bad," I said, dropping a section of intestines into the last tub for final rinsing.

"Not even fried?" Edward asked, scratching his head.

"No, not even fried," I said with stark finality.

Ronald Jr. looked at Edward with a smirk on his face. "Hey, man, do you want to make a quick twenty dollars?"

Edward looked puzzled and said, "Shit yeah, but what do I have to do?"

Ronald Jr. turned to face me and grinned. He gestured his head my way. Now both brothers stared me in the face.

"If you make Marilyn eat a piece of chitlin', I'll give you twenty dollars."

"I'm sorry, Marilyn," Edward said, "but you're gonna eat some chitlin' today."

Mama and I had only cleaned about a third of the first set of innards. I dropped another piece, about a foot long, into the third tub of clean, warm water for the final rinsing.

"I will not eat chitlin's today, tomorrow, or in the future," I said. "Besides, Mama said they're going into the freezer, and she ain't cooking them until Christmas."

I began to bounce another foot-long section of chitlin's up and down in the first tub of water. I didn't notice Edward's stealthy movements as he got closer to the tub of guts, until it was too late.

"Who said anything about them being cooked?" Edward said, and he reached down, grabbed a piece of raw chitterling from the tub, and slammed it against my face. The grayish hog gut, although cleaned, still stank and dripped with water.

A Head of Cabbage

I darted out the back door, skipping a few steps, and ran toward the nearest tobacco barn to hide.

Edward ran after me with the string of raw chitterling dangling in his hands. He eventually caught me, put me in a headlock, and practically dragged me back to the house for everyone to witness.

I clenched my teeth and pressed my lips together as tightly as I could. Edward rubbed the raw chitterling all over my mouth.

"Why don't you talk now? You always got something to say. Talk now," Edward said. "Please, say something. Just say anything." Edward held the chitlin's over my mouth. I began to cry, but I kept my mouth tightly closed.

"Edward, you can let her go," Ronald Jr. finally said, and he reached into his back pocket. "She didn't eat 'em, but seeing them covering her mouth is good enough for me." He gave Edward a twenty-dollar bill.

I complained to Mama that she let the boys do whatever they wanted and that it was not fair.

"My boys was just having a little fun," she said.

Less than six hours later, the sausage had been put into the grinder; the pork chops and ribs were in the freezer; and the hams, shoulders, and side meat had been salted and hung in the smokehouse.

I took a bath and called my former classmate David, whom I'd had a crush on for two years. When David pulled into the driveway in his baby-blue 1966 Chevelle, I forgot about my brothers and the chitterling.

David took me to listen to music at his home. His family's unpainted wooden house was relatively small and didn't look sturdy, almost as if a strong wind could easily have blown it over. But I found the interior of the house immaculate and different. I had never seen wallpaper before. There were hundreds of black decorative metal tacks running down the sides of tan wallpaper to hold it in place. The floors were covered with glossy, new-looking brown-and-beige linoleum.

In the family room hung pictures of Dr. Martin Luther King Jr., John F. Kennedy, and Bobby Kennedy, and on the opposite wall hung several portraits of deceased relatives. A single lightbulb hung from the ceiling. Beautiful brown-and-white lace curtains graced the three short windows.

I sat on a multicolored sofa, when David's aunt Autry walked into the cool room. She didn't say anything to me, nor did I say anything to her, and David did not introduce us. Instead, his aunt lit up a Newport cigarette and started on David.

"David, I'm almost out of cigarettes—and what good is you to me if you ain't nowhere to be found when I need you to take me to the store?"

The expression on David's face was one of surprise and guilt, as if he had done something wrong. He told his aunt he could take her to get cigarettes right away. And he did. I went with them to three different stores. They purchased cigarettes at one store, Pepsi-Cola at another, and groceries at a third.

The next day, before I left to go back to school, I decided to have a womanly talk with Mama. She was in the kitchen, washing a few dishes, when I walked in. I told her I thought it was time for me to start taking birth-control pills.

"Birth control?" Mama hollered. "Here I was thinking you was a nice girl, thinking of nothing but education." She shook her head. "But now I see you thinking 'bout something else."

Mama wiped her hands on the terry-cloth dishrag and walked over to the kitchen table. She dropped her body down hard into one of the chairs, sighed, and looked up at me. "Do you know what girls do when they take birth-control pills?"

Her face rippled with painful-looking frowns as she squinted. I flushed with embarrassment and turned my head away from her line of sight.

"Mama, all the girls at school are taking them. I think I should too, just in case," I said almost inaudibly. "I'm going on twenty."

"Just in case of what?" Mama snapped. "Oh Lord. Have mercy on my child."

I wanted to ease her angst, so I said I didn't really need birth control.

CHAPTER 32

WASHINGTON, DC

In August 1971, I accepted an assignment in Washington, DC, with the office of the Equal Employment Opportunity Commission (EEOC) through the work-study program at Bennett College.

I arrived in Washington, DC, totally unaware of what big-city life was like. The nonstop traffic, constant sirens, honking car horns, crowded buses, dirty streets, and crowds of people everywhere caused me to instantly dislike the city. In addition, I found it unacceptable to see only hazy streetlights instead of stars when I looked up toward the night sky.

On my first day of work, I was introduced to the manager as one of eight underprivileged college students. The manager was a handsome Afro-American man professionally dressed in a dark suit. He remained seated while his white female assistant and I stood in front of his big, glossy desk. Unfortunately, I forgot his name, and I was glad I did.

The first thing he said to me was "I heard you lived on a farm in North Carolina."

I nodded. "Yes, that's true."

In a derisive tone, he asked, "Do you like driving tractors and picking cotton?"

He looked over at his assistant, took a sip of his coffee, and chuckled. His assistant blushed and looked embarrassed. I wanted to cuss and spit in his face, but I stood there, forcing myself to remain calm and respectful.

"Ah, no, sir," I said. "We raised tobacco, not cotton, and I have brothers who drove the tractor."

As I spoke those words, I became angry at myself for not walking out of his office and the program. I'd had no idea or warning and no reason to think that a professional northern black person would denigrate southern blacks. I had incorrectly assumed that all black people in the United States had empathy for one another, no matter their plight.

Now I realized that was not the case. So I resolved never to be in this manager's presence again.

As most people did, I went to work at 9:00 a.m., but many employees took two hours for lunch and left around four in the afternoon. I also noticed that many of them started drinking coffee mixed with vodka or some other type of alcohol as soon as they arrived, and I was the only one who appeared to be surprised. I wondered if President Nixon was aware of his employees' behavior.

Paranoia eventually set in, and I trusted only Sue, one of the students in the program. Sue was from Springfield, Ohio. She was pretty and sophisticated and had more worldly experiences than I.

One evening, after work, Sue and I walked down the business district on our way to a Chinese restaurant, when a man approached.

"You ladies are walking too fast for a man from New York," someone from behind said.

I began to talk to the man, just being friendly. Sue told the man to get his New York ass away from us, and the man moved to the other side of the street. Sue rolled her eyes at me as she picked up the pace.

"Marilyn, that man was looking for a prostitute. And while I'm at it, let me tell you about pimps," she said. "They are always looking for innocent young women they can turn into whores to make money for them. So don't think a smile means a friend."

There were eight of us in the program for underprivileged students: two black males, two black females, one Native American male, and three Native American females. One day all eight of us were taken to Capitol Hill so a few of the congressmen could see and talk with us. We were told beforehand that we should be pleasant, smile, and appear grateful.

Our first stop was to a certain congressman's office. This man looked strange to me in a white suit and with a long, waxed mustache sticking out on each side of his upper lip. He grinned and hugged us, hugging the girls much too long. When I saw him hugging Sue, I was afraid he would molest her in plain view, but she managed to wiggle away from him with her dignity intact.

After the visit, our supervisor told us we had done an excellent job with the congressmen on Capitol Hill, and he thought the appropriations bill would be passed to provide continuity in everyone's salary.

A Head of Cabbage

I returned to campus early in January 1972 and fell ill. I called my friend Linda over to my room. I told her I thought I had stomach cancer, because I could not stand the smell of fried foods and could not keep anything down.

Linda sat in the only chair in my sparse room. "Girl," she said, "I thought the only thing you did was study. It sounds like you're pregnant."

I laughed for a bit before the laughter cascaded into fear. "I can't be pregnant. I haven't had real sex."

"Marilyn, are you sure?" she asked.

"During the Christmas holidays, I fooled around a bit with my boyfriend, David, but we didn't have real sex. There was no penetration."

"Uh-huh." Linda rolled her eyes. "Well, I know of a case where a girl got pregnant, and the man wore a condom. You can get pregnant without actually doing it, you know."

I didn't know.

"You need to see a doctor, but you can't go to the infirmary here." Linda paused. "If you are pregnant, they will kick you out of school."

My dream of a college education was within my grasp, but I was afraid I had blown it. Another week passed before I called my first cousin Virginia and told her about playing around with David. There was silence on the telephone before I heard a heavy sigh. "You need to go see a doctor," Virginia said.

A few days later, Dr. Hughes, a gynecologist whose office was not far from campus, confirmed the pregnancy. The baby was due in September.

I discreetly asked around and found out it was OK to be pregnant if the student was married. However, the college expelled all unwed mothers.

I began to daydream about how happy David, the baby, and I could be together. David and I would get married, and he would get us a place somewhere near campus for me to continue my education. I would enroll the baby in the on-campus nursery while I was in class, and after I picked the baby up and studied, I would have dinner ready before David came home from work. I could hardly wait to tell David about the baby.

David picked me up the following Friday evening at the Greyhound bus terminal in Danville, Virginia. He preferred going directly to his house, where he had the latest music and could dance with some of his cousins. He never enjoyed dancing with me, because he said I lacked rhythm.

Growing up in the Holiness Church had prevented me from normal teenage behavior. I seldom listened to rock 'n' roll or rhythm and blues, except when Daddy had the radio tuned to a station out of Nashville, Tennessee, in the wee hours of the morning. Mostly, we listened to country music because we could only get one station. Occasionally, we would watch *American Bandstand* and *The Ed Sullivan Show*, but I never went anywhere to dance or just listen to music. The Holiness Church had taught me that dancing, wearing makeup, and curling my hair were of the devil and would send me straight to hell.

About five miles before we reached David's home, I told him we needed to talk. He drove down an unpaved road and parked in the driveway of an old abandoned house. I took a deep breath and turned to face him.

"David, we are going to have a baby."

In the semidark car, I could hardly see, but I clearly saw the panic on David's face. He looked away without saying a word. I sat motionless, watching him, hoping he would accept some responsibility for the predicament I was in.

"Wow," he finally said, "a baby. A real live baby. Well, get rid of it."

His cold response jarred me out of my pleasant reverie.

David popped a Colt 45 beer, took a long gulp, and turned to face me. "You do know abortions are legal now, right? So get rid of it, OK? We can't have a baby."

While waiting for my answer, he finished off the sixteen-ounce beer. I laid my head against the window and held back tears.

Without looking at him, I said, "I know abortions are legal, and I will get one."

Sunday night, after I got back to campus, I called my cousin Virginia again. I told her what had happened with David.

"Marilyn, it's not all your fault. Men are just not men anymore, and a lot of women are to blame. Some mamas encourage their sons not to get married, because they think they will lose their sons. It's kind of like their sons are surrogate husbands for them."

"But David's mother does not know about my pregnancy; plus, she has a husband," I said. "Please just tell me what to do."

A Head of Cabbage

Virginia was one of my smartest cousins, and I trusted her.

"Don't forget that Mary got pregnant with Jesus before marriage," she said. "If it was so wrong, would God have done that to Mary? At least you have choices."

I did not want to talk about Jesus. "Believe me," I said, "I feel bad enough without you bringing up Jesus."

Virginia sighed and asked, "What are you going to do?"

"There is not much of a choice," I said. "Staying in school is important. If I graduate college, other members of my family will do the same, and then we will have generations of college graduates with opportunities to attain middle-class status."

Arrangements were made to have the abortion in Chapel Hill, North Carolina. Virginia's oldest sister, Shirley, picked me up and took me to Chapel Hill Hospital for the abortion early one cold February morning. The receptionist asked a series of questions and then sent me to see a psychiatrist. He checked off boxes on a sheet of paper as fast as he could and then asked me if I could live with myself if I had this abortion.

"I'll have to," I said in a whisper while crying.

He asked about my background and which school I attended. I lied and said I attended Greensboro College, for fear he might contact the dean at Bennett College and have me expelled.

"Marilyn, please calm yourself," Shirley said when I returned to the waiting room. "You are doing what is best."

CHAPTER 33

PREGNANT AND AUNT V

Shirley's encouraging words made me feel better, until the nurse called my name to come with her. We walked down a long corridor into a cold, sterile room. A stainless-steel table and a mechanical device sat in front of a small bed. The device was plugged into an electrical outlet.

The nurse gave me a gown and asked me to undress. I felt the sensation of fluttering butterflies in my abdomen as the nurse stepped out of the room. After a few minutes, the nurse returned. I was sitting on the padded bed, fully dressed.

"Miss Abbott," she said, annoyed, "you must disrobe before the doctor can begin the procedure. I will step out to give you a little more time."

I could hardly breathe. I thought of my baby.

My voice was cracking, so I whispered to the nurse, "May I ask you a question before you leave?"

"Sure," she said, and she turned around.

"How is the doctor going to give me this abortion?"

"He is going to insert a saline solution into your cervix and then suction it all out. It will take only a few minutes, and it will not hurt," the nurse said. "Then you can get on with your education."

I started to pray. *God, please forgive me*, I said about four or five times, and then an overwhelming feeling of calmness came over me, and I heard an inner voice that sounded like the whisper of a child.

Mama, don't kill me, the voice said.

I jumped off the bed and put on my shoes. I didn't question the voice, because I didn't believe my conscience had played a trick on me. I said to the inner voice, "I'm not going to kill you."

Just then, the door opened, and the doctor and nurse walked in.

"I've changed my mind," I said. "I'm going to have my baby."

My heart throbbed faster and harder as I watched the doctor's face change colors. It went from white to pink to an angry red. I felt as if my heart were going to jump out of my mouth.

"You're supposed to have this abortion," the doctor said.

The nurse took my arm. I snatched it away from her weak grip and rushed past both of them.

"Miss Abbott, the papers have been signed. You are—"

I was out the door before the doctor could finish. He and the nurse dashed out behind me. I kept looking back, wondering if they could force me to have the abortion since I had signed the medical procedure papers. I started to run.

"Shirley, let's go! Let's go!" I hollered, rushing through the swinging exit doors.

Once we were outside, I told Shirley I had changed my mind and wanted to have my baby, no matter what people thought about me.

"Well," Shirley said, "it ain't nobody's business. It's your decision. Stick to it."

I started to cry.

"What's wrong now?" Shirley asked.

I wiped my tears before I tried to explain how I felt. "I thought one day I would work in some capacity to influence young women to stop becoming unwed mothers. So they wouldn't stay poor. Now I'm becoming one."

We got back to Yanceyville late in the afternoon. I called David from Shirley's house and told him I hadn't had the abortion.

"Well, OK," he said, "but I ain't getting married."

I hung up the phone and thought about Mama and Daddy. I was the one child who'd screamed and fought with all my might about getting an education. Now I had to acknowledge my failure and face my shame.

Within a few months, the campus closed for the summer. I was too ashamed for Mama and Daddy to see me pregnant and unmarried. So I moved in with my sister Mildred and her husband, Reginald, in Greensboro.

Three days after giving birth on September 4, 1972, I handed over my baby girl to my aunt V, who had agreed to keep her so I could remain in college. She held my baby tightly and pointed a finger in my face just as I was about to leave for Bennett College.

"Don't you start having a bunch of babies without a husband. Birth control is available."

"It won't happen again," I said.

I worked on campus during the week through the work-study program. Every Friday, my cousin Virginia, who worked in Greensboro at the telephone company, picked me up from campus and took me to her mother's house to spend time with my baby.

In the middle of October, I arrived at Aunt V's house on a Friday night. She was distraught.

"Marilyn, that boy David came up here and brought a bunch of hand-me-down baby clothes. I don't want him coming to my house," she said emphatically. "He acts funny to me, and I think you ought to stay away from him."

Two weeks later, David suggested we get married. "Marilyn, I think we should get married and raise our own baby. What do you think?"

"OK," I said, "but I need to complete my senior year, so I can get a good-paying job."

"Yeah," David said, nodding in agreement.

On November 11, 1972, David and I married in the home of David's Baptist pastor, Reverend Singletary. It was a simple ceremony with only David's aunt Autry and Mrs. Singletary in attendance.

We lived with David's aunt and uncle for a few months before David bought us a beautiful mobile home and had it placed on his mother's land across the road from where his aunt Autry and uncle Hunter lived.

CHAPTER 34

UNHAPPILY MARRIED

In early August 1973, I started to make plans to return to college to complete my senior year. I would be a college graduate soon, the first in my family. I was happy, but David was not.

"You're one sorry mother," David said one Saturday morning as I sat reading over some correspondence I had received from Bennett College. "I hate mothers who don't want to take care of their own children." He stared across the table.

I laid the material down and practically screamed, "What is your problem? I cook, clean, and take good care of Sherondalyn, and all I want to do is graduate from college. It's only nine more months, for Christ's sake. Don't you understand that I will be able to get a job to help us have a better life? What's wrong with that?"

David stood up and screamed even louder. "You want to know the problem?" He threw both hands in the air and took a step backward. "The problem is, I don't want a part-time wife. I want a full-time wife and mother for my daughter. All you think about is Bennett College." Then, in a feminine voice, he mocked me. "I've got to get my degree."

"Shit," I said, "David, you promised me before we got married that I could finish college. It's only nine months."

David walked up close to my face, as I'd seen his aunt Autry do with her husband on several occasions. He jerked his neck this way and that before he spoke. "That was then, and this is now. If you don't want to take care of your child, then you shouldn't have had her."

David stormed out of the house and left with his first cousin Salmon, who lived next door.

Sometime before daybreak, David returned home. I pretended to be asleep. He slipped into bed and, after a few minutes, sat up.

"Marilyn, it's time for breakfast. How about fixing me some bacon and eggs?"

Neither of us mentioned that he'd spent the night away from home.

I grabbed my robe, went into the kitchen, and cooked him a full breakfast. I returned with his food about twenty minutes later, but David was asleep. I placed the food on the dresser and sat on the edge of the bed. I shook him to wake him up. I wanted to talk.

"David, you and Sherondalyn are very important to me and will always come first in my life, so I'm not returning to school in the fall," I said.

"That's good," David said. "Now, let me sleep, please."

A couple of weeks later, as we sat at breakfast, David was not his usual self. He didn't look at me directly but gave all his attention to Sherondalyn sitting in her high chair.

"What's wrong? I thought you would be happy now that I'm not returning to school," I said, "but I see you've still got something on your chest."

David stood up, grabbed his car keys off the bar, and said, "You need to get a job," and then he left for the evening.

With help from my cousin Virginia, I was hired by Southern Bell Telephone Company as a telephone operator. I made a little more than fifty dollars a week and saved twenty-five dollars per month. I paid the telephone bill and bought groceries. David took care of the mortgage on the mobile home, the car note, and the electric bill.

Early one Monday morning, I overheard David asking to borrow five dollars from his aunt. I told him I had saved some money he could have.

"You ain't making any money as it is. You need to wait until you start making real money before you try to save some," David said with displeasure before he walked over to his aunt Autry's house.

I thought of Meimei, my previous African boyfriend, and the advice he had given me: strive to save more than 10 percent of what I earned. I vowed to continue saving money for a rainy day or when I would be able to return to college.

As days and weeks went by, David appeared unhappier. We argued over simple, stupid little things, such as the choice of meat I cooked for dinner. If I cooked chicken, he wanted pork chops. If I cooked pork chops, he wanted fish. When I vacuumed, it was too early or too noisy. I couldn't do anything right. He made me feel like I would never be able to please him, no matter how attentive I was to him and Sherondalyn.

Late one Saturday morning, I had already fed the baby and eaten myself, when David came into the kitchen and sat at the table.

"Marilyn, you ain't cooked breakfast yet!" he yelled over the sound of the vacuum cleaner.

I stopped vacuuming and walked into the kitchen. "David, let me know when you're ready for breakfast."

David snorted his response. "You don't tell me what to do. What kind of wife won't cook for her husband?"

He gave a haughty laugh, as though he had stumped me with his cleverness. I tried to follow the mantra "Be nice, don't talk too much, and speak softly," as Mama had advised. I bent down near David and spoke in a soft tone.

"David, I don't know what kind of wife won't cook for her husband, since I'm not that kind of wife."

"Well," he said, standing up, "I will tell you the kind of wife you are. The sorry kind."

Later that evening, after David left, I called my cousin Virginia and told her about my conversation with David.

"Welcome to married life," Virginia said, and then she suggested I join the Silhouettes, a women's club she belonged to.

There was not anything to do in Yanceyville but go to church. Many elderly citizens couldn't even do that, because they needed assistance and transportation. So the Silhouettes raised money to take a different person out to dinner and a movie once a month. One member would pick the elderly person up. The other members met them at the agreed-upon location, usually a restaurant in Danville, Virginia, or Burlington, North Carolina.

"Well," I said, "I suppose I should join. It will give me something to do when David is out with Salmon on the weekends."

"Oh," Virginia said before pausing too long. "David hangs out a lot with Salmon on the weekends?"

"Sometimes," I said.

Virginia sighed. "Oh, I see."

CHAPTER 35

SOUTHERN BELL

Soon after I got to work on Monday, I found myself sitting in my supervisor's office. But before our meeting, I was on a bronze swivel stool, waiting for the switchboard to light up, when I heard Susie, the operator who sat next to me, struggling with a customer's request.

By the questions Susie asked, I knew the customer was male and black and lived off Rahut Street—the ghetto in Burlington, North Carolina.

"Sir, I cannot understand a word you're saying. Raw Street?" Susie said. "I've never heard of that street before."

I tried to be helpful by inserting my incoming cord into the same lit cell to hear and interpret for Susie. I listened for a while and then told Susie that the man wanted to place a collect call to his mother, who lived on Rahut Street.

Susie, a seasoned telephone operator, completed the call and then slid off her stool and threw her headset hard against the frame of the cord board.

She looked at me and said, "I can have your job for that. You don't interfere with a call I'm handling. Who does that?"

I was surprised by her demeanor. My attempt to assist her had been an insult to her. The switchboard lit up like stars on a clear night, but no one answered any calls. Instead, they were all listening to Susie and me.

Finally, Brenda Burnett, a Communications Workers of America (CWA) job steward, slid off her stool and came to where I sat.

"Marilyn, what happened?" she asked.

I sighed and watched Susie speed-walk toward the supervisor's office. Her blonde hair bounced up and down around her round, florid face. Her high heels barely made her look five feet tall.

"I don't know what I did wrong," I said. "I was trying to help Susie, but she said she could take my job away."

I felt a sense of doom well up inside. Brenda told the other operators, all sitting in a straight line, that the show was over and to get back to work before she had to represent them in a union meeting.

I saw Mrs. Lamont, Susie's supervisor, walking toward me. Susie stood a few feet outside Mrs. Lamont's office, looking at her painted fingernails.

"Marilyn, I need to see you in my office," Mrs. Lamont said.

Brenda, the job steward, stooped down and picked up her black leather briefcase. As she did, she whispered, "I'm going to represent you. They might try to fire you today."

I thought about Daddy telling me how undermining some white people were and how they seemed to enjoy hurting black people. Brenda and I walked with Mrs. Lamont toward her office, and I saw Susie standing there with a smirk on her face.

"Brenda, I ate before Southern Bell, and I will eat after Southern Bell. I don't need you to represent me. I can speak for myself," I said. "If the truth fires me, then I'm fired. I want Susie to know that she may take away my job but never my dignity."

Brenda turned and walked away, shaking her head. "Marilyn, just call me later, OK?"

I nodded and watched Brenda return to her seat. Then, finally, I garnered up enough courage to enter Mrs. Lamont's office alone.

Susie sat at one end of a small, glossy mahogany table. Mrs. Lamont, who appeared to be nervous, went to the head of the table. I slid into the middle seat.

Mrs. Lamont cleared her throat before speaking. "Marilyn, Susie told me you interfered with her work. That is not acceptable behavior. If any operator has difficulty in handling a customer, she will call a supervisor over for assistance. Operators should not rely on peers."

She looked at Susie for a moment. Susie gave a fake smile and nodded.

"What you did was a terminating offense," Mrs. Lamont said. "I'm not firing you today, because you have been on the job for only three months. Instead, I'm going to put an entry in your records." Then she placed both of her hands on the table and said, "You need to apologize to Susie."

I looked at Susie and then at Mrs. Lamont, but I couldn't apologize. They looked at each other in bewilderment. I felt humiliated and was willing to leave my job before I apologized to someone who'd threatened to have me fired for trying to be helpful. I looked away.

For a few tense moments, no one said anything.

"Mrs. Lamont," Susie said, "I will apologize first." Susie shifted her body and tilted her head toward me. "Marilyn, I'm sorry this happened. I was hoping we could be friends." She placed her hands on the table and looked at me with her big, wide gray eyes.

"I feel the same way," I said, "except I'm surprised you have any friends, much less expect me to be one. You wanted to get me fired, when I was only trying to help you and that black customer. I need this job, but I will quit and find another one if I have to."

Mrs. Lamont bowed her head as though she were at her wits' end. Then she looked over at me. "How do you know the customer was black? Did you see him through the phone?"

I forced myself to remain composed. I took in a few quick breaths and exhaled slowly. I looked over at Susie and then at Mrs. Lamont. "I could tell he was black by the way he spoke—the broken English, the texture of his voice. And no white people live on Rahut Street in Burlington."

Mrs. Lamont nodded. On the other hand, Susie twitched in her seat and tapped her glossy red fingernails on the cold wooden table.

Finally, Mrs. Lamont got up and opened the door. Susie rushed out, and by the time I got back to my stool, Susie was already sitting on hers, telling another coworker that Mrs. Lamont had put an entry in my record.

When I got home, I didn't mention my frightful and stressful workday to David.

CHAPTER 36

TROUBLED WATER

By late March 1974, I began to accuse David of having an affair, because our romantic life had become nonexistent. He insisted that the only woman he had ever touched was me and demanded an apology. I gave him one, but our late-night conversation left me with more questions than answers.

"Marilyn, the reason I don't have sex with you as much as I would like is because my doctor told me that vigorous sexual encounters may cause my leg to be amputated." David asked, "Do you want a peg-leg husband?" He stood, dropped his pants, placed a hand partially over a long scar on his left leg, and then began to rub it gently.

I had seen the scar many times but still glanced at it. Finally, I undressed and sat down on the bed. I didn't believe him and still thought he had someone on the side. I had thought David was an honest man. Now I knew he was an incredible liar.

"I was on my way to see you when the accident happened. I got T-boned." He sighed heavily. "Now I have a steel pin in my leg and can't have sex with you without losing my leg. I swear." He sat down at the foot of the bed near me and cupped his chin in his hands as he stared down at the floor.

I took in a deep breath. "David, can't we have sex once a week? The accident happened three years ago. You work and walk OK, and you dance for hours with your cousins!"

David yelled, "I swear, you're unbelievable! I just told you what my doctor said, and you're still thinking about sex. It doesn't make sense for a woman to want it as much as you do. Something is wrong with you. It really is."

I began to wonder if something was wrong with me. Maybe I was not attractive enough. Perhaps I was too skinny. But unfortunately, I couldn't determine the problem.

"David, do you realize that we haven't had sex for almost two years? I think you're messing around with somebody. Mama said men always want to do it. You ain't doing me, so that leaves somebody else."

David stood up and propped himself against the doorframe. He gave me a vacuous look for a few seconds and then went into the living room and turned the volume up on the stereo. The music was so loud that the windows in the bedroom shook. Finally, he lit a cigarette and returned to face me. He blew a puff of smoke upward and then looked down at me.

"I should have known something was wrong with you," he said. "You need to get yourself checked out. It just ain't normal for someone to want sex as much as you. I bet you're going to have an affair."

I managed to control my disappointment. I got up and turned the stereo down. "David, I married you for better or worse, and it's worse, but I don't want you to lose your leg. So I have no choice but to remain faithful."

David turned the music up even louder and asked me not to touch his stereo, because he wanted to listen to his music loud.

I felt dejected as I crawled under the sheet with two pillows stuffed around my ears.

The stereo began to emit a thick grayish smoke early the following day. David slept while I watched and waited for it to catch fire. The stereo never blazed, but the overheating caused irreparable damage.

A couple of weeks after the stereo overheated, David's first cousin Salmon brought an expensive-looking floor-model stereo into the living room one Saturday evening. Salmon said, when I questioned the cost and whether we could afford it, "It's a gift to David from me."

While Salmon waited in the living room, David changed into a stylish cream-and-burgundy popcorn-knit shirt and a pair of burgundy flared-leg polyester pants. David's square jaw added a hint of mystery to his face. His tinted glasses made him look as handsome as any male model.

David told me that he and Salmon were going to the Country Palace, a disco club on the outskirts of Yanceyville. He apologized that I couldn't go with them. I had to stay home to look after the baby.

Something in the back of my mind told me that there was something else going on. I thought this was my chance to catch him with his girlfriend. So I asked Aunt Autry to watch Sherondalyn for me. She agreed, and I went to the club an hour later.

A Head of Cabbage

I found the most inconspicuous spot and sat and watched David dance with different women. I felt better that he and Salmon sat alone when they were not dancing. I started to sneak out, when I heard the crowd begin to chant, "Go, David. Go, David." I peeped through the crowd and saw a woman lying on the floor with David straddling her, gyrating, but their bodies were not touching.

I watched him dance for a few more minutes before I left, feeling confused, angry, jealous, and rejected. When I got home, I called my cousin Virginia and told her about David's fancy rhythmic movements, yet he was unable to have sex.

"I believe you," Virginia said. "He's the best dancer I have ever seen, and I have seen quite a few."

I was in tears as I spoke. "He told me he couldn't perform sex because he was afraid of losing his leg." I raised my voice a couple of octaves. "But his pelvis was gyrating all over the place."

"I know," Virginia said. "It will all come out in the wash. Just hold your peace. Promise me."

"OK, I'll hold my peace," I said before I hung up.

I waited in the guest bedroom for David. I couldn't sleep. When he came home in the wee hours of the morning, he went into our bedroom and lay down on top of the bed. I waited until he went to sleep, and then I poured a bucket of cold water over him.

He jumped up. "What the fuck is wrong with you?"

"I saw you at the Country Palace," I said, "and I don't think anything is wrong with your fucking leg. I think you're having an affair with that big-assed woman I saw you dancing with last night." I stood near the bed with the empty bucket in my hand.

David raised a hand as if to hold me back. "Marilyn, I just want to get some sleep right now." He lay down on my side of the bed, and I went to the guest bedroom.

Around four thirty in the morning, I woke up to a cold liquid splashing over me. I opened my eyes and saw David standing near the bed with an empty orange juice carton in his hand.

He looked down at me. "I started to piss on you," he said, and he walked out of the room.

During Sunday breakfast, David didn't speak. I was still confused and angry. I asked him about his ability to make such wild, gyrating dance moves. He ignored me and grabbed a beer from the fridge.

After a few minutes, he focused his eyes on me and slowly said, "You are not normal." Then he finished off his beer.

"David, my girlfriend told me that her husband chases her around the house for it day and night. What is wrong with me that you don't want to have sex with me?"

David popped another beer and began to drink it in big gulps. I watched his Adam's apple rise and fall. After finishing the second beer, he set the empty can on the table's edge and stood up.

"You want to know what's wrong?" He hiccupped. "I will tell you. First, I don't like you approaching me for sex, period. That's my job. I'm the man. Second, you don't keep Sherondalyn's hair neat, and another thing, I would like for you to cook me rabbit once in a while. And one more thing—you get on my nerves by trying to save every penny you make. It doesn't make sense. I'm sick and tired of you squirreling away every cotton-picking dime. You're just too stingy, and it turns me off. Are those reasons enough for you?"

I sat across the table with a horrified scowl on my face. "In other words," I said, "you're cheating."

Seven more months went by, making it two and a half years since we'd had sex. Then, one warm Saturday night in early October, David came home earlier than expected. The scent of marijuana and alcohol reached my nostrils before David peered into the guest bedroom, where I pretended to be asleep. He staggered into the bedroom and shook me. I didn't move or make a sound.

"Marilyn, you're a good wife," he said. "You deserve a much better husband than me. And you deserve some sex, and I'm going to give you some tonight."

I continued to lie on my back and pretended to be asleep. David's manhood was flaccid, just about four inches long. He straddled me, rubbed his privates across the bottom of my lower abdomen for about fifteen seconds, and then fell over and went to sleep.

The next day, I called Virginia and told her about the fifteen-second encounter with David the previous night. She puffed on a cigarette.

A Head of Cabbage

"Child, I have heard of the sixty-minute man, but the fifteen-second man takes the cake." We both had a good laugh.

I became ill within a few weeks and could not keep anything down. I went to the doctor and found out I was pregnant. *Life is so unfair*, I thought. *I'm pregnant again without even having had an enjoyable sexual experience in over two years.*

After two months, I told David the news. "David, we need to talk," I said early one Sunday morning as we sat down for breakfast.

"Yes, we probably do." David sighed and held his head down as though he were dreading the pending talk.

"I'm pregnant again."

David looked terrified. He got up from the chair and walked to the refrigerator, blinking as though something hindered his vision. Then, after taking two beers out of the fridge and opening one, he sat down.

"Marilyn, I have something on my mind that has been bothering me for a long time. I need to get it off my chest," he said, and he gulped down the remainder of the first beer.

I braced myself, thinking he would tell me he was having an affair with the big-butted girl I had seen him dancing with at the Country Palace. But instead, he closed his eyes for several minutes.

Finally, he said, "I've been having homosexual thoughts."

I gasped. "Homosexual thoughts! I've never heard of anyone having homosexual thoughts," I said, shocked. I felt dizzy, as if someone had dropped fifty pounds onto my chest. Finally, I somehow managed to ask, "Have you acted on those homosexual thoughts?"

"No, of course not," he said, and he opened his eyes.

"Well," I said, "as long as you don't want to act on those homosexual thoughts, I guess you're not a punk."

David began to sweat, although it was cool in our mobile home. He wiped the sweat from his brow. "Whew," he said, "I feel so much better now that I got that off my chest. I sure hope the baby is a boy."

He grabbed the second beer and left without eating his breakfast.

CHAPTER 37

YOUR HUSBAND LOVES A MAN

Six months had passed since I had become a member of the women's social group the Silhouettes, and it was my turn to host. I wanted to impress my new friends and have everything go well. I had an assortment of drinks, finger sandwiches, fruits, nuts, and desserts sitting on the kitchen table. I set a rustic old utensil caddy in the middle of the bar, along with white napkins, glasses, and thick paper plates.

The red shag carpet stood up straight and fluffy as if it were new. I was proud of our mobile home, with its beautiful Spanish decor. Red-and-black curtains with golden tassels hung from the double window in the living room. The room was small but clean, neat, and stylish. A large conquistador picture hung on the back wall, and a small Spanish ship with two large red ceramic anchors on each side sat on the coffee table. An extralong black leather sofa sat across the back wall.

I had heard ugly jokes about trailers and people who lived in them. I tried not to fit the stereotype. I walked from one end of the trailer to the other to check on cleanliness. I was determined to have a fun-filled meeting.

It was almost three o'clock, and everything appeared perfect, so there wouldn't be anything for the group to gossip about behind my back. I heard cars approaching and looked out the window. A six-car caravan pulled into the long driveway.

I thought it was odd that everyone arrived simultaneously, but that was good. We could get started on time. I welcomed everyone and offered a drink. Everyone declined, and the usual chatter and hugs were missing.

Chubby, the club's president, remained standing. She cleared her throat and walked over to me but refrained from looking me in the eye. Her voice trembled as she spoke.

"Marilyn, please sit down for a moment," she said, taking the tray of drinks from my hand. "How are you and David doing these days?"

All eleven ladies looked over at me and stared at my big pregnant belly. I sat at the bar and allowed my eyes to roll over each doleful face before I turned to face Chubby. "David and I are doing just fine. Why are you asking about my husband?" I was perturbed.

Chubby walked into my tiny kitchen and set the tray of drinks down. She took a deep breath and then walked back into the living room and stood in front of me.

"Marilyn, that's just too hard to believe. Uh, we know that you're pregnant and all, but someone needs to tell you."

She lowered her head and paused for a few seconds, looking at all the other ladies in the room, before continuing. They were squinting and nodding.

"What is it?" I asked.

"We all met earlier and, ah, decided that—" Chubby looked around the room again. "We are your friends. I hope you realize that."

"Yeah, I suppose so," I said, looking around the room at all the members. But my gut questioned these new friendships.

"We think it's our duty—ah, our responsibility—to tell you the truth." Chubby paused again. She looked at my cousin Virginia, who nodded her approval.

My jaw tightened, and my throat began to swell. I had to speak. I turned and looked directly at Chubby.

"I want you to tell me what you all met about if it concerns me." I screamed, "Just tell me!"

Chubby closed her eyes and began to shake her head. "Marilyn, everybody in Yanceyville knows that—" She paused again. "Oh God, help me, Jesus," she moaned. "Marilyn, I'm so sorry—I truly am—but you need to know that Salmon, that faggot, has taken your husband away from you. Your husband loves a man."

The room was quiet and motionless. The only sounds I heard were a few singing birds outside the window and the constant hum of the window air conditioner. I let out a short, nervous laugh as fear and angst gripped my thoughts. My limbs went limp. I felt nauseated.

"You guys are crazy," I said. "Salmon is a man and David's first cousin, for Pete's sake!" My voice trailed off to a whisper as I grabbed the rail of a barstool to steady myself.

Chubby put her arm around my shoulders. "Lord knows we didn't want to tell you. But somebody had to. You needed to know the truth about your husband. Just think back over the past year, and try to remember changes in David's behavior."

"Amen, sister," someone said, and the other women mumbled in agreement.

"Marilyn, it's true. They are both fags, plain and simple," Virginia said. "You shouldn't say anything to David until after the baby is born. Fags can be quite temperamental."

It took all the strength I could muster, but I walked over to the front door and said, "I want all of y'all to leave, except Virginia. Please leave. Now."

I opened the door and watched the women as they walked out. I was beyond embarrassment and humiliation.

The women looked at me with pity in their eyes. Each one touched my arm and told me how sorry she was—as if giving condolences at a funeral. Some of them whispered to one another, saying I should kill the SOB. Chubby was the last to leave. She apologized as she walked down the seven concrete steps to her car.

"Marilyn, I'm so sorry to be the one to tell you. I really am."

I nodded and closed the door and then turned to my cousin Virginia, who stayed with me.

Virginia said they'd had suspicions for quite some time but did not want to break up my marriage. She lit a cigarette and blew the smoke away from me.

"Marilyn, there are some real awful diseases out there that are being transmitted by these nasty, low-down homosexuals. We didn't want anything to happen to you." She grabbed a napkin from the bar and dabbed her eyes.

"Do men actually fall in love with each other?" I asked.

Virginia said, "Yes, it's a strange phenomenon, and it happens all the time in big cities like New York and Los Angeles, but most people keep it a secret."

"But I've never even seen a homosexual, Virginia," I said, and I started to cry.

"Oh, you've seen them," Virginia said. "Everyone has. You just didn't know it." She took two swallows of her iced tea. "Marilyn, promise me that you won't say anything to David until after the baby is born."

"I won't say anything right now," I said in a whisper, "but after the baby is born, I will get David to go see a psychiatrist to help him change back to a normal man."

Virginia said, "Homosexuals don't change. You must move on. I'm sure he didn't ask to be a faggot. Prayer and psychiatrists can't change who he is."

I went into the bedroom, lay down, and cried. Everyone had known but me. I imagined everyone laughing at me for not knowing David was homosexual. I finally understood why David found so many faults and why his sexual interest in me was nonexistent.

Later that Saturday afternoon, David told me that he and Salmon were going to the Country Palace to get their weekend started. David got dressed in a white suit and walked across the lawn to Salmon's house. When I saw Salmon standing beside his white 1974 Chevrolet Impala, also dressed in a white suit, I knew he and David were lovers.

I sat on the sofa and, for a few minutes, contemplated what I should do. I drove to the Country Place a little while later. When I saw David and Salmon walking toward the entrance, the thought crossed my mind to run David over.

I waved to David and asked him to get into my car because we needed to talk. David came over and said that our talk had to wait, and he walked away.

I leaned out the window. "David, are you a goddamn faggot?" I yelled with the utmost vulgarity. I wanted my ugly words to dissipate the disgust, deceit, and humiliation I felt.

David responded with equal disgust and anger. "Yes, I am," he said, "but I much prefer the term *gay*." He rolled his eyes with a flutter of blinks. "Now, if you don't mind, I don't want to keep my lover waiting."

He started to walk toward the club's entrance again, where Salmon stood patiently. Gravel and dust flew into the air as my green Grand Prix headed straight for David. I screamed, "I quit college for a goddamned faggot! I want you dead!"

David stopped and turned around without moving.

I heard a voice inside my head: *Mama, who is going to take care of me?* I felt my unborn child talking to me. I slammed on the brakes and turned the car, just shy of hitting David. People were looking at us in horror.

"Marilyn, I don't care if you kill me!" David screamed. "Go ahead and do it!"

I made a sharp right and exited the gravel parking lot. I drove to his aunt Autry's house and told his aunt and uncle that David and Salmon were dating each other. His aunt Autry was not upset. On the contrary, she had a look of complete acceptance and did not say one word to me. Then I started to tell David and Salmon's cousins about the affair.

"What can I do? What's going to happen to me and my baby?" I asked as hot tears rolled down my angry face. The baby kicked inside me as I wrapped my arms around my swollen belly. No one said anything. I felt their abject silence; their coldness and stonelike eyes enveloped me.

Someone finally said, "Marilyn, you got to know that blood is thicker than water."

I felt as if someone had thrown a brick against the side of my head. I knew I was no longer part of this family. So I drove across the road, where I no longer had a home, and called Mama.

"Stop it!" Mama yelled twenty minutes later as she entered the mobile home and caught me trashing the place. "You've done enough. Get yo' stuff, and let's go home."

Sunday morning, I awoke in my old upstairs bedroom to the sound of voices and the smell of sausage and fried apples. I tiptoed down the stairs. The door to the den opened just enough for me to see my brother Edward as he talked. I stood outside and listened.

"Man, I'm telling you what I saw with these two eyes." Edward pointed his index and forefinger toward his face. "Salmon has moved into Marilyn's house. I ain't seen or heard nothing to beat that shit."

Daddy took a swig of whiskey from a glass jar sitting on the table just as I stepped inside the room. Everyone stopped talking and looked at me.

Ronald Jr. wiped his mouth with a handkerchief before he spoke. "Marilyn," he said, "take a seat, and just listen to what we're going to do." He pointed to the same old sunken sofa I had sat on a hundred times. "We're going to kill him for you and the baby. Do you still have life insurance on him?" Ronald Jr. rubbed the lower part of his chin as he waited for my answer.

I nodded.

"Good," he said. "It'll just take a split second; he won't feel or see a thing."

"I don't want you to harm a hair on his head," I said. I knew I wanted to be the one who killed David. I just wanted to get some ideas on doing it without using a gun.

I fixed Sherondalyn's breakfast. Then I listened while Ronald Jr. and Edward talked about the best possible ways to send David to his Maker.

Ronald Jr. poured himself a glass of moonshine and lifted it to make a toast. Edward and Daddy raised their glasses.

"David has got to die for what he has done to our family," Ronald Jr. said. "He can't stay on top of this earth."

I spoke up. "You both have wives and children. Who will look after them if you get caught and go to prison? Everyone is expecting you to do something to him anyhow. Don't jeopardize your own families. I need you to promise that you will do nothing."

Ronald Jr. looked at Edward and then said, "We'll let things cool down a bit and wait for Marilyn to change her mind."

Early Monday morning, I headed to Greensboro to ask my sister Mildred and her husband, Reginald, if I could live with them for a few weeks.

Sherondalyn, who was two and a half, was curled up on a pillow asleep as I cruised up Highway 158 West. After about fifteen minutes, I heard sirens and saw flashing blue lights behind me. I pulled over and cut the engine. A white deputy sheriff came up to the driver's-side window. He peeped into the car and asked for my registration card and my driver's license.

The deputy looked at the documents and flashed a broad smile. "Ah— aren't you the girl who's married to that he-she man?"

I was so scared I would get a speeding ticket that I ignored his question. He handed my driver's license and registration card back to me.

"Didn't you know he was a he-she before you married him? Some people are just born with both sets of genitals and swing both ways, I guess."

I felt as if the whole world knew David was a homosexual. Tears began to roll down my face. All I wanted to do was get out of Yanceyville and never return.

"I think you've got enough problems on your hands," the deputy said. "I'm not going to give you a speeding ticket, but you've got to slow this Grand Prix down." The deputy patted the top of the car.

"OK," I whispered.

The deputy stood watching as I pulled off for Greensboro, North Carolina.

CHAPTER 38

MY DADDY'S SHOES

My sister Mildred sat in her living room, shaking her head in disbelief. "It's the most disturbing thing I have ever heard in my life," she said. "Two men dating each other like a man and a woman? You have got to be kidding me."

I took a few minutes to tell her about the fifteen-second encounter with David that had left me pregnant, and she gasped. "Oh my God."

"I just can't understand a man who don't like pussy," Reginald, my brother-in-law, said as he walked into the living room, where Mildred and I sat.

Mildred looked up at her husband. "Reginald"—she spoke his name slowly with a deliberate drawl—"don't you need to go work in the garden?"

"Oh, I'm sorry," Reginald said, and he walked outside.

As soon as I got to work on Monday, I went directly to my new supervisor, Hilda, a slender woman with short, wavy blonde hair. Her blue eyes seemed kind, and she had always treated me well.

She motioned for me to sit down. "Marilyn, I'm so sorry to hear that your husband prefers men," she said. "I know that must be a terrible shock to you."

I held my head down in shame and wondered how she knew David was gay. I wanted to go through the roof and never be seen again by anyone who knew about my situation. It had only been two days since David confirmed he was gay, but the news had already reached my workplace. I did the best I could to keep my composure. I didn't respond to her statement.

"I need a week's vacation," I said softly.

"I'm not authorized to grant you an unscheduled week of vacation," Hilda said, "but I will check with our general manager."

Edith, the general manager, was a rapid-fire, hot-tongued redhead who looked like Lucille Ball but had a deeper voice. She seemed intimidating, although I had never spoken to her. She bounced into the office in three-inch black heels with a wisp of a smile on her taut face. Her black-and-white pantsuit showed off her svelte body. She stood directly in front of me.

I could not explain the misery I felt to Hilda, Edith, or anyone else. If misery could have been rated, mine would have hit the top of the scale. With lowered eyes, I stared at the blue-and-gold-carpeted floor, waiting and hoping that Edith would make an exception and allow me to use my vacation.

"Well," Edith said, "I understand that you're having family issues—to be specific, that your husband likes men." She gave a sympathetic smile and looked over at Hilda. "I can't imagine what you must be going through right now."

I could not speak because my brain was shutting down from shame. I thought I must have been the only person in the world in this situation—and it was getting worse by the minute.

Edith walked two steps closer to me and touched my shoulder. "How did you find out, dear? Does he really have two sets of genitals? It's so unfortunate. Did you catch them in bed together?"

After a few minutes of silence, I somehow found the courage to answer her questions, after which she told me she could not grant me a vacation, but I could take early maternity leave.

I declined early maternity leave and went to my workstation amid stares and snickering from my coworkers. I often went to the bathroom to cry and pray, but since I was pregnant, my excessive health breaks were acceptable to management.

The following day, I reported to work as usual and tried my best not to look or feel upset. However, the workstations were buzzing with talk of "Marilyn's husband likes men." My coworkers talked about my life within my hearing range as though they were talking about their pets.

Louise, a big, hippy woman from New York with a superior attitude, leaned over to my workstation and asked, "How do you feel losing your husband to a man?"

I didn't respond, but the sting of her words made an indelible scar on my psyche. I wanted to slap Louise, but I couldn't fight while pregnant. I jumped up and went to the bathroom to cry in private. While I was sitting in the last stall, two coworkers walked in. I recognized both voices.

A Head of Cabbage

"Damn," Louise said. "Minnie, that takes the cake. Men are fucking men. And they said that Marilyn caught them in her bed."

Minnie's voice was loud and raspy. "If he was my husband, letting some man poke him in the ass, I would shoot both of 'em."

I waited until the bathroom was empty and then let out a wail before proceeding to Edith's office. "I want to take early maternity leave, effective right now," I said.

Edith looked startled for a moment and then said, "That's a good decision, Marilyn."

When I told Mildred I had taken early maternity leave, she suggested moving the trailer that David had purchased a couple of years ago into a mobile home park. I initially frowned at the idea because I thought only poor white racists lived in mobile home parks, and they might give me even more trouble. But I needed to provide a home for Sherondalyn and the baby I was carrying.

Later that night, I called David and told him I wanted the mobile home so the children and I could have a place to live.

"You want my mobile home?" David sounded surprised. "Salmon has moved in, and I don't want to ask him to move out. We are so happy together."

His words cut me to the quick. I tried to modulate my breathing to speak without crying over the telephone. "David, are you telling me that you want to provide a place for a fucking man to live and not your own child?"

David spoke more slowly, as if he thought I hadn't heard him the first time. "I'm saying that my lover is living here with me, and I don't want to mess that up."

I thought I would have a mental breakdown and wished my brothers had killed him. I eased the phone onto the hook without saying another word and stayed out of Mildred's sight for the remainder of the night. I didn't want her to see me in such an angry and pitiful state.

The next day, I told Mildred what David had said to me.

"Find an attorney, and call him right now." Mildred brought her big yellow-pages telephone book to me.

Later in the week, after meeting with an attorney, I called David again and told him I had an attorney to help me get the trailer and had checked on the cost to relocate it.

I stayed with Mildred and Reginald for another week before David relocated the mobile home. Then, afterward, he asked to move home with me, and I agreed.

Ten days later, I saw all of David's clothes piled high on the bed. I knew he was leaving. I walked into the room and sat down. I didn't say anything; first, I just watched him as he stuffed his clothes into a duffel bag.

Veins protruded from his neck and temples, and sweat rolled down the side of his forehead. He threw his hair back and said, "Marilyn, I'm sorry. I'm really sorry, but I cannot stand to be away from my lover another minute."

I finally had clarity about David's being gay. It was not something he'd chosen like a pair of shoes. I had read every book on homosexuality I could find in the library, and I knew there was no hope for a real marriage. But still, I wanted him to stay with me until the baby was born.

"What if I go into labor with no one here to take me to the hospital?" I said. "I need you to stay until after the baby is born. Please."

The fear I felt of being alone and nine months pregnant was indescribable. David grabbed his clothes and placed them in the backseat of his car, and then he came back and took the TV.

"I want something to show for my labor," he said, and he left.

I knew that was the last time David and I would sleep under the same roof. So I locked the door behind him. Sherondalyn, who was awake, saw me closing the door and started to cry. She ran to me, screaming and carrying one of David's shoes in her arms.

"Mama, don't lock my daddy out. Please don't lock my daddy out. You're keeping my daddy from coming home."

My heart broke even more as I unlocked the door. Sherondalyn's little lips quivered in anguish as she clung to her father's shoe. I didn't know how to console her, so we both sat down in front of the unlocked door until we went to sleep.

Sherondalyn and I developed a ritual since we no longer had a TV. We went to the library several times during the week and checked out as many books as allowed. Whenever she thought I was sad, she would bring me one of her books.

A Head of Cabbage

"Mama, I will make you feel better," she said. "I'll read to you."

She made up stories about the pictures she saw, and I pretended to be interested in what she pretended to be reading. Sometimes, in the middle of her story, she would ask about her father's whereabouts. I often lied and told her he was working and would see her soon. I felt horrible that I had allowed the wrong man to impregnate me, and I'd made things even worse by marrying him. Her misery was all my fault.

During the day, Sherondalyn walked around the house with David's shoes in her arms. When she went to bed at night or took a nap, I had to lay his shoes nearby, or she would scream, "Give me my daddy's shoes!" After one of her crying spells, I walked to the pay phone down by the clubhouse, called David, and asked him to see her. David asked if he could keep her for a few days. I wanted to say no to make him suffer a little, to make him want something he couldn't have, but then I remembered how Sherondalyn's face lit up whenever he was around.

I watched David and Salmon as they drove off with Sherondalyn in the backseat of Salmon's car. She grinned and waved to me. My heart exploded with resentment and hate. My resolve to kill David grew more substantial like a wild weed in an unattended flower garden.

CHAPTER 39

A HEAD OF CABBAGE

Monday, June 23, 1975, was a beautiful summer day. I dropped Sherondalyn off at Mildred's home at ten o'clock that morning and headed to my 11:00 a.m. appointment with my ob-gyn in Burlington.

As I sat in the doctor's office, I looked around the room and saw several other pregnant women. Their husbands sat beside them, flipping through magazines and sipping coffee. An image of David and Salmon drinking coffee flashed in front of me. It was unbearable. I grabbed a magazine and started to flip through it, when the nurse came in.

"Mrs. Jamison," the nurse said, "this way, please."

Within seconds, I was in stirrups, and I was shocked when Dr. Long said I had already dilated four centimeters and needed to get to the hospital.

I drove myself to the hospital, and two hours later, I had a baby girl. I wanted to give her an uncommon, beautiful, romantic name because I didn't think I would ever have much of anything else to give her. I named her Paris.

In mid-August, Southern Bell called a working surplus. Unfortunately, I could not yet return to work, but I could receive unemployment benefits. I had a total of fifty-three dollars stashed in a peanut butter jar under my bed, so I had to make that meager sum last for as long as I could. Eventually, I made out a simple budget. I paid forty dollars to the mobile home for lot rent, ten dollars for food, and three dollars for gasoline for the car.

After paying the rent, I went to Food Town in Greensboro. Sherondalyn, now three years old, walked beside me. I got baby formula first and then a head of cabbage, a five-pound bag of flour, and a large slab of fatback pork.

Sherondalyn noticed other women with their grocery carts overstuffed with all kinds of food and drinks. She looked into our cart, frowned, and rolled her eyes up at me. At the checkout counter, I gave the clerk my last ten dollars. She gave me three dollars and twelve cents back. I drove home feeling good that I had some money for gasoline.

Teary-eyed, Sherondalyn dragged the small grocery bag with the cabbage into the house and said, "Mama, you said we would get groceries today."

I tried to mask our poverty and stooped down to face her. "Baby," I said, "we got food. This is all we need right now."

Sherondalyn dropped to the floor in a crying fit as the head of cabbage rolled down the hallway. She kicked and screamed and finally said, "But it's one head of cabbage."

I cooked a quarter of the cabbage, one long slice of pork side meat, and two biscuits for dinner. First, I set the table for one. Then I held Paris and gave her a bottle at the table while I waited for Sherondalyn to finish eating. Later, I ate her leftovers.

Mildred usually came to check up on me twice weekly, and I always pretended I had adjusted to becoming a single mama. However, I could hardly wait for her to leave, so I could crawl back into bed and cry. I became obsessed with killing David first; then I wanted to kill myself. I thought my misery and poverty were because of him. If only he had admitted that he was gay and had not deceived me early on, I would not have quit college or had two fatherless children living in a trailer park without adequate funds to care for them.

David's next visit came a week after Mildred's. He looked tired and worn but didn't sit down. Instead, he went into the back bedroom and kissed both sleeping children on the forehead before returning to the living room.

"Marilyn, I've got to tell you something," he said, standing near the front door.

I thought, *What more can he tell me?* I wanted him to say his piece and leave.

"What is it now, David?"

"Marilyn, the bank called about your car. I told them where they could pick it up."

"But," I stuttered, "I need my car. I have to find a job."

"Well," David said, "they're going to pick up your car on Monday." He repeated himself more loudly, lurching toward me. "Do you hear me?"

A Head of Cabbage

I was in shock. "Can you make one payment for me? My unemployment checks should start in a few weeks," I said. "I've already applied and will get eighty-seven dollars and seventy-five cents weekly."

David took a piece of paper out of his pocket and laid it on the bar. It was the bank's telephone number. "Marilyn, I have to live too," David said. "I can't make a payment for you, and there is no need to let them get further behind."

I struggled to stay composed. I reached for David's arm, but he snatched it away as if he could not stand for me to touch him.

"David, what can I do? I'm in this trailer park alone with two babies!" Even though I knew he didn't love me, I expected him to have enough compassion to pay the car note at least once.

He mocked me. "What can I do?" Then, twisting his mouth into an ugly grimace, he said, "You can call the loan officer in Danville and tell them what time to come pick up the car—that's what you can do." David turned and walked out, slamming the metal door behind him.

The following day, I went to the pay phone and called the bank. The loan officer told me to bring $100 to them within three days to cover the interest, and they would defer my loan payment of $117 for two months. I assured the bank officer that I would have $100 to him by Friday.

I deposited another twenty cents into the pay phone and called my sister Mildred. I told her what the loan officer had said and asked if she could loan me $100. She said she would let me know after discussing the situation with Reginald, her husband.

Around ten o'clock the next night, car lights flickered in my bedroom window. It was my brother-in-law's yellow Ford Torino. I was happy to see that car pull into my driveway. I grabbed my robe and rushed to open the door, thinking Mildred was bringing me the loan. But instead, it was Reginald, and he was alone. He had a big smile on his face. I looked beyond him.

"Where's Mildred?" I asked. Reginald had never been to my home before without my sister, so I was surprised.

"Oh, Mildred didn't come," he said, "but she did tell me that you need us to loan you one hundred dollars so you can keep your car."

I nodded. "I promise to pay you back as soon as my unemployment checks start."

Reginald's grin widened. "Well," he said, "I ain't got a hundred dollars to loan you, but I have a hundred dollars to give you if you have something to give me."

I was stunned and wrestled with my choice of a response. I wanted to cuss, but I feared Reginald might lie and tell my sister I had propositioned him.

"I don't need the car that bad, Reginald," I said, "and if you want to fool around, it would be wise not to try it with your sister-in-law."

He left, humming a tune I didn't recognize. After Reginald left, I checked on the girls. They were sound asleep. I left them alone and went to the drugstore, where I purchased a bottle of sleeping pills.

When I returned, I went into my bedroom and put on my best outfit: a lime-green A-line dress with big black double-breasted buttons down the center. I put on white pantyhose, lime-green platform shoes, and heavy makeup. I decided life was just too hard. It was time to die, but I wanted to look as good as possible when they found my body.

I walked into the girls' bedroom to see Sherondalyn and Paris one last time. They looked peaceful and sweet. I kissed them goodbye.

> Dear Mama,
> I think I'd rather be in heaven than here on earth. I can't stand to live anymore. Mildred, please take care of the girls for me; their daddy is not fit to raise them. The Social Security they will get from my death should feed them. Love them, please.

I didn't sign the suicide note. I didn't know why. I just pinned it to the top of my dress.

I took all the sleeping pills with a small glass of water. I felt that no one would miss me, which was all right with me. I lay down on my back, careful not to mess up my heavy makeup and hair. I felt happier now that I would not have to suffer any more heartache, humiliation, disappointments, hardships, or rejection.

Sometime during the night, I heard Paris screaming at the top of her lungs. I got up, changed her diaper, fed her, and rocked her in my arms until she went back to sleep. I laid her down in the crib, and then I went back to bed.

I woke up the following day, again to the baby's screams. I was groggy. I managed to get out of bed, fed Paris, changed her diaper, and fixed Sherondalyn a bowl of grits. As I watched Sherondalyn eat, I had a moment of clarity. I had almost killed myself! I jerked the attached suicide note from the top of my dress and tore it up. Then I started to drink as much water as I could force down. I wanted to flush the sleeping pills out of my system. While Sherondalyn ate breakfast and Paris slept, I went to the mobile park office and called the loan officer at the bank in Danville, Virginia.

A week later, my brother Ronald Jr. came to visit me unexpectedly.

"What the fuck is going on up here? Marilyn, you got family. Why didn't you tell somebody that you needed help to keep your car?" Ronald Jr. bellowed as soon as he walked inside.

I was shocked and ashamed. I hadn't known my brother Ronald Jr. was aware of the repossession.

"I didn't want to burden anybody with my life, and I don't want to beg." But I didn't mention to my brother that I had already asked Mildred and Reginald for a loan a week earlier or that I'd asked David to make one car payment until my unemployment started.

"Marilyn, Marilyn," he said, shaking his head, "you got two kids. You can't be up here in this dead-blame trailer park with a bunch of rednecks without a car." He stood just inside the door, looking me up and down, making me feel uncomfortable and stupid. Finally, he closed the door and said, "You got a problem, and it's called pride. You better kill pride 'fore it kills you."

Since Ronald Jr. had returned from Vietnam, his communication style had become one of insults and intimidation. I stared across the room to avoid his deep brown eyes as they rolled over me. I didn't speak but waited to hear what would spew off his tongue next. Finally, he got up close to my face and started to rub his beard.

"You don't know how to do anything. You picked a goddamn faggot for a husband." Ronald started to pace the short distance of the living room floor; briefly stopped in front of me; and, in a feminine voice, said, "I want a man. I want Salmon." He checked his watch. "Shit. Put some clothes on the kids; we're going to Danville. I'm going to get your car back."

Minus the insults, I was startled by his generosity. I didn't move. He started to pace the floor again, as if in deep thought, and then he shot me a glance.

"That's right," he said. "I'll pay for your car till you get on your feet, so get a move on. We got to get to the bank."

On the drive to Danville, Ronald Jr. continued to scold me for not asking the family for help. He talked about the family sticking together and said I still had a family without the faggot. I hated that he thought I had not tried to help myself, but to make the trip as peaceful as possible, I agreed with everything he said as we traveled up Highway 29 North, speeding toward Danville, Virginia.

In less than an hour, we pulled into the bank's parking lot. Ronald Jr. told me to stay in the car. About five minutes later, I saw my brother walk out of the bank. Another man walked a little slower behind him.

"I know y'all ain't sold her car that quick," I heard Ronald Jr. say to the man, who I assumed was the loan officer or security personnel minus a uniform. I didn't hear the other man speak.

"Ah man, git out of my face. You ain't nothing but a liar and a thief," Ronald Jr. said as he scratched his head. "Go kiss your mama's ass, and find a way to kiss your own white ass."

I sat in Ronald Jr.'s car with Sherondalyn and Paris, keeping them quiet, with my head lowered but not too low. I saw several people exit the bank. Some stood and listened to Ronald Jr. as he hurled insults at the man.

Ronald Jr. shared his theory with me on our drive back to Greensboro. "The bank knows they can get more for your car than what you owe, so they're going to sell it and keep the profits. They do that kind of shit to us all the time."

I nodded in agreement.

Driving with one hand, Ronald Jr. zoomed by every car on the highway and talked for the drive's duration. On the other hand, I kept a sharp eye on the side-view mirror to see if a highway patrolman was behind us. Forty-five minutes later, he pulled into my driveway much calmer.

"Marilyn," he said, "do you remember that American flag cake you sent me when I was in Nam?" He cracked a wide grin, showing a small gap between his two front teeth.

I gave a slight nod. I felt let down because I hadn't gotten my car back.

"That damn cake was crumbling like sawdust by the time it reached me in the field. The red part had turned orange, the blue frosting had turned gray, and the white part was green with mold." He cackled and coughed, and his eyes teared up. "But my buddies and me—shit, we ate the mold and every damn crumb."

I forced a smile.

Ronald Jr. opened the car door, stepped out, and lit a cigarette. "Well, I just wanted you to know that I appreciated that damn cake. I'm going to find you a car so that you can get on your feet."

CHAPTER 40

THE STALKER

Mildred came to visit two days after Ronald's failed attempt to reclaim my car. Again, she took me to the grocery store, and again, I purchased baby formula, a few heads of cabbage, and a slab of pork fat with twenty dollars that David had sent me. During our return drive, Mildred told me that one of her church members sold cars, and she would help me get one cheap so that I could look for a job.

Within a few weeks, she and Reginald picked me up to go look at a car. I bought a sky-blue 1962 Chevrolet Bel Air. Reginald negotiated the price for $100.

The hood was rusting, the door on the passenger side was a dull black, and the trunk had been spray-painted white to camouflage bubbling rust and multiple dents. The ceiling was bare except for a few frayed, dangling strings resembling cobwebs. The front window on the driver's side was missing. A thick layer of semiclear plastic was taped around the opening. Unfortunately, the key was a poor duplicate of the original. It took about fifteen minutes to start the engine. I had to keep wiggling the key until it hit the right spot.

The neighborhood children laughed at the car whenever I drove by. The adults waved and cringed as though they could not bear to watch.

One day I returned home from a job hunt and saw my middle-aged next-door neighbors Melvin and Mamie planting yellow mums in front of their trailer. I waved and started toward my front door, when I heard Melvin say to Mamie, "Will you look at that? She actually drives that thing!"

Blanche came to visit me a few days after I got the car. She was still with her husband, Slim, but had a clandestine relationship with a handsome boyfriend.

"This is Randolph, the best-looking man in the world," she said as her introduction. She ushered him into my small mobile home and then pulled me aside. "Child, child, child," she said excitedly, "he has a good-looking brother, and I've already made arrangements for him to meet you. Just wait until you see him."

She giggled, and I allowed a bit of hope to rise in me.

I was interested but afraid I would be rejected since I was not as attractive as Blanche. I shook my head.

"I don't think I should be dating. I'm still married," I said, making an excuse that I thought Blanche would accept.

"Girl, he's even taller than Randolph, and he's got muscles to spare just like my man."

Blanche glanced at Randolph, who was grinning like a Virginian opossum in heat. She squeezed one of Randolph's muscular arms, fluttered her eyes, and rested her head on Randolph's chest for a few seconds. Then Randolph lifted Blanche and planted a long kiss on her waiting lips. When Randolph let her go, Blanche waltzed over to where I stood.

"Honey," Blanche asked, "do you mind if I speak to my sister alone?"

Randolph shook his head and grabbed an old magazine off the coffee table.

Blanche took my hand and led me into my back bedroom. "Girl, I apologize for not coming sooner to see you, but I've been busy." She wrapped her arms around my waist and said, "I know how to help you get over that faggot husband of yours."

"Blanche, the correct term is *gay*," I said, more enlightened.

My sister glared at me for a full minute and then said, "Don't you ever cry over a faggot. There are a lot of men out there. Get yourself another one. The fastest way to forget one is to get another." Blanche squeezed me tighter while sharing her words of wisdom.

I didn't argue. Instead, I nodded in agreement because I wanted Blanche to leave. I wanted to get back into bed and cry myself to sleep since David had the girls for the weekend.

"I ain't going to let one man drag me down and wear me out," she said as she twiddled a few strands of hair.

"Blanche, do you realize that you have a husband? What if Slim finds out?" I asked, afraid that Slim would beat her again if he knew.

Smiling, Blanche sat down on the bed and crossed her legs. "He has a girlfriend and won't stop seeing her." She threw up both hands. "Well, do you want to meet Randolph's brother or not?"

"I still feel married," I said, sitting down beside her.

Blanche lost her dainty smile. "I got news for you," she said in a curt tone. "You ain't got a husband, and you never had one. You better learn to have some fun instead of sitting around this place wasting away over a faggot." She rolled her eyes around the small room and then said, "When I leave this world, it won't owe me anything."

I told Blanche I would think about it.

When she was ready to leave, she pointed to my car. "Why on God's green earth do you have that piece of junk sitting in your driveway?"

I said, "It's my new car."

"New car?" she scoffed. "I don't think so!"

Blanche giggled as Randolph slipped one arm around her waist and opened the passenger door of his black Cadillac.

Mildred came to visit me within a day or two after Blanche's visit to tell me she had a coworker who wanted to meet me. When I told her that Blanche would introduce me to her boyfriend's brother, she became more determined to persuade me to meet her coworker first.

I didn't want to meet anyone, because I didn't trust any man. I had begun to believe all men were closeted homosexuals, yet I agreed to meet Mildred's coworker to appease her.

Before Mildred left, she looked in my refrigerator, gasped, and quickly closed the door, apparently surprised at the bareness. I had a few bottles of baby formula, a pitcher of water, and two giant heads of cabbage.

The following Friday evening, a new-looking yellow Lincoln Continental pulled into my driveway. A well-dressed man in a dark green suit introduced himself as Donald, Mildred's coworker. He walked with an intentional limp as part of his swagger. Once inside my home, he looked me up and down, and then his eyes roamed around the room. The look on his face was one of wonder—as if the roof might cave in on him.

I extended my hand. Donald took it and said, "It's good to finally meet you. I've heard a lot about you."

Donald invited himself to go from room to room as though searching for something. I felt violated, but I remained silent. I didn't know what to say to this man my sister thought was a gem. I wondered what Mildred had told him about me.

Finally, he opened the door of the refrigerator. His eyes darted about as though they were recording an image.

"Stop it!" I yelled, rushing over and slamming the door.

"Oh." He jumped back and said, "Don't worry; we're going to the grocery store tonight."

Donald continued to look around the kitchen, shaking his head and making mental notes, and even though I took an instant dislike to Donald, I allowed him to take me to Food Town. He bought me more groceries than I had ever had at one time. But as he carried the food into the house, I started to worry. I knew men didn't spend money on women for nothing.

The following week, Donald had a telephone installed, and then the next week, he took us clothes shopping. A week after that, he told me we needed to have a serious talk. A sick feeling came over me because I knew he expected something I didn't want to give.

He told me he would be a good father to the girls and a real husband. He rubbed his groin area slightly and gave me a lascivious grin. I told him that the girls had a father and that I was still married.

"Yeah, but I'm a real man," he said, "and will be a real husband."

I cringed. My dislike for Donald grew.

He smiled broadly, and I noticed his lack of dental care. I thought of Daddy showing off his new truck to make people think he was better off financially than he was. Even though I felt repulsed, I couldn't ask him to leave. After all, he had filled my refrigerator with enough food to last more than a month, he'd had a telephone installed, and the babies had shoes. Another two weeks went by before I told Donald that we didn't click, and I began to date a man Blanche introduced me to.

After three weeks of my dating this new man, my neighbor Mamie approached me early one Saturday morning. I was sitting in my car, wiggling the key in the ignition, when she walked up.

"That big red man you're seeing is a stalker, and he's dangerous," she said. "You need to get rid of that jackass fast. Every night, after I pick up Melvin, we see his ass parked two lots below my trailer, watching yours. Leave him alone." Mrs. Mamie stomped her cigarette and walked back to her trailer.

After that, I had the jitters, and it took me twenty minutes to crank the car.

CHAPTER 41

A TIME TO KILL

One Sunday, Mildred picked the children and me up to visit Mama. When we returned late in the evening, I saw my new boyfriend, Jake, was parked just where Mrs. Mamie had said, two vacant lots below her home. With Sherondalyn in tow, I carried the baby to the back bedroom and put the girls to bed, thinking Jake would soon ring my doorbell.

"Charcoal, who the hell brought you home?" Jake hollered as he stepped inside my home. Then, incredibly, he closed and locked the front door, sidestepped me, and went to the back of the trailer. I followed him as he looked under the beds and checked the closets and both bathrooms.

He looked puzzled and tilted his head. "I know you were hiding a man. He must have run out the back door before I got here. You better be glad he bailed."

Jake rushed back to the living room. I followed a few steps behind, thinking of my next-door neighbor. How I wished I had listened to Mrs. Mamie's advice. After putting a few items from the baby's bag into the refrigerator, I turned to face Jake.

"I just got home from visiting my mother. She lives in Caswell County. I put my children to bed, and here you are, yelling at me. Do you just walk into someone's home without an invitation?"

Jake lifted me up and carried me into the living room a few feet away without answering my question. He dropped me into my black-and-white love seat and then squatted in front of me and laid his head in my lap. I felt his hot breath on my legs.

I was in over my head and had no idea how to handle the situation but knew better than to agitate him. I didn't try to move his head because Jake was a big man. I guessed he was on the far side of 270 pounds and about six foot five. He was handsome, with hazel eyes and a pronounced jawline that made his short dark hair stand out against his light skin.

"Charcoal," Jake said, raising his head, "I love you, and I want to take care of you and the girls." His deep-set eyes darted around like those of a wild, frightened animal. "Charcoal, Charcoal." Jake called me twice again, using the nickname he had given me when we first met, because of my dark skin. "Do you love me?" he asked.

I didn't want to lie, but I was too afraid to speak the truth. "Let's take things slow and see where they lead," I said, still taken aback by Jake's accusatory verbiage and angry demeanor.

"Who are you sleeping with, Charcoal?" he asked.

The question shocked me. I didn't know how to respond, so I didn't. Then Jake slapped me hard across my face. The quickness and force of the strike sent me sideways in the chair. I saw dancing stars as I raised both hands to my face.

Finally, I dropped both hands from my face and looked into his menacing eyes. "I'm not sleeping with anyone," I said, glancing at the red telephone on the wall.

I was too scared to move toward the phone and thought he might use the cord to strangle me if I tried to call the sheriff. I didn't care if I died, but I wanted my children to be raised by someone who loved them, and that was me. So I forced myself to stay calm, think, and not retaliate.

"You ain't sleeping with me, so who is he?" Jake asked, grabbing my shoulders and repositioning my body to sit up straight in the chair. "I can easily break a man's jaw if I want to." He paused as perspiration ran down his face. Then he said, "And I can snap your neck just like that." He started popping his fingers in rapid succession all around my face.

I tried to conceal my fear while stealing a glance around the room to see if there was anything I could use as a weapon. Nothing was within reach. I thought of my three-year-old and three-month-old babies, who depended on me to keep them safe. Looking down into Jake's square face, I knew lying was my only option if I was to survive the night.

With the back side of my hand, I gently stroked Jake's face and neck. "Jake, honey," I lied, "I like a big, strong man like you. And if you will wait a little longer, until I get my divorce, I think you can be my man—my only man. I have not and will not ever mislead you."

Jake stood up, smiling, and pulled me up close to him. I leaned in closer against his big, muscular chest and began to massage his back. I stood on tiptoe so I could whisper in his ear.

A Head of Cabbage

"When I'm ready, you'll know it, but right now, I just want to go to bed and think of you. Please let me get some sleep. The girls got the best of me today."

Jake's eyes glowed as he started to place wet, soggy kisses all over my face and neck. I felt disgusted but faked enjoyment to gain his trust.

"Jake," I said, "since I found out that my husband is gay, I have not wanted to be with anyone, but when I'm ready, you are the one man for me."

"Hush, my darling," Jake said, touching my lips with four big fingers lightly. "Your husband is a sick fool, but don't worry about him, because you got me now. Our love will grow, just like your sister and my brother's love."

I looked up, smiled, and lied again. "I know our love will grow." Then I faked a yawn. "Oh, I'm so tired, honey!"

"Darling," Jake said, "you do look exhausted. I'll go and let you get some rest."

After I locked the door behind him, I spat into the bathroom sink and called Blanche. I told her that Jake was handsome, as she'd said, but he was a psycho, and I wanted his brother, Randolph, to tell him to leave me alone.

Blanche didn't believe that Jake was anything like my description. Instead, she chastised me for not knowing how to handle men.

"Well," Blanche said, changing her tone, "what on earth did you do to him? Or should I ask what did you do with him? Girl, you opened up his nose mighty fast." She giggled. "I swear, I didn't think you had it in you."

Finally, Blanche agreed to have her boyfriend intervene on my behalf after I told her that Jake had slapped me hard enough to cause an aneurysm. Then I called my conservative sister, Mildred, for advice. Unbelievably, just as Mildred answered the telephone, Jake pulled back into my driveway.

I told Mildred that she should send the sheriff to my house unless I called her back within ten minutes and that my life might depend on it. Then I hung up the phone.

"Marilyn, open up," Jake said, banging on the door.

I rushed to the kitchen, grabbed my hammer from underneath the sink, and then cracked the door but left the security chain fastened. Jake forced his foot inside the door. While he talked, I watched the clock above the stove as I coaxed Jake to leave within the ten-minute time frame.

Somehow, I convinced him to go. When I saw his car lights fade from sight, I called Mildred back and told her the whole story.

The following Saturday, around one o'clock, David, my ex-husband, came to visit the girls. He walked into the house nursing a sixteen-ounce Colt 45 in one hand and with several more dangling from his other hand.

He gave me twenty-five dollars and started to talk about his bills and how he wished he could give me more money for the girls. The more he talked and smoked, holding his cigarette in the air with his pinkie finger extended, the more I despised him. He blew smoke upward in little puffy circles.

I wrestled with my innermost thoughts about whether it was time for me to act. I psyched myself up to think of all the reasons I should kill David. The children would be better off without a homosexual father. David's behavior was sure to embarrass and humiliate the children, and they would not want to bring their boyfriends around. David might find their boyfriends attractive and make a move on them. The kids at school would tease them about their father's sexuality. I wondered if it was possible that David's lifestyle could cause them to be homosexual. It was time to kill.

I decided to do what needed to be done while the children were still babies. I stood in front of the refrigerator, gathering courage. It might have been my imagination, but I heard the voices of friends, family, and coworkers, all telling me to kill the miscreant. He deserved to die for what he had done to my girls and me.

David gulped down one beer, popped open another, and then slid off the barstool and cleared his throat. "Marilyn, may I use the bathroom, please?"

"Sure, you can," I said, thinking the timing was perfect for my vengeance.

David went to the bathroom and left the open can of beer sitting on the bar. From the refrigerator, I retrieved the syringe and vial of insulin I had stolen from Mama, a diabetic, when Mildred and I visited her the previous weekend. I injected forty cubic centimeters of insulin into his beer without touching the can. Mama had told me once that taking too much insulin was dangerous, and if someone ingested it without being diabetic, it would be deadly.

When David returned from the bathroom, he took the open can of beer and raised it to his mouth. My entire body began to sweat, and my heart pounded hard and fast. I felt nauseated, but I kept my eyes on him. I prayed silently for composure but also for forgiveness: *Dear God, forgive me for what I now do. I know I can't create life and should not take it, but I have no other choice—it's for the sake of the children.*

I watched and waited for David to drink the insulin-laced beer.

Uncharacteristically, David lowered the beer without taking a swallow. "I don't need to drink any more today," he said. "I have to drive home." He walked over to the sink and poured the beer down the drain.

CHAPTER 42

MR. SANCHEZ

I had put in more than thirty-seven job applications within eight months, so when I got a call back from the Montgomery Ward department store's personnel manager at Carolina Circle Mall, it was not a surprise. I was interviewed over the telephone and was offered a job as an interviewer.

I was elated and agreed to report to the job the next day. My hair was in a round, fluffy Afro. My makeup was impeccable, and I had on a new dark green pantsuit and dark green heels to match.

As soon as I walked into the personnel office and introduced myself, the white female manager said good morning and immediately excused herself. By the look on her face, I knew the job offer would be rescinded. I looked out the window and waited for her return. My heart raced, while fear and doubt plagued my mind. I thought, *Will I ever get a job that pays enough for me to take care of my children?*

Ten minutes later, another manager, a white male, came in and told me they were in dire need of someone who could work the switchboard, and since I had experience with the telephone company, he believed I would be a better fit for that position. He apologized and asked if I was OK with the new opportunity. I needed a job and was afraid to say no, but I felt he wanted me and my Afro tucked away from the public's view. I accepted the job as switchboard operator, even though I felt humiliated.

I called to tell Mildred about the job switch.

"Well, the Lord answered your prayers. You didn't get the job you wanted, but you did get hired. Be grateful," she said.

"You're right," I said. "At least they didn't treat me like the people at Gilbarco."

"What happened at Gilbarco when you went in to take your typing test last week?" Mildred asked.

I tried to sound chipper or at least feel less disappointed before I answered her question.

"It was a living nightmare," I said. "As I began to take the typing test, this big white man came into the room and sat on the desk next to me and the typewriter. He read a newspaper, making sure it rattled as much as possible when he turned the pages. I'm sure I didn't do well on that test."

"Jesus, Jesus!" Mildred said. "Why are white people so evil? Don't they know we just want to make a living?"

Three weeks after I got the job at Montgomery Ward, the girls and I were headed to the grocery store in my old, beat-up car. We'd been on the road for about ten minutes, when Sherondalyn spotted low flames shooting up from under the hood. It scared me so much that I stopped the burning vehicle in the middle of I-85. I thought the car would explode in an instant like I'd seen on TV. So I grabbed the girls and started running down the middle of the interstate. Cars blew their horns, but no one ran over us.

A truck driver stopped his rig directly behind my burning car. "Hey, lady," the man hollered, "stand on the side of the road while I push your car off the highway."

The man raised the hood and put the flames out. Then he called his wife on a CB radio, asking her to come and take us home.

"I hope someone would help my wife if she got into a bind when I was not around," he said, and then he climbed back into his rig and drove off.

I wanted to tell Daddy that there was at least one good white man around, but I called David instead and told him about the car burning up and that I couldn't go to work. Later that evening, David and Salmon drove up to my mobile home in separate vehicles. David told me that he could ride to work with Salmon since they had gotten an apartment together. When David handed his car keys over to me, Salmon spoke.

"Hey, Marilyn, how are you doing?"

I pretended not to see him and looked away without speaking.

David gasped at my rudeness. "Marilyn, I didn't know I could be so happy."

David turned and got into Salmon's car. I watched them drive off together as my hate for them doubled.

The following day at work, after I put my purse in the bottom drawer of my desk, I heard my name: "Marilyn, we have a code twelve in electronics. Hurry, please." It sounded urgent.

A Head of Cabbage

I grabbed the phone and repeated, "Code twelve in electronics," as my boss rushed toward my desk, huffing and sweating.

"He's getting away! Damn. Marilyn, you're too slow," Mr. Sanchez said with unmistakable anger and revulsion. He stood in front of my desk with clenched fists.

"Code twelve. Electronics department," I called over the PA system several more times. I was unsure what code twelve meant since I hadn't had any training. I eventually found a brochure inside the desk drawer with all the codes. I looked up at Mr. Sanchez. "What happened?"

"That crook got away with a twenty-seven-inch color TV," Mr. Sanchez said, and he took off his brown jacket and threw it across his shoulder. "He just picked it up and walked out of the goddamn store." Mr. Sanchez started back to his desk across the hall. He paused and looked back at me. "Is that what southern black men do?"

"No, sir," I said. "He's probably from New York and learned to steal from the white folks up there." I watched several white coworkers laugh out loud at my comment.

"The next time we have a code twelve, I need you to be Johnny-on-the-spot," Mr. Sanchez said, rolling his eyes over me.

"I thought I was pretty quick," I said. "I made the announcement as soon as you told me we had a code twelve, sir."

"Do you know him?" Mr. Sanchez asked.

"Know who, sir?" I played dumb but thought Mr. Sanchez was dumber than I was to think I knew every black person who walked into Montgomery Ward.

He waved a hand, took the few steps to his office, and closed the door.

One of the older white women came over to my desk. "You know that Mr. Sanchez is Spanish, don't you? That's not a tan. He came from Arizona. They don't know how to relate to black people like we do," she said, and then she whisked back to her desk across the room.

I nodded and wondered how long I would keep this job.

CHAPTER 43

I'M NOT AFRAID

After three months, I quit my job at Montgomery Ward and started to work for Cone Cotton Mill in Greensboro, North Carolina, as a spinner because it paid a higher hourly wage.

My sisters Blanche and Mildred worked at the same mill. I rode to work with Blanche, which enabled me to save money on the cost of transportation. In addition, with a pay increase, I was able to buy a few more groceries—several heads of cabbage instead of one—and I was able to save ten dollars every two weeks.

After working the third shift one Monday morning, Blanche asked me to go home with her. She told me Slim would not be there, because he finally had gotten a job in one of the mills in Burlington. I didn't agree to go, but Blanche zoomed past the exit to my home. I rolled my eyes.

"What?" she said with a smirk on her face.

I stared out the window and refused to talk until we pulled into her driveway. I had an uneasy feeling, but I followed Blanche into her bedroom. I didn't like to visit Blanche's home with Slim standing around grinning at me, and I still felt angry about what he had done to me when I was just a little kid. But that day, he was not home. Cold beads of sweat rolled down my face as I looked around her bedroom. In a corner near the bed stood a shotgun. The uneasy feeling soon graduated to a sense of doom. I told Blanche I had to go home and get some sleep. My gut screamed, *Get out!* She got a large manila envelope from the top of the dresser, and we left. On the drive back to Greensboro, I told Blanche to be careful of Slim, because I had a bad feeling about him.

Blanche smiled and looked over at me as we exited Highway 54 onto I-85 South.

"I'm not afraid of Slim. I got me a piece, and I will burn him," she said. "Look inside."

On top of her wallet was a pistol. I didn't know what model or type.

"What if Slim takes it away from you and shoots you with it?" I asked, more frightened for her safety.

Several weeks went by without my seeing Blanche outside of work. Then, late one Saturday evening, Slim called and said, "Marilyn, let me talk to Blanche."

I knew Blanche's habits well, and I surmised that she had told Slim she was coming to visit me so that she could spend some time away from home, possibly with Randolph.

"Slim, Blanche is not here," I said, noting the time on the clock above the stove.

"What time did she leave?" he asked.

I felt he wanted to hem her up when she got home. I didn't want to lie, but I had no choice. Otherwise, I feared, Slim's jealousy might end with his beating Blanche when she got home.

"She just left a few minutes ago," I lied, "but she said something about stopping at the store." I hoped my lie would give her time to get home before his suspicions notched into a rage.

Blanche picked me up Sunday night, and we headed to Cone Mill in Greensboro for the third shift. I mentioned that Slim had called me Saturday evening, asking for her.

"Oh really?" she said, sounding surprised. "What time did he call?"

"It was around four o'clock," I said. "Blanche, please don't put me in the middle of your dallying around. I don't want Slim to think you've been with me when I haven't seen you."

A part of me admired Blanche for her charm and magnetism, which captivated men. I wished she would show me how to develop flirtatious boldness. I didn't think of Blanche as a beauty queen, with her five-foot-one frame, big butt, and round face, but something about her was not ordinary.

CHAPTER 44

POOCHIE

Mama called one day, sounding worried and demanding. "I need you to come home for an important meeting next Sunday."

"What kind of meeting?" I asked.

As usual, Mama did not mince words. "You just make sure yo' ass is here," she said. "That's all you need to know for now."

Mama hung up without giving me an idea of what to expect. I didn't call any of my siblings to question them, because I would have incurred long-distance telephone charges. I could only afford to pay the local telephone bill.

I heard Daddy's harsh voice six days later when I entered the hallway of my parents' house. "Y'all's mama done lost her mind."

My stomach began to churn as I turned the doorknob to the den, where my siblings stood around the hot wood-burning cast-iron stove. It was late October, and the old house had a chill. Daddy looked up at me as soon as I entered the crowded room. He scooted his old rubber-bottomed chair farther away from the stove.

"Maylyn, yo' mama done lost her mind. I swear, she's gone crazy, accusing me of everything under the sun."

I didn't say anything right away. Instead, I looked around the room and gazed over the solemn faces of my brothers and sisters.

Not sure how to take Daddy's comments, I finally asked, "What's going on?"

"Ain't nothing crazy 'bout me. I just ain't gonna take it no more. Yo' daddy is giving all his money to his shit-ass women," Mama said, and she started calling out female names.

"I ain't got no shit-ass money to give nobody, Nora," Daddy said, throwing up his hands. "Where is all of this money 'posed to be coming from? I work at the Williamsburg Plant, and they ain't paying that much money."

"Well," Mama said, "I'll live in a ditch before I keep living here wit' y'all's daddy. I've had 'bout all I can take. Y'all chillums got to find me somewhere to live," she said before walking out of the room.

We all looked at one another. I didn't know if everyone was in shock or not, but no one spoke. I took a seat on the sunken brown sofa in the back of the spacious den.

"I don't know why Nora is trying to turn y'all chillums against me. Somethin' is wrong wit'—" Daddy stopped talking midsentence as he looked over at the opening door. We all saw Mama rush back in with a navy-blue hand towel. She walked around the room and waved it high in the air.

"Y'all's Daddy is into voodoo. He thinks I'm gonna take whatever he dishes out. This here towel is one of the things he's been using to put a root on me," she said, walking over to stand by Edward and Ronald Jr.

Knowing that Mama had always been superstitious, Edward, the oldest child present, ignored Mama's comments about Daddy putting roots on her and began to question us.

"Do y'all know anything about Daddy and a bunch of women?"

We all stayed quiet. I noticed Ronald Jr. rolled his eyes back and forth as if he wanted to say something, but he didn't. I knew a thing or two about Daddy's womanizing, but I too remained silent. I hoped Mama would stay with Daddy, even though I had driven Daddy to Roxboro several times to see women after he lost his driver's license due to drunk driving. My mind went back to one of those times.

It was a Saturday afternoon, and Daddy said he needed to go to Roxboro. I'd just gotten my driver's license and was honored that he had confidence in me. I was eager to drive anywhere. Daddy told me to drop him off at a little white stucco house just before the city limits. I did, and then I drove downtown and parked his truck, thinking I would have to wait about an hour. Three hours went by, and Daddy had not returned. I walked to a hamburger grill and got a cheeseburger and a grape soda. On my way back, I saw a big-busted woman I didn't know standing in the doorway of a launderette. As I got closer, she yelled down the street.

"Where is yo' good-looking daddy?"

I didn't say anything to the woman. Instead, I looked behind me,

A Head of Cabbage

thinking she must have been talking to someone else. I kept walking, and as I got nearer to the launderette, she stepped into my path.

"Yes, ma'am, you is one good-looking child, looking just like Poochie Abbott. Ain't he yo' daddy?"

I nodded and kept walking.

"Poochie is one good-looking man. Now, you tell 'im Martha is waiting on 'im to come see her," the woman said.

Before I reached Daddy's parked truck, I saw another woman letting Daddy out of her car.

I never told Mama or anyone else about the incident, and I didn't see the need to say anything now. I felt sorry for Daddy, who looked pitiful, and his jug of moonshine did not boost his spirits.

My siblings and I all remained silent until Edward called our names. "Ronald Jr., do you know of anything that Daddy has done that is bad enough for Mama to leave him?"

Ronald Jr. glanced back at me sitting on the sofa for just a second and then shook his head and said nothing.

"Mildred, have you ever seen Daddy do anything that was bad enough for Mama to leave him?"

Mildred stood up and walked closer to the heater. "I can't think of anything."

"Inez, you know of anything bad about Daddy?" Edward asked.

Inez shook her head. "Naw, I don't," she said, pulling her sweater tighter around her body.

"Marilyn, what you know about Daddy that's bad enough for Mama to leave him?"

Edward turned his whole body to face me because he couldn't turn his neck. Daddy looked over at me. He opened his mouth, but no words came out. I wanted to say that I knew of nothing, but I remained silent.

"Well, y'all look at that," Edward said. "Marilyn don't have anything to say. She used to talk a mile a minute, and now the cat got her tongue. So what do you know?" Edward walked over to where I sat on the sofa. He looked down at me and raised his voice an octave or two higher. "I asked you a question."

"The only thing I know is Mama should have left a long time ago when Daddy wouldn't let us go to school." Then, taking a cue from Ronald Jr,

I denied knowing anything about Daddy's womanizing. I looked up at Edward. "I don't know about anything else," I said, forcing myself not to talk too much. Instead, I stared down at the broad-planked floor.

"Well," Edward said, walking closer to Mama, "seems like there ain't a good enough reason for you to leave Daddy."

"Shit, boy," Mama said, and she moved away from Edward. "I ain't staying here another day wit' y'all's daddy. I got enough chillums for somebody to take me and Terri in. Now, who is it going to be?" She took her time to ponder each of us.

After the family meeting, nine of Mama's children pooled enough money together to purchase her a mobile home, and she moved into a mobile home near me.

Unfortunately, I had no money to give, but Mama and Terri stayed with me for about three weeks until her mobile home was purchased and delivered.

CHAPTER 45

YOU GOT A CAR

In January 1976, on a blisteringly cold Saturday night, I got an unexpected visit from David. He immediately told me that he could not stay long, because Salmon was waiting in the car. The reason for his impromptu visit was to take his car back.

"Everything is great between Salmon and me. We will be working different shifts starting next week." He took the keys off the wall rack, paused, and lowered his head for a few seconds. "Marilyn, I didn't mean to hurt you. I didn't even know what was wrong with me until after we got married. I don't know why I'm the way that I am," he said before gulping the remainder of the Colt 45.

"You know, David," I said, "no, you didn't mean to hurt me, but you did. I have two children without a father, and I doubt any other man will want a woman with two children."

"Well," he said, walking closer to the door, "I don't want to keep Salmon waiting."

I watched both cars leave, and I began to ponder the best way to kill David and how soon. I was still angry, too bitter and hurt to pray. I couldn't think of God, who I thought had not helped me have a better life. I asked myself what I had done to deserve this hard life. *How can I help myself without a way to get to work?* Finally, I went to bed and cried myself to sleep.

The next day, I called my brother Ronald Jr. and told him that David had come and taken his car back, leaving me with no way to get to work. I hated to bother him, but he had said he would keep an eye out to get me another car when my Grand Prix was repossessed. I hoped he would keep his word. Uncharacteristically, Ronald Jr. did not give me a lecture.

On Monday, it started to drizzle. I was looking out the window, when I saw a brown Chevrolet Nova and an orange Volkswagen pull into my driveway. Ronald Jr. and his wife, Mercy, rushed inside the house just as it started to downpour.

"Marilyn, you got a car. That Nova is yours," Ronald Jr. said, and he dropped the keys onto the bar. "You try to get on your feet, and take care of these dead-blame children."

I wanted to grab and hug my brother, but that would have been weird since we didn't show affection or appreciation. I felt it, but I didn't know how to express it.

"How much do I owe you for the car?" I asked.

"The car cost eight hundred dollars, but don't you worry about paying me back right now," Ronald Jr. said. "You get on your feet."

He looked at his wife, and I looked her way too. I saw a smirk on Mercy's face as she eyed her husband objectionably. After that, I told myself that to reimburse Ronald Jr. for the car was my priority.

Ronald Jr. looked around the cold room. He saw three-year-old Sherondalyn bundled up like a little Eskimo, sitting quietly in her red rocking chair beside her eight-month-old sister, who was in her blue bassinet, wrapped up in several colorful blankets.

Shaking his head, Ronald looked at his wife, Mercy. Their eyes met, and I knew he was going to say something mean.

"Marilyn, I sure hope y'all don't freeze to death up here."

"I was trying to save on my heating bill," I said, pulling my old wool sweater closer.

They both zipped their black leather jackets and headed out the door. Ronald Jr. looked back and said, "I know you're trying."

Now I understood why many people in the church became emotional and jumped around screaming, "Thank you, Jesus!" repeatedly. I wanted to do the same thing right now.

CHAPTER 46

THE CHAIN GANG

Three months after receiving the car, I applied to return to Bennett College to continue my quest for a college degree. Excitedly, I shared my plans with Blanche as she drove me home from work.

"That's a good thing, Marilyn. When you get your college ring, I want your high school class ring."

"Sure," I said, pleased that Blanche had given me her blessing.

"Let me wear it now, and you wear this one." Blanche slipped her pear-shaped crystal ring off her finger and handed it to me. I gave her my high school class ring.

Blanche pulled into my driveway, turned off the motor, and asked. "Do you know what today is?"

"No," I said as I opened the car door and slid out.

Nothing of importance came to mind, and all I wanted was to get some sleep after standing up all night. Blanche gave a little giggle, one I'd heard many times when things were going her way.

"One week from today is the day Slim has to be out of my house. He will be out of my life for good."

"Where is he going to live?" I asked, thinking that Slim was not bright enough to find a place to live independently.

"I don't know, and I don't care." She shrugged. "The separation papers say he has to go. Then I can get on with the pursuit of my happiness." Blanche rolled her neck in a twisting motion, smiling. "I will get my divorce."

"I'm glad Slim has to move out. I've been scared for you since the last time he beat you up," I said. "Are you sure you're going to get a divorce?"

Blanche leaned out the window as she backed out of my driveway. "Just watch me."

I was too tired and sleepy to take a shower, so instead, I lay across the bed and dozed off to sleep. An hour or two later, I woke up in a cold sweat.

I'd had a disturbing nightmare about our uncle Gene, who was married to Mama's sister Aunt Ola. In the dream, Uncle Gene had asked me to tell Blanche to be careful because he saw her coming after him. I lay awake for a few minutes, thinking that Blanche would have an affair with our uncle. Finally, I was so upset about the vision that I called Blanche and told her about it.

"So you haven't heard?" she said, yawning.

"Heard what?" I asked, thinking she might have already started an affair with Uncle Gene. My stomach began to churn, but I thought to myself, *I can't judge Blanche, because I still plan to kill David.*

Blanche yawned again. "Marilyn, Uncle Gene died last night. So your dream doesn't mean diddly-squat. Now, let me get some sleep, please." She hung up the telephone.

I was disturbed about the dream. It had been so vivid. I crawled into bed and pulled the sheet up around my shoulders. Instead of counting sheep, I began to pray about everything that bothered me. Naturally, my dream was at the top of the list.

A week went by, and early one Friday morning, after a long, hot night of working the third shift at Cone Mill, I lay in bed half asleep. The telephone rang four times before I answered.

"Aunt Marilyn, get Grandma, and come to Chapel Hill Hospital right now. Come now! Aunt Marilyn, please come now."

A cold chill ran down my body. I slid out of bed, stretching the long cord as I entered the bathroom. My stomach began to boil, as it usually did when something upset me.

"Who is this?" I asked, unsure of the voice on the other end of the phone.

"It's Claudia. Please hurry. Daddy shot Mama this morning."

I heard her, and my gut felt the awful truth of her words, but my brain was operating in slow motion.

Amid painful outbursts of crying and a few moments of clarity, Claudia began to tell me what had happened.

"Mama was outside on the porch, when Daddy drove up. They started to argue, and then Mama asked Daddy if he had completed packing and reminded him of the court order to leave." Claudia started sobbing. "Daddy raised his shotgun near Mama's head." She let out a long wail.

"Daddy said, 'I'm ready to leave now. I'm going to the chain gang, and you're going to hell.' Then he shot Mama in the head. She's at Chapel Hill Hospital."

There were no empty seats in the waiting room as Mama and I squeezed through the crowd of people. The room was filled with relatives and other people propped up with pillows and blankets. Someone told us the doctor should be coming in any minute to update us on Blanche's condition. To my surprise, Daddy was there, sitting quietly in a corner chair. I had not seen him since Mama moved out, leaving him alone.

Mama went over and sat beside Daddy. Unfortunately, he appeared too drunk to give Mama much comfort. Daddy's eyes were beet red, and he looked as if he had aged twenty years.

Daddy gestured for me to come to him. "Maylyn, don't you let some shit-assed joker turn yo' head," he said, his voice quivering. "Do you hear me?"

A tear rolled down his face, and my heart broke at seeing him this distraught. It was the first time I thought Daddy might love me just a little bit, even though he had never said so. I nodded and glanced around at my other relatives in the room. Everyone seemed to be engaged in private conversations.

"Don't let menfolk twist yo' head so you end up like—" Daddy's voice cracked, and he stopped talking, as though it were too painful to go on speaking. He lowered his head, and Mama wrapped her arms around him. They held on to each other in silence.

I cleared my throat and managed to say, "Daddy, I won't," just as the doctor walked in.

Ronald Jr. raised a hand to quell the loud conversations. The doctor's face was grim and grave. He told us that Blanche's head wounds were extensive, and it appeared the blast had been at close range. Her brain continued to swell, and it had nowhere to go. He assured us that he and his team were doing all they could to save her life, but it did not look good for Blanche.

Only a few of us could visit her at a time. I was in the second group. On my way to the ICU, I recognized Randolph. He stood facing the wall at the end of the hall, near the elevator. I lingered behind the others because I wanted to speak with Randolph alone. I touched his shoulder. When he saw me, he grabbed me and held me tightly. I didn't want my relatives to see him or find out who he was to Blanche, so I pleaded with him to go home. Reluctantly, Randolph released me and asked that I tell Blanche that he loved her and wanted her to fight and come back to him. I promised to say that to her, and I did.

CHAPTER 47

HEAVEN OR HELL

Mama and I arrived at Blanche's house just a few minutes before the funeral director. Family, friends, and neighbors were standing around the kitchen table, eating and talking. A few were mournful, but most were in a festive mood.

Mama gestured for me to follow her into the bedroom, where Claudia stood with two documents in her hand. She handed them over to Mama.

"Grandma, I found these two insurance policies," she said, and she started to cry silently.

Mama looked at one of the policies and then gave it to the funeral director, who now stood in the doorway.

"Sorry, folks, but this insurance policy will not pay off," Mr. Fulton, the funeral director, said. "It was never signed by Blanche."

He handed it back to Mama and began to read the second policy. Finally, he handed the second policy over to Mama, telling her that a finance company in Roxboro was the primary beneficiary.

Mama gaped at the funeral director. She shook her head and sighed. "The insurance policy won't pay off?"

She walked over and asked me what to do. I took the policy out of Mama's hand, signed Blanche's name, and then gave it to the funeral director.

Mr. Fulton nodded. "Yes, Marilyn, I think it will pay off now, but I still need to have Claudia sign it over to me since she is the beneficiary." He unbuttoned his black suit jacket and looked over at Claudia.

Mama asked Claudia to sign the insurance policy over to the funeral director.

"These papers say I'm the beneficiary. I'm supposed to get the money!" Claudia shrieked, confused and distraught. "I ain't giving away my money!"

Mama failed to make Claudia understand that she needed to sign the policy over to the Fulton Funeral Home to help pay for Blanche's funeral expenses. Finally, Shirley, Mama's niece and Blanche's best friend, spoke up.

"If Blanche didn't want Claudia to have the insurance money, then she would not have made her the beneficiary."

Mama shook her head and rolled her swollen eyes at Shirley. "She's dumb to say that," Mama whispered to me.

I walked over to Claudia and wrapped my arms around her. "You are the beneficiary, but life insurance is for the beneficiary to take care of the dead person's funeral expenses."

Claudia frowned. She looked at me with a smirk, as if she thought she was being swindled out of her money.

"As you can see," I said, "there is not enough money here to even bury your mama. Please sign the papers over to the funeral home. We have to get her buried, and that costs money." Reluctantly, Claudia signed the papers.

Mama grunted and lit a cigarette. "You know, death brings out the worst in most people and the best in just a few. But if you want to create a lifetime problem for a family, involve some money. Two dollars will do the trick."

Eve, Blanche's second-oldest daughter, stood in a corner, crying. Neither Claudia nor Eve said much for the remainder of the evening, but I noticed they kept staring at me. I dismissed their demeanor as grief.

Blanche's funeral took place about three days later. It looked like a revival at Mineral Springs Baptist Church in rural Caswell County. The parking lot was packed, and the newly paved road was lined with cars as far as I could see. The church overflowed to standing room only, and there were people lined up along both sides of the walls. Others, who could not enter the overcrowded church, stood outside. Some no doubt had come thinking they would see a sideshow, and others were genuine in their condolences. It was hard to believe that all those people had known Blanche.

The processional started with Blanche's children, Mama and Daddy, and then her siblings. As we walked by, I heard whispering.

"There go her sisters. Look at their pretty legs, but Blanche had the prettiest, poor thing."

I turned slightly to my left, hoping to see the person talking about us.

Instead, I saw Randolph sitting near the front in dark sunglasses, holding a white handkerchief to his eyes.

The family didn't know who Randolph was, and when his sobbing became noticeably loud, my siblings began to stir, whispering and quietly asking about the crying man. I thought they were suspicious that he was her boyfriend, but fortunately, no one asked me about him.

The eulogist said he didn't have a heaven or hell to place Blanche in, but one thing was for sure: everybody needed to get his or her own soul right before it was too late.

People talked about Blanche and her supposed many lovers during our walk across the highway to the burial site. One woman I didn't know said to another, "I'm sorry to say, but right about now, Blanche probably is busting hell wide open. I bet half the men here have—"

I stopped in front of the woman and turned around. She stopped talking and looked away.

CHAPTER 48

I WANTED TO HELP

May 8, 1977, was one of the happiest and most beautiful days of my life. I sat in the shade of magnificent magnolias in the quadrangle at Bennett College, waiting for a degree in sociology to be bestowed upon me. I kept looking behind me, searching the crowd to see if Mama was present. When my name was called, I paused and looked back once more and saw someone waving a white fan. It was Mama. The exhilaration I felt was beyond words. Mama had come to see me graduate!

Within two weeks, I got a job with the Greensboro sheriff's department. It was the cruelest and most boring job I'd ever held.

One night, as I viewed the black-and-white monitor in the control room, I saw two police officers kick a young handcuffed person lying on the concrete floor in the basement of the sheriff's department. I wanted to go scream for them to stop, but I was afraid to say anything. I wanted to keep my job until I found another one.

After several minutes of butt-whipping, the poor person was exhausted and stopped wiggling and mouthing back at the deputies. The sergeant on duty assigned me to make the booking. I was in shock when I saw the person up close. The suspect was not a light-skinned black male, as I'd thought, but a young white woman with short, curly dark hair. Her battered face was black and blue, and her eyes were almost swollen shut. Between sobs, the woman told me she was diabetic, and her glucose level had dropped. She'd been trying to make it home to get something sweet to eat, when she'd become dizzy and weak. She'd swerved, and the police had pulled her over.

I looked at her hands. Her fingers were swollen and red as though they were ready to pop. The woman admitted to resisting arrest. She was afraid of going into a coma.

Mama had gone into a coma once due to a low glucose level. So while the woman was still in the holding cell, I went into the kitchen and got her a small glass of orange juice and a wet cloth. She gulped down most of the orange juice, and after a few minutes, her shaking and sweating ceased.

My stomach began to ache as soon as I started to take her to the showers. I saw one of the deputies, a big sandy-haired man, standing on the top step with a wide grin.

"Do you need help with her?" the big deputy asked.

"No. She is not a problem," I said, and I stopped in front of the deputy, waiting for him to remove himself from the stairs or at least move to one side so we could pass.

"She's a real wildcat. I think you need some help," the deputy said, and he then grabbed the woman's breasts.

I was scared of the deputy and didn't know what to do. I was the only female on the night shift. Finally, it dawned on me to lead the lady into view of the surveillance camera attached to the ceiling. The deputy walked away immediately and gave me a hateful stare. The incident frightened me so much I could hardly lock the cell behind the lady. I wanted to tell the on-duty supervisor but felt that might bring wrath down on me from the other deputies.

The lady told me she was going to sue the city for police brutality. I whispered in her ear, "I will testify on your behalf. I saw how they kicked you around on the floor in the basement. I'm quitting this job pretty soon."

The next day, thunderstorms were soaking the streets of Greensboro and everything in sight as I ran into the sheriff's department. I had planned to write down the name and other information of the brutalized woman and call her later, but when I looked in the filing cabinet, I found she had been released. I never saw or heard anything about her again.

I walked over to the monitors to see what was going on at different sites in Greensboro. Crane, a stocky blond deputy who appeared to be in his early fifties, stood up and walked over to where I stood.

"Who do you think you are, running in here late, dripping wet, with sexy black stockings on?"

I felt as though he were calling attention to me. I believed he wanted our supervisor to know that I was a minute or two late. I sat down and crossed my legs.

"What business do you have looking at my legs?" I asked.

The other guys in the room roared with laughter as Crane's face turned a deep, embarrassed red. The supervisor looked over at me and cracked a smile. He never mentioned my tardiness.

Later in the evening, the sky remained dark, and the streets remained wet, when a prominent socialite was arrested for lifting a necklace—her terminology. She was a well-dressed white lady who lived in one of Greensboro's upscale neighborhoods, Irving Park.

I was told to book her. After she was fingerprinted, I put all her personals into a large manila envelope and typed up all her information. While I was processing the lady, she told me she would give me a hundred dollars if I would go to her house and get enough money out of her husband's safe for bail. She pleaded, cried, and told me how embarrassed she would be if her friends and husband found out she had been arrested.

I felt sorry for her and wanted to help. I gave her a tissue to blow her nose. She took it gracefully, and between blowing her nose and wiping her eyes, she told me she never had wanted for anything. Her husband took excellent care of her and their children. She raised her big gray eyes up at me.

"I just needed some excitement in my life. I did lift that necklace from Thalhimer's department store, but I have more than enough money to pay for it."

"Yes, ma'am, I'm sure you do," I said.

"My husband could purchase every necklace in that store," she said, full of pride, "but I just wanted the thrill of lifting it." She dabbed each eye with another tissue.

"You're entitled to make a phone call for someone to go get your bail," I dutifully said to her.

"All I need is a hundred dollars more," she said. "I can give you the code to my husband's safe. You can go to my house and be back within an hour. Please, miss, help me."

I looked around to see if anyone was listening. Everyone seemed to be busy with his own work and watching the monitor.

"The spare key is located outside the house, under the brass cactus planter, the small one," she whispered.

I needed an extra hundred dollars. That was enough to buy enough groceries to last a whole month. My mind told me to take the hundred dollars, but something in the pit of my stomach warned me against going to this woman's house.

"Ma'am, I think you should call one of your children," I said.

"My children are away," she replied.

"I don't think I should go to your home, but I will allow you to make as many telephone calls as you need to find a bail bondsman." I inserted her belongings in the filing cabinet and then slammed the heavy metal drawer shut.

Then she said, "I will give you two hundred dollars. My husband will be returning in two days. I need all of this settled before he comes home."

I wanted the $200, and I wanted her to make bail without any embarrassment. She seemed to be a nice lady, just bored. I started to write the code down, when Crane walked over to where we were. He pretended to read something on the bulletin board near us. I took that as a bad omen and whispered to her that I couldn't go to her home.

The deputy left our space after a short while. The socialite started to sniffle.

"I'm sorry your people have been treated so poorly by some of my people, but my family is not prejudiced. Please help me."

I wanted to help the woman but was afraid. I felt her neighbors might see me go into her house and call the police. I would be arrested for sure or possibly shot on the spot for breaking and entering. I grabbed the big telephone book and turned to the yellow pages. I found her a long list of bail bondsmen.

"I suppose you are right," she said in a soft, whispery voice. After making about fifteen phone calls, she found one that pleased her.

The next day, I got reprimanded for allowing her to make more than one telephone call.

CHAPTER 49

RALEIGH, NORTH CAROLINA

In the spring of 1978, one year after I started working at Greensboro's sheriff's department, my former employer, Southern Bell, called me back to work. I was apprehensive about the reception I would receive, since everyone knew the circumstances of why I had left.

Around ten forty-five, I stepped inside the one-level brick building across from Holly Hill Mall on a Monday. First, I saw a few black employees standing over in the hallway, eyeing me suspiciously. Then, finally, Brenda, a black job steward, made her way through.

"Hey, girl, welcome back," Brenda said, and then she began to tell me all about the changes that had taken place and the grueling computerized training I would have to take.

The other black ladies began to walk toward us. Brenda turned and faced them. "I got this," she said, and the well-dressed ladies stopped and began to whisper among themselves.

The job steward said, "Marilyn, several white people failed this computerized training. We can't have you fail and embarrass us."

"I intend to pass whatever I need to pass. But I need my old job back," I said, looking over at the group of black women bunched together staring at me.

"You got to pass this training and every test they throw at you!" someone yelled from behind.

I didn't say anything to them, but my heart quickened, and fear set in. *What if I can't perform my old job?* I got a drink of water from the fountain to calm my nerves and ease my burning throat.

"I've had the training, and I'll review most of it with you, just to make sure you pass," Brenda said. "So far, all six of the black employees have passed. The white people are mad because they think the NAACP will

229

start a lawsuit if the company doesn't let us pass." Brenda stopped talking as several white women walked by us. She eyed them. "Can you believe they're saying that? They know we never get a fair shot at anything. The instructors let us pass my ass."

I spoke loudly enough for the cluster of black women to hear. "I will pass the tests and not embarrass y'all."

Brenda seemed satisfied with that and gave me a pat on my back. "All right then," she said, "I'm depending on you."

I passed all the required tests, but we were required to handle each customer's request within an average time of twelve to fifteen seconds.

After a couple of months of speeding through customers, I applied for a higher-paid position. I got the job but relocated to Raleigh and had another six weeks of training.

There were six of us in class: four white females, one white male, and me. One day, after class, we sat around the table and talked as we waited for the heavy beltway traffic to die down. I mainly reviewed the day's lesson.

One of the female students asked the class, "Did you all see the news this morning? This nigger garbage collector pushed this lady down in my neighborhood. Can you believe a nigger actually pushed her down?"

I continued to review the lesson. I slyly glanced over at the other students' faces and saw one of the women pointing with her head toward me. She was trying to remind them that I was still in the room.

The instructor changed the subject and started to talk about her husband, Louie, and their colored yardman. I thought she was trying to make me feel better. But then she said, "Colored people don't care if you don't remember their names." The other students nodded. That did not sit well with me, but I said nothing. I didn't want the instructor to find a reason to fail me in class.

At that point, I knew I had to leave. It was better for me to wait in heavy traffic than stay in class. So I stood up and said I had to pick up my baby from day care. I thought my job would be over if I said what I wanted to say.

After six weeks, I passed the training, along with the other five students, and was assigned a desk.

It didn't take long for me to find out that my supervisor was a hellion. First, she told me I couldn't put any customers on hold for longer than three seconds, but I noticed the experienced and new coworkers would put their customers on hold for two to five minutes and sometimes longer for various reasons.

After I complained about my supervisor to Jannie one day, she said, "Marilyn, get it through your skull: your supervisor does not like you. She never will, no matter how good you are. Carly only likes white people like her."

Jannie, a shapely, curly-haired coworker with chocolate-colored eyes and skin, was a seasoned universal customer representative, which meant she sold services and telephone equipment and collected delinquent telephone accounts, as I did. We had a monthly sales quota to meet and had to collect the money on overdue bills, make satisfactory payment arrangements, or temporarily deny telephone service within specific parameters.

"I do a good job. I'm the best salesperson on Carly's team. She will come around to see that I'm just like everyone else. She's going to stop riding my back pretty soon," I said, and I took a large bite of my crisp Granny Smith apple.

"It does not matter how competent you are or how well you sell," Jannie said. "This is North Carolina. You can't change what's been drilled into her. She has been groomed to be racist." She rolled her eyes and shook her head at me. "And for God's sake, you need to stop calling her Mrs. Carly. Do you hear me calling her Mrs. Carly?" Jannie took in a deep breath, unwrapped her candy bar, and took a bite. "Call her Carly."

A few days after my talk with Jannie, I asked Carly a question about the job. Instead of helping me, Carly wrote me up for lack of job knowledge. Unfortunately, she did not know the answer and sent me to another supervisor to get the information I needed.

After a few weeks of feeling stupid, I started to ask the smartest supervisor in the office for help when I needed it. That created a hot situation in the office because other reps did the same thing.

The manager called a center meeting and said, "From now on, everyone has to seek help from his or her immediate supervisor unless that supervisor is busy or out of the office."

CHAPTER 50

SLOW WALK TO HELL

My slow walk to hell began on a Friday two weeks after the manager's meeting. I stood in fear and watched Carly as she pulled the drawer from my desk and carried it away. It was my entire work file. I figured there was only one reason she would have done that.

"Please tell me. What did y'all do to that woman? Why does she hate me so much?" I asked Jannie during our last fifteen-minute break the following Monday.

"We showed up for work on time every day—that's all," Jannie said as she popped the lid off her soda. Then she pointed a finger. "You be careful. Carly has been quite successful in getting most of the black employees fired. She's building a case on you right now."

I said, "Jannie, I'm sure you're right. She took all my work files home with her last Friday."

Jannie set her Pepsi down and said, "That bitch is in overdrive looking for something on you that warrants discipline or termination."

I tried to harness my thoughts as my heart fluttered, and I began to panic and doubt myself. Would Carly find something to justify termination in the work files she had taken home?

"Girl, watch your back. I know her well," Jannie said. "She's planning to get rid of your ass real soon."

I was so afraid of getting fired that I wanted to quit. But I forced myself to take long, deep breaths, trying hard to conceal my fear. I hoped Jannie was wrong about Carly's plan to get rid of me.

After we returned from break, Carly came to my desk and told me I should be glad she had not found any discrepancies in my work files.

I felt a puke coming on. I rushed to the bathroom and hung my head over the sink. I didn't throw up, but I tried to as bitter bile stuck in my throat. I began to rinse my mouth, when someone entered the bathroom. I was so paranoid that I thought the person was one of Carly's spies.

That afternoon, after work, Jannie and I walked out of the building together. Jannie pointed a finger at me as she headed to her car.

"Whatever you do, be careful."

"I'm watching my back," I said. "I'm going to be the best employee Carly ever had. She will never find anything that will warrant firing me."

Jannie stopped. "Marilyn, it has nothing to do with the quality of your work." She shook her head. "Man, you just don't get it. It's the color of your face."

"Jannie, I don't believe that people are prejudiced for no reason."

Jannie opened the door to her car and said, "You don't have to believe it. You will see for yourself soon enough."

When I arrived at work the next day, Carly was standing at my desk. "Marilyn, I need you to accompany me to Mr. Bradshaw's office."

I covered my mouth to muffle an awful groan. I thought today was the day I might have a heart attack or lose my job—maybe both. What if Carly had found something that warranted some form of discipline? I could hardly breathe, and my legs trembled, but I managed to follow her into Mr. Bradshaw's office.

I sat next to Carly, facing the office manager. He cleared his throat and said, "Marilyn, I understand that you are putting every customer you handle on hold for about three seconds."

"No, sir," I said. "The only time I put customers on hold is if they ask me a question I can't answer. Then I put them on hold long enough to get the correct information, and I hurry back."

Mr. Bradshaw, a tall, balding white male, looked from Carly back to me. "Well," he said, "you'd better be glad you didn't put any customers on hold while I was listening to you late yesterday; otherwise, I would have fired you. Carly has already told me that she has warned you about this tendency."

I nodded and willed myself to remain calm. I wanted to scream and cuss them both because I knew it was just a matter of time before Carly successfully fired me. I walked out of Mr. Bradshaw's office feeling scared and embarrassed.

I saw Jannie standing at her supervisor's desk. Then, after a few seconds, she walked by me with long strides and whispered, "Meet me for lunch."

A Head of Cabbage

Three hours later, Jannie and I had lunch at Daryl's restaurant across the street from where we worked.

Jannie said, "So the bitch is taking it up a notch."

Feeling defeated, I said, "Mr. Bradshaw threatened to fire me on the spot. He said Carly told him I put every customer on hold for three seconds. She's been timing me."

Jannie blinked. "She actually said you put every customer on hold for three seconds?"

"Yep, she said every customer."

"Well, do you?" Jannie asked.

"No, but I do put some on hold long enough for me to find the correct information."

Jannie and I ate in silence for a while, and then Jannie said, "We've got to get you some help with that bitch."

A month later, things had not gotten better. I was filled with angst each day that I went to work. Whether I had a positive or negative attitude did not matter because I could not change my supervisor's perception of me. I knew that something simple could cause me to lose my job, lose my ability to take care of my children, and lose my hope of getting out of poverty.

Right after lunch one frightful day, I saw Moxi Ann, Mr. Bradshaw's secretary, coming out of his office. I felt her eyes on me and smelled her perfume before she stopped to speak to one of her friends.

My heart began to race. My thoughts became convoluted when I saw my supervisor, Carly, leaving the manager's office as well. I tried to think about what I had said or done during lunch. I had eaten with a couple of my white coworkers. Had they later said something negative about me to Mr. Bradshaw or Carly? By the time Moxi Ann reached my desk, I could hardly breathe. I reached down into my big green canvas bag and got out my composition tablet.

"Marilyn, Brad would like to see you in his office now," she said politely. She then wiggled back to her desk outside Mr. Bradshaw's office.

I followed behind her and waited just outside Mr. Bradshaw's office, since he held his telephone between his shoulder and his chin, talking to someone. I looked around the sizeable open-spaced workroom to see if Jannie was anywhere in sight. I didn't see her, and that made me more anxious. I told myself to remain dignified. *Don't scream, cuss, or storm out of his office, no matter what he says to you.* I reached down and held my right leg to stop it from shaking.

"What happened this morning with Mr. Turner?" Mr. Bradshaw asked, gesturing for me to come in and take a seat.

Before answering, I quickly reviewed the conversation in my mind as to what had happened with Mr. Turner, a customer who had not paid his telephone bill. The call had not gone well, but I was confident I had followed Southern Bell's protocol.

"Good morning. This is Ms. Jamison with Southern Bell Telephone Company," I had said. "May I speak to Mr. Jimmy T. Turner, please?"

"This is Mr. Turner. What do you want?" the angry voice on the other end of the telephone had said.

"Sir, I'm calling on behalf of Southern Bell regarding your past-due telephone bill. When can we expect your payment?"

Mr. Turner had said, "I will not have a nigger tell me that my bill is late or ask me when it's going to be paid." *Click.* The telephone had gone dead.

I had noted in his records that he'd hung up while refusing to give a date to expect payment. So I'd issued the paperwork to turn his telephone service off until he paid his account.

"Marilyn, do you remember this customer?" Mr. Bradshaw asked with a raised brow.

After collecting my thoughts, I told Mr. Bradshaw precisely what had happened. "The account came in as a delinquent referral to call and secure payment. Mr. Turner refused to make payment arrangements. He hung up on me, and I temporarily denied his service."

Mr. Bradshaw said, "Well, from now on, I don't want you to ever call this customer again."

"What if he is late in paying his bill?" I asked. I knew Carly would write me up if I didn't handle a nonpaying customer within the appropriate time frame. She had already taken my files home to check them over, looking for mistakes or anything worthy of termination.

"In that case," Mr. Bradshaw said, "take the delinquent referral to your supervisor to deal with him and to determine the next step."

When I walked out of Mr. Bradshaw's office, Jannie bumped into me.

"Is everything OK?" she asked as she kept walking.

I nodded.

Two months later, Mr. Jimmy T. Turner's account was delinquent again. Reluctantly, I took the paper referral to Carly to handle, as instructed by Mr. Bradshaw. When I handed it to her, she jerked the delinquent referral from my hand and quickly scanned it.

Carly said, "I do not do craft work. You will call this customer."

I pointed to the permanent notations on the referral made by Mr. Bradshaw, which stated that only a supervisor should call to talk with Mr. Turner. I felt I was heading toward termination at breakneck speed. Finally, I said, "But Mr. Bradshaw said I was never to call this customer again. He told me to give the referral to you, for you to decide the next step."

Carly stood up and asked, "Who gives you your appraisal?"

All I could think of was keeping my job and dignity. So I chose my words carefully.

"I earn my appraisal. You and Mr. Bradshaw sign it," I said in a whisper.

"Oh no, I give you your appraisal, and Mr. Bradshaw concurs with me," Carly said, dragging out the word *concurs* much longer than necessary. "You call Mr. Turner, and ask for payment now."

I picked up the referral, and on the way back to my desk, I discreetly peeped around the corner to see if Mr. Bradshaw was in his office. He was not. Instead of going back to my desk to call the delinquent customer, I went to Mrs. Raven, another supervisor, even though I was not supposed to. I told Mrs. Raven the story and asked her what I should do.

Mrs. Raven read all the pertinent information in the customer's file.

"Well, I think Carly should make the call, but if she told you to call, you have to follow her directions. Otherwise, you could be written up for insubordination."

I went back to my desk and called Mr. Turner. He hung up as soon as he heard my voice.

Less than an hour later, a sandy-haired white man walked onto the floor space, and someone directed him to Mr. Bradshaw's office. I knew the devil had stepped inside.

CHAPTER 51

I'M NOT OK

Two days later, Carly was standing at my desk, waiting for my morning arrival.

She said, "Marilyn, BellSouth security team is here from Charlotte, waiting to interview you." She pointed to a small conference room, where some recording equipment was sitting.

I wanted to say, "Fuck you, white bitch. Kiss my black ass. Whatever this is, it's because of you." I believed she had said or done something to get me in trouble. However, my desire to say such ugly words slowly died as I looked toward the conference room window, where I saw one of the men drawing the blinds.

"Don't take a call," Carly said. "You need to come with me now." She turned and strutted to the conference room.

I didn't say anything. I couldn't speak. I got my purse and composition tablet from my bag. As I followed Carly, I looked at the few black employees across the room. They looked back at me with pity in their eyes, as if they knew I was about to be fired. I thought so as well, but I would tell the truth, and if they fired me, I would leave quietly, not screaming or cussing.

The office job steward, a well-dressed blonde woman who looked to be about thirty, got her briefcase to accompany me.

I held up a hand. "It's not necessary for you to come with me."

The steward said, "Marilyn, please don't go in there alone. You can trust me, and you need union representation."

I didn't believe she would or could help me. I eyeballed the job steward for a moment, and then I cut my eyes over to Carly, who was entering the conference room.

"I don't trust you," I finally said. "I've been told that you party with Carly on weekends. So I will speak for myself, whatever the outcome."

I raised my eyebrows high and stuck out my chest. I was determined not to embarrass myself or my black coworkers. I walked into the conference room alone. The angst I felt was overwhelming when my feet crossed the threshold. I thought about saying to them, "You all are a bunch of white-ass racists of the worst kind: stupid," just before resigning my job. But of course, I didn't say it out loud, nor did I quit. Mr. Bradshaw excused Carly from the meeting, making me think I had a slight chance to keep my job.

There were three white men dressed in dark suits standing in the room. On the long, polished table were a tape recorder the size of a small TV, four microphones, and a folder in front of three chairs. One of the men pointed to a chair for me to sit.

I gazed over at the three stone-faced men as they took their seats. Their attire appeared coordinated to deliver some fright technique, and it was working. I told myself not to overthink this, and if they fired me, it wouldn't be the end of the world.

One of the men lowered his head to the mic. "Do you object to having this interview recorded?"

I said, "No, I don't object. Record away."

The machine made a low buzzing noise that I found irritating, but I said nothing about it since the noise camouflaged the sounds of my nervous rumbling stomach. Finally, the tallest and heaviest of the three men began to speak. I assumed he was in charge. He cleared his throat, grabbed the microphone, and brought it closer to him.

In a crisp baritone voice, he said, "Mr. Jimmy T. Turner called the consumer services director of Southern Bell, Raleigh, North Carolina, and filed a formal complaint against Miss Marilyn A. Jamison. Are you Marilyn A. Jamison?"

"Yes. I'm Marilyn A. Jamison." I sat as straight as possible, thinking about how I could prevent the security team from seeing my fear.

The heavyset interrogator went through the formalities one by one—my date of hire, my job title, and the address where I worked. Of course, I said yes to all three.

"Mr. Jimmy T. Turner has alleged that a Marilyn A. Jamison has been harassing him at his residence after hours by calling and hanging up on him and his frail wife."

His baritone voice cut into my sense of well-being as all three men stared at me.

"No, sir, I have not called Mr. Turner after hours or harassed him or

A Head of Cabbage

his frail wife." I managed to respond softly without sounding scared, even though I was about to piss on myself.

One of the men adjusted the microphone to pick up my voice better. I could hardly talk. My palms were sweating, and my heartbeat was so fast that I was afraid I might look guilty. I knew I needed to speak louder before my voice became a whisper. I looked around the small conference room—three rough-looking white men, my white manager, and me. I remembered the words Daddy had often said to me years earlier: "Gal, you don't know nothin'. That white man is the devil himself. They'll try to stop you from doing well in life. They pure evil."

Under the table, my legs shook uncontrollably, and I thought I was facing three devils all alone. I placed a hand on each knee to hold my knees as still as possible. I turned my head slowly and looked at each man, trying to find enough courage to speak what I knew was the truth.

Mr. Bradshaw sat in the back of the room in a dark gray windowpane suit with a sky-blue shirt and a dotted burgundy tie. His crossed legs and shiny black shoes made him look more than professional. He looked confident and stylish. But he chewed gum, which made me think maybe he too was a bit nervous.

Perspiration rolled down the sides of my face, back, and underarms. My stomach churned and ached, but I mustered enough courage to speak my thoughts.

I asked, "Do you think any black woman, a single mother, would harass a Nazi or a Ku Klux Klansman? Really?" I held my legs underneath the table a little firmer. I remembered Daddy telling me that white people would rather hear a lie from another white person than the truth from a black person. I hoped Daddy was wrong.

The men looked at one another but said nothing. I continued to speak as some of my fear began to dissipate.

"No woman is that dumb. That man is a Nazi. I saw the swastika tattooed on his arm when he went into Mr. Bradshaw's office. Either he is lying, or someone else is harassing him and his wife."

I stared at the heavyset man directly and waited for his response. No one verbally responded, but two men nodded in agreement with me. The stocky man was most arrogant. He gave the other two men a disapproving glance. Then he turned back to me.

"Someone is definitely harassing this customer. We will find out who that person is. We don't allow employees to harass our customers, Ms. Jamison."

I felt a tinge of hope since two of the men seemed to be reasonable. I said, "I hope you find the person who is harassing Mr. Turner. It's not me."

The heavyset man with the baritone voice began to act like a bully. Finally, he stood up, twisted his head toward me, and then lurched closer to my face. "I understand that your manager—ah, Mr. Bradshaw—asked you not to call this customer again. Why did you disobey his direct order?"

I looked over at Mr. Bradshaw sitting in a corner seat a few feet away from the interrogators. He appeared to be intently listening as he watched the scene.

I said, "Carly, my supervisor, made me call Mr. Turner. I showed her Mr. Bradshaw's notations, but she forced me to call that customer."

I knew shit would hit the fan soon, and I would lose my job—if not now, then in a week or two, as soon as Carly heard about my telling the truth about her orders.

The interrogator had a questionable look on his face. He opened his mouth in disbelief and briefly looked back at Mr. Bradshaw.

Mr. Bradshaw stopped chewing. Both his feet were flat on the floor and wide apart as he asked, "What did you say?"

I said, "It can be proven. I wrote on the customer's account in green ink the date, time, and reason for the call and that the call was made at the insistence of my supervisor."

The three men looked at one another while the humming tape recorder continued to record, and then they all looked back at Mr. Bradshaw.

I thought there might be light at the end of the tunnel after all. I eased up out of my chair and asked, "May I go to my desk for a moment to get the referral on which I made the notations?"

Mr. Bradshaw and Mr. Baritone said yes simultaneously.

I hurried to my desk to get Mr. Turner's file. I quickly flipped through it twice. Unbelievably, someone had cut the notations off the document. I brought the file anyway and showed the men, including Mr. Bradshaw, where I had written the inscriptions in green ink. They looked at the file dubiously but saw several cuts made. They also saw a few dots of green ink.

A Head of Cabbage

"We can't conclude anything with this," the heavyset guy said, and he laid the customer's file on the table and stared at me.

My heart started to flutter again. Then I smiled because I remembered something else. Mrs. Raven, another supervisor in the office, could help me.

I glanced over to Mr. Bradshaw and said, "Please check with Mrs. Raven. She knows all about this. She was the one who told me I should do what my supervisor asked me to do but to make thorough notations on the account as to why I called the customer, disobeying your direct order."

Mr. Bradshaw left the room, walking relatively fast. I didn't know if Mrs. Raven was at work or if she would tell the truth. I tried to look through the blinds, but all I saw was the bare wall. The wait was excruciating. One of the men tapped the table with his pen. I looked at the wall clock. Mr. Bradshaw had been gone for seven minutes.

Finally, the door flew open. We all looked, but it was the secretary.

"Mr. Bradshaw said he would be back in a few minutes. Can I get anyone anything?"

Mr. Baritone declined her offer and said we all were OK, and one of the other men resumed tapping on the table.

Shit no. I'm not OK. They're in here to take away my livelihood, I thought.

Mr. Bradshaw sidestepped his secretary and entered the room just as she left. He gave a big sigh. "Mrs. Raven said Marilyn is telling the truth. She didn't want to call Mr. Turner and tried not to. She was afraid of getting into trouble."

He stood at the table and looked at me as if he wanted to apologize, but he didn't.

Finally, the heavyset man told me to return to my desk. He cracked a faint smile. "I'm happy we could resolve this so soon," he said, and the other two men nodded.

I started to leave the room, when a thought came to me. I stopped and turned around. "Mr. Bradshaw, is it against company policy to destroy customers' records?"

He gave a resounding "Absolutely."

I said to the security team, "Somebody has been destroying customers' records around here. Can you find that person?"

CHAPTER 52

VENGEANCE IS THE LORD'S

The Sunday before Halloween, I heard a faint knock at my door. Standing on the concrete stoop were two attractive women clutching Bibles. They said, "God loves you. Do you know him?"

No one had ever greeted me in such a way, and I immediately felt at ease and invited them in.

"Vengeance is the Lord's." So my two impromptu guests told me an hour later after I had shared the details of my miserable life, broken marriage, and stressful and hostile work environment. When I told them my ex-husband was gay, they read Leviticus 20:13, assuring me God would punish David. When I told them about my racist boss, they said that God was not partial to one group over another and that I should take comfort in knowing that each evil person would get his or her reward.

In November, my two children, their cousin Ernest, and I attended our first all-day social event with the Jehovah's Witnesses. I loved it. There were several six-foot tables with more food than I had ever seen at any gathering. I wanted to stay awhile longer, but Sherondalyn, my seven-year-old, had gotten sick.

I told Brenda, my newly made friend, that I was leaving because Sherondalyn was not feeling well, just when a soloist began to sing. The songs were not traditional Negro spirituals or gospel songs, but I stopped in my tracks for a moment and stared at the soloist. The man, a tall blond probably in his thirties, had a clear tenor voice that sounded magnificent.

Two handsome Spanish-looking men accompanied the soloist with acoustic guitars. Although the building was bubbling over with people, it was quiet, and every child was well behaved and sat quietly with his or her parents or friends. I was impressed with this group of Christians.

An hour later, I was home. I gave Sherondalyn a teaspoon of Robitussin cough syrup and put her and Paris to bed. I finished rolling my hair with big pink foam rollers and started to brush my teeth, when I heard tiny footsteps running down the hallway.

"Sheron won't read to me. Mama, make Sheron read to me." Paris couldn't pronounce the name Sherondalyn yet and called her sister Sheron.

Five minutes later, Sherondalyn came into my bedroom as I was reading Dr. Seuss's *The Cat in the Hat* to Paris. I noticed that Sherondalyn's breathing was laborious, and she was panting as if she had run a marathon. I grabbed my purple terry-cloth bathrobe and puffed-up green bedroom slippers, threw a blanket over Sherondalyn, grabbed my purse, and headed out to Community Hospital, a fifteen-minute drive from where we lived on Buffaloe Road.

By the time I reached the hospital, Sherondalyn was delirious. She started to spell words at random and say things that didn't make sense. Her breathing was scary, as if each breath might be her last.

The receptionist at admitting told me I must take her to Wake County Hospital because Community Hospital didn't have a pediatric department. I'd lived in Wake County for about six months but did not know my way around town. Also, I had no idea how to get to Wake County Hospital.

A policeman stood just inside the door and heard me pleading for help. Eventually, he came and stood several feet behind me.

I cried out to the lady at the desk. "Please help my child! She's so sick."

I kept an eye on the policeman. I was afraid he might arrest me for disturbing the peace. But then he walked closer as I begged for help.

The policeman said, "Miss, they can't help you here. Your little girl does appear seriously ill. You must take her to Wake County Hospital."

"I don't know how to get there!" I screamed louder than I wanted to. I bent over heaving, and Sherondalyn began to slide out of my arms onto the floor.

The policeman lifted her from my arms and started toward the exit. He said, "Follow me."

He placed Sherondalyn in my car. Then he ran to his squad car and turned on his siren and blue lights. I skipped first gear and took off in second. My red Audi's tires squealed as I turned out of the parking lot behind the police car.

The emergency room staff were waiting for us. A young doctor introduced himself as Dr. Hanson. He took one look at Sherondalyn and made a diagnosis. I heard him say to the nurses that her lungs had collapsed. Then, without hesitation, he gave orders to several other people who worked with him. Sherondalyn, barely conscious, was wheeled away in a bed.

"Miss, do you need some help in taking care of this financial obligation to the hospital?" Dr. Hanson asked me as we walked down the hallway.

I felt insulted, but I understood why he made the assumption. My hair was in big pink foam rollers. I should have thrown out the green bedroom slippers I wore months ago. Indeed, I met every poor-woman stereotype. I remained calm but was fearful that they might not save Sherondalyn if they thought the hospital wouldn't get paid. I prayed, *God, help these doctors save my child. Give them knowledge and talent that will save her life.*

I said, "Save her life, please. I have insurance on her, and so does her father. You will get every penny you charge."

Dr. Hanson said, "Miss, I didn't want you worrying about your daughter's health and this financial obligation. No offense intended."

When I was not permitted to accompany Sherondalyn, I found my way back to admission to give my Blue Cross Blue Shield insurance card, but I couldn't find it.

The admission clerk had a smirk on her face as she extended her hand for me to give her the insurance card. She eyed me as if she didn't believe I had insurance. I finally remembered that I had changed purses because of the Jehovah's Witness social earlier in the evening.

"I left the card at home, ma'am. It's in my other purse. I'll go home and get it. I'll be right back," I said, and I rushed out of the hospital.

My home telephone was ringing before I opened the front door.

"This is Dr. Hanson, Ms. Jamison. We have to perform emergency surgery on your daughter right now if she is to have a chance of survival. I need you to give us verbal consent to operate. We cannot wait for you to get back to the hospital."

I let out a groan or maybe a wail. Dr. Hanson's words were painful to hear. Immediately, I said, "You have my consent to do whatever you need to do to save her life."

I fell to my knees and prayed for Sherondalyn for several minutes before finding the insurance card. I checked on Paris and Ernest; they both were sound asleep. I started back to the hospital, when a yellow light popped up on the fuel gauge, warning me to refuel. I pulled into the nearest service station off US Highway 1. Unfortunately, it was closed and would not reopen until the next day at 7:00 a.m.

I returned home and called David. I told him about Sherondalyn's being hospitalized and asked him to see if his aunt Autry could keep Paris and Ernest, because I planned to stay at the hospital with Sherondalyn. Then, even though it was after eleven o'clock, I called my new Jehovah's Witness friend, Brenda, and asked her to pray for Sherondalyn's healing.

The following day, I was sitting in front of the gas pump when it opened at 7:00, and I staggered into Sherondalyn's room twenty minutes later. She was in the intensive care unit. A large black rubber tube was sticking out of her right side and into a suction pump sitting on the floor beside her bed. An oxygen mask covered her nose, and her tiny wrist had an IV taped to it. I held on to the side of the door, listening to the machine beside my daughter's bed pump and make a sucking sound. Finally, I made my way to her bed and kissed her forehead. She looked frail and afraid, but she smiled when she saw me.

I was with her for only two or three minutes before someone told me I must wait in the waiting area. Half a dozen Jehovah's Witnesses were present. First, they prayed for Sherondalyn, and that made me feel better. Then one of the female Jehovah's Witnesses took me to get breakfast somewhere, and when we returned, the doctor was waiting for me.

"Ms. Jamison," he said, "we need to talk right now about your daughter. She needs a blood transfusion, or she will die. Her red blood count is extremely low. She has internal bleeding and has lost a lot of blood."

One Jehovah's Witness elder said, "No blood, Doctor. Find another way."

The doctor looked frustrated. He looked at me, and so did all the Jehovah's Witnesses.

"No blood, Doctor. Find another way." I repeated the words of the elder.

The doctor left, shaking his head in disbelief.

Less than fifteen minutes later, the doctor returned to the waiting room to talk to me. He appeared exasperated. "Ms. Jamison, how can you sentence your own child to die?"

I looked around at my friend and the other Jehovah's Witnesses praying for Sherondalyn's healing and for me to be strong enough to do what was in Sherondalyn's best interest. I wanted to relent and allow the doctors to give her the needed blood transfusion. But I felt powerless to say so. I felt that God would not be pleased.

I said, "She will not die. We are praying for her to live."

Each Jehovah's Witness gave me a nod of approval, and I felt as if God had given me his consent as well. Finally, the doctor left again, shaking his head in disbelief, and I was afraid Sherondalyn might die.

Two days later, a social worker came to talk to me while Sherondalyn slept. She told me they were in the process of getting the state to assume custody of Sherondalyn since I was not making decisions in her best interest. I told her to do what she needed to do. Then the social worker asked me about Sherondalyn's father, and I began to panic, thinking the social service department might have authority to give David custody. I told her he was not in the home.

Then she asked, "Ms. Jamison, do you believe in corporal punishment?"

"Yes, I do."

"When was the last time you punished your daughter?"

I said, "I don't remember the last time, because Sherondalyn is a sweet child, and I seldom have to punish her."

The social worker began to speak intensely. "Well, the doctors can't determine why she has internal bleeding. You know, Ms. Jamison, sometimes we hit or shake our small ones just a little too hard and—"

I immediately stopped her. "I don't abuse my children. I do correct them, and I sometimes whip them on their legs with a switch or use a belt on their butts but not so hard as to cause internal bleeding. I don't know why she has internal bleeding either. I was told she had pneumonia, and her lungs collapsed."

The social worker checked a few blocks on her clipboard and then looked at me and said, "The bleeding is consistent with abuse. Well, that's all for now."

CHAPTER 53

NO BLOOD

I knew it would happen sooner or later. When I returned to work a couple of days after Sherondalyn's admittance to the hospital, Carly called me into her office. She said, "I am officially warning you that your employment with Southern Bell is in jeopardy due to your absenteeism. We understand that your little girl is ill, but we have a responsibility to our customers not to keep them waiting. We have to answer to the utilities commission, after all."

I was aware that we were required to answer 80 percent of all calls within twenty seconds. Both management and craft workers tried hard to keep the utilities commission happy with the level of service provided to customers. After all, AT&T, the parent company of Southern Bell, was a monopoly and was being challenged in US district court. I assumed the utilities commission would share information with the US district court about the quality of service provided. I had been in several meetings where the name of Judge Harold H. Greene, who had to make a ruling, evoked unpleasant feelings and fear. We didn't know what to expect if the verdict was unfavorable to AT&T. That was why I was not upset with Carly for warning me about my attendance.

I tried to put things into perspective. I heard Carly, but I was thinking of Sherondalyn. It finally dawned on me not to fear losing my job but to fear losing my child. I saw Carly staring at me with a questioning look. It took me a minute to give her a response.

I said, "I will not miss any more days." As soon as the words left my lips, I regretted saying them. I knew they were a lie, because I needed to stay with my daughter in the hospital for a few more days.

"Good then," Carly said. "I'll just note in your records that we've had this conversation and that you fully understand the consequences."

When I got back to my desk, Jannie stood nearby, watching me. Then she sauntered over. "What did that bitch say to you?"

"She warned me about my attendance."

Jannie rolled her eyes. "Marilyn, don't you have some vacation left?"

"Yes, two weeks."

"Then you need to march your ass right back into her office and tell her that you need to take a week of vacation right now." Jannie started to walk off but then stopped, grabbed my arm, and said, "Due to sickness in your family. I'll be praying for Sherondalyn."

When I entered Sherondalyn's room Tuesday morning, Dr. Hanson was in her room and said, "Your daughter will probably die unless you allow us to do this experimental procedure."

I shook my head. "No blood. No experimental surgery. Find another way."

Dr. Hanson walked out of the room with his frustration showing. His words resonated with me for hours. I felt guilty and ashamed that I might be dooming my child to a slow death.

Suddenly, the phone beside her bed rang.

"How are you holding up?"

"I'm fine. Just a little tired," I said, recognizing Mildred's voice.

"How is Sherondalyn?" she asked.

I told Mildred that the doctor wanted to do an experimental procedure to open Sherondalyn's chest enough for a man's fist to be inserted to see what was going on inside. They had determined she had pneumonia, but she was losing blood, and the doctors didn't know why.

Mildred asked, "Are you going to let them give her a blood transfusion?"

I had talked with Mildred on numerous occasions about the blood issue, and she was doing her best to keep calm. However, I could tell she was angry with me by her crisp tone.

I said, "No blood transfusion. I don't want to displease God."

"Marilyn." Mildred paused for a second. "God doesn't care if Sherondalyn gets a blood transfusion or not. It's those Jehovah's Witnesses you are mixed up with who care about blood transfusions. They have brainwashed you. Just think for yourself for a change. Don't let your child die because of Jehovah's Witnesses. They are a misled people. Believe me, it has nothing to do with God."

I didn't respond to my sister. Instead, I hung up the phone and watched Sherondalyn's vital signs fluctuate on the monitor. I was confused and scared. I could hardly think. *Am I condemning my child to die? Am I being tested by God? If so, for what? Do I need to deny her a blood transfusion to please God? Or am I just too weak and brainwashed by Jehovah's Witnesses to do the right thing for my child? Do I want their approval and acceptance so much that I can't make a sensible decision regarding my child's life?* Finally, I sat back down in the chair. Sherondalyn stirred, and I took her hand.

She turned her face toward me. Her sunken dark eyes pierced my soul. She could hardly speak but slowly asked me, "Mama, am I going to die?"

I raised her hand to my chest and said, "Sherondalyn, there is a God in heaven who will not let you die. Don't worry. You are coming home soon."

The following day, I arrived at the hospital and found several doctors and the social worker waiting in Sherondalyn's room. They took me to a small conference room, and one of the doctors told me that the hospital board had met and had decided no longer to treat Sherondalyn.

I screamed and begged, but the board had made their decision. Never had I felt such fear, not even when Daddy had threatened to shoot me with his shotgun. I thought I would collapse, but I didn't. Finally, I said, "Hospitals are supposed to help people. What kind of hospital is this? Please help my—"

An older doctor interrupted. His blue eyes were stern and unblinking. He spoke in a deliberate tone. "Arrangements have been made for your daughter to be transported to the UNC Medical Center in Chapel Hill. A team of doctors have been briefed, and they are waiting for your daughter's arrival. The ambulance is ready for her transportation."

He turned and walked out the door. The others followed. I felt sick with guilt and fear as I watched them walk out of the room.

The social worker remained behind. She touched my arm. "Ms. Jamison, you may want to follow the ambulance to Chapel Hill."

During the drive to the hospital, I tried to bargain with God, although all my religious teaching had taught me that no one could. I told God that if he spared Sherondalyn's life, I would give up my plan to kill David and remove all evil thoughts from my heart to hurt or harm any of his creations.

By the time I reached Sherondalyn's room, doctors and medical students were already there. I counted thirteen people standing in her room; all wore white coats. The younger ones were taking notes. A middle-aged doctor sat down and put a stethoscope on Sherondalyn's chest. I stood just outside the door, observing them and thinking about life.

People existed for thousands of years before organized religions, written words, and languages—before doctors and scientists had the knowledge and technology to save lives. Man's laws are not God's laws. Man restricts and limits, and God allows free will. God allows man to increase knowledge for the benefit of his creation. These thoughts stayed with me, and I closed my eyes and prayed.

I thanked God for entering into my thoughts and helping me to understand that it was all right to use the knowledge of science and technology for the benefit of his creation.

When I opened my eyes, I noticed that the suction pump the doctors at Wake County had hooked up to Sherondalyn was no longer connected. The calmness I'd felt earlier was no longer with me, and I screamed, "You need to hook up her pump! Her lungs will fill up with fluid without it. Please connect the pump."

I leaned against the wall to steady myself. The sitting doctor stood up. The others remained silent and looked toward him.

"Are you Ms. Jamison, this child's mother?"

I nodded.

"This pump no longer has any value for her health. We will be taking the tube out of her side shortly."

I told them the pump was suctioning fluid from her lungs so she could breathe. I begged them to reconnect it.

"Ms. Jamison," the doctor in charge said, "after listening to her breathing, I'm quite certain the pump isn't necessary."

Nine days later, I stood in the middle of Sherondalyn's room, saying what I never had thought I would ever say: "You can give her a blood transfusion if you have to. Just don't let her die."

Once I said those words, I felt better. I felt free.

The doctor said, "We don't need to give her a blood transfusion. We know what caused the internal bleeding." Finally, he asked, "Do you think your daughter is getting better?"

"I know she is."

"How do you know that?" he asked.

"Her voice is much stronger, her eyes are not as weak, her skin looks better, she stays awake longer, and she is well enough to smile."

I looked away from the doctor and toward Sherondalyn. She smiled.

The doctor said, "I think she is better too. We sometimes ask the parents what they think. They know their children much better than we do."

"What caused her internal bleeding?" I asked.

The doctor said, "When the tube was inserted, one of her arteries was accidentally cut."

For a moment, I wanted to cuss out loud. The doctor and social worker at Wake Medical Center thought I was abusing her. It turned out the doctor had cut her artery.

"So that doctor at Wake Medical Center cut her artery and caused her to have internal bleeding and almost die?" I asked the doctor.

"Medicine is not a perfect science," the doctor said, "but we do the best we can to save and prolong lives."

I said, "I should sue them for threatening to take my child away and accusing me of child abuse. Would you say the doctor at Wake Medical Center almost killed my child?"

The doctor looked at me and sighed. "Ms. Jamison, I'm saying the Wake Medical doctor saved her life. That tube the Wake doctor inserted drained the fluid from your daughter's lungs. Had he not done so, she would not be with us today." He made a few notes on her chart and hung it at the bottom of the bed just as David stepped into the room.

David looked feminine in a long-sleeved, silky Carolina-blue shirt. The top two buttons were open, exposing the top of his chest. I wanted to slap him and vomit on him, but I restrained myself. His Carolina-blue pants were much too tight. He flung his long black hair back out of his face, exposing his clean-shaven face.

"Hello," he said. "I'm Sherondalyn's father."

David left his lips slightly apart as he twitched and then posed with one hand on his hip and bent down to kiss Sherondalyn on her forehead. He did not speak to me right away. He saw me rolling my eyes and shaking my head in disgust. Finally, David turned his backside to me, flung his hair around a second time, and then took a seat near Sherondalyn's bed. I sat on the opposite side, closest to the door.

The doctor looked at me and then at David. "You're Mr. Jamison?" The doctor hesitated for a moment. "The child's father?"

David said, "Yes, I am."

The doctor did a good job of trying to conceal his shock and said, "Your daughter is improving, but we need to keep her here a little longer to make sure."

After the doctor left, I said, "I can imagine the conversation the doctors are going to have this afternoon. It won't all be about Sherondalyn's health."

David sprang up like a jackrabbit and said, "Marilyn, I don't care what people think about me. You should see who walks into some of the gay nightclubs where I go." He smirked. "A lot of them are doctors."

David saw my anger and displeasure. Veins popped out on his neck as he tried to contain his temper. Finally, after about an hour, he looked at his watch and leaned closer to Sherondalyn. "Baby, I have to leave now, but Daddy will be back to see you soon." He kissed Sherondalyn, turned his head away from me, and left the room.

As David's footsteps faded down the hallway, I realized my hate for him had not lessened, even though I had made a promise to God.

CHAPTER 54

LEVITICUS 7:26

I awakened to one of those days when I wanted to turn over in bed and pull the covers over my head. Sherondalyn was still in the hospital, and I was at the lowest point of my life. I was afraid of losing my job and my child. I had not gotten paid for the days I missed from work. My car payment was late, and I had not paid any household bills. I had $100 earmarked for travel back and forth to the hospital and work.

I didn't make it to my desk before my supervisor, Carly, said, "Marilyn, I need you to go to the conference room before you take any calls."

I hung my head down and followed her across the office floor. I was tired and ready to accept whatever my fate was. I had prepared for the inevitable. I stepped inside the conference room, looking back for Jannie.

"Surprise! We're having a hot dog sale for you today, and all the money is going toward your children's Christmas," Dee Shanks, a white coworker, said to me when I walked in.

That week before Christmas, my coworkers restored my faith in humanity. I looked around the room and saw Carly standing with the other office supervisors. I was shocked when Dee Shanks handed me $800. I accepted the money, thanked everyone, and rushed to the bathroom to cry. I had expected an awful day but received the opposite.

That evening, before I went to the hospital, I paid bills and bought groceries with the money my coworkers had raised. I didn't buy the children anything for Christmas. Instead, I explained to Sherondalyn that Christmas was a day when Christians celebrated love and showed appreciation to family and friends. God had sent Jesus to teach love and show humanity how to behave toward one another.

Sherondalyn nodded and said, "Mama, I understand. I know you love me and get me what I need."

The hospital staff gave her some toys, which she shared with her younger sister, Paris. I did buy a boom box for my nephew Ernest out of the Social Security check I was receiving for him.

It was snowing big, fluffy flakes when Sherondalyn returned home after three months in the hospital. We drove from Chapel Hill back home to Raleigh in forty-five minutes. As soon as I put Sherondalyn to bed, I called my Jehovah's Witness friend Brenda and told her the good news. She said she was coming right over to see us.

"I have something to tell you all," I said nervously when Brenda and two more ladies sat down.

The oldest woman of the three said, "Yes, yes, yes. God does heal. We're so happy that your little girl is home and doing fine without taking blood."

I took in a few deep breaths and said, "I don't think I can be a Jehovah's Witness, because I have come to believe that God gives and allows knowledge to be used to benefit all people, even the knowledge of saving lives through blood transfusions." Those words, once I spoke them, were spiritually liberating. It was as if someone had opened my chest and taken a constricting weight out of it.

The women looked at one another. Finally, the oldest woman opened her Bible. She found the book and chapter she wanted and read a verse to me.

"Leviticus 7:26 says, 'And you must not eat any blood, in any place where you dwell, whether that of fowl or that of beast.' Blood transfusions are the same as eating the blood of people."

The other two women nodded in agreement.

I shook my head. "You know," I said, "men have made God out to be some mean, cruel God who will punish people for just about everything, even for wanting to live. Fortunately, I no longer believe that."

The oldest woman said, "Your daughter did live without a blood transfusion. God saved her."

I nodded. "Yes, I believe he did. And I thank him for allowing the hospital staff to use the skills and knowledge they acquired by studying medicine and science. In my heart, I know I will not make the same decision I made before. Instead, I will allow a blood transfusion in the future if either of my children needs one."

The lady responded, "You're right about two things. It's your decision to take blood, and you can't be a Jehovah's Witness." She closed her Bible, and they left. After that, I never saw or spoke to Brenda again.

CHAPTER 55

THANK YOU

In May 1979, I read in the *Raleigh News and Observer* that a plastic surgeon from New York City, Dr. Jessup, would be at Chapel Hill Hospital for a few weeks and accept new patients. I called the 800 number in the ad and arranged for a consultation about the scars on my face.

The doctor explained that people of color sometimes overhealed, which caused a keloid to develop. Therefore, he was unsure if he could minimize my scars or if a procedure would make them worse.

"I'm willing to take any risk," I said casually.

"What is the origin of your scars?" the doctor asked, leaning forward to get a closer look.

I tilted my head and leaned in so he could see every quarter-and-dime-sized dimple along with dozens of smaller pox holes.

"Mama said that when I was about three months old, my face broke out in bumps. She burst the bumps to make them go away, and they got infected."

Dr. Jessup began to prod, pinch, and touch my face. Occasionally, he scribbled a few words down on his notepad.

After telling him that Daddy wouldn't let Mama take me to see a doctor until gobs of flesh fell off and that the white people's hospital in Danville, Virginia, had refused to see me, I detected pity in Dr. Jessup's eyes.

He asked, "Did your parents ever find a doctor for you?"

"Mama said they later found a black doctor, but he didn't know how to treat me. He just put some type of cream on my face."

Dr. Jessup sat up straight in his chair and stared at me for a few seconds. Then he pushed the hanging light away. Several tense seconds passed before he spoke.

Then he said, "The white people's hospital probably didn't know what to do either. I'm sure your mother and father did what they could."

I thought of Daddy telling me that some people had to be ugly. I had wondered if my scars were the reason Montgomery Ward had wanted to hide me away from the public and the reason the Gilbarco manager had sat next to me ratting the newspaper while I was taking the typing test.

Chills ran over my entire body as disappointment set in. Then, as I stood up, I told myself that I had lived twenty-eight years with these scars and would continue to live with them if I had to.

I looked back and said, "I'm not trying to become a southern beauty queen. I just want these scars removed."

Dr. Jessup said, "I will try to improve the appearance of the scars—make them smoother. If they heal the way I think they should, we both will be pleased with the results."

The next day, when I asked Carly if I could change my last week of vacation, she said, "Marilyn, I cannot grant you vacation. There are at least twelve senior people who also want vacation in June, and they can't get it either. It can't be changed."

"But the date has been set. Please reconsider."

Carly looked up at me and said, "May I remind you that your attendance has not improved that much since your daughter was ill?"

I walked out of Carly's office, went to the bathroom, and prayed for a few minutes. On my way out, I saw Mr. Bradshaw walking down the hallway. I walked into his office right behind him.

"Mr. Bradshaw, I need to change my vacation for a medical procedure. It's urgent."

He asked, "What kind of medical procedure?" He pointed to a chair for me to sit.

"It's cosmetic surgery. A visiting plastic surgeon from New York will be at Chapel Hill Hospital for a month. He has agreed to do some cosmetic work to improve the appearance of my face." I watched Mr. Bradshaw's eyes rove over my facial scars.

Mr. Bradshaw said, "I can see that you need to do something with your face." He leaned across his desk so he could get a better look, all the while gesturing for me to come closer toward him.

I stood up, placed both my hands on his desk, and leaned over with my face angled so the overhead light would make it easier for him to see.

The feeling was uncomfortable. I felt as if I were naked, and I wondered if he required someone needing a tooth extracted to show him the cavity.

I then said, "The doctor said he could help me, but it has to be done next week." I sat back down and silently prayed, reminding God that everything was in his hands.

Mr. Bradshaw stood up and opened the door. "I think the office can manage without you for a couple of weeks. I'll talk with Carly."

In early June, my sister Mildred drove me to have the outpatient procedure. I returned home with the right side of my face heavily bandaged. I felt no pain but could only open my mouth wide enough for a drinking straw. My nephew Ernest ordered pizza for his and the girls' dinner.

Forty-five minutes later, the pizza man rang the doorbell. I opened the door, and when he saw my face in bandages, he started screaming, and then he jumped off the concrete steps. The pizza flew into the air and landed in the grass. The pizza delivery man sprinted to his car, locked his car doors, and drove off.

I called the pizza restaurant and slowly explained the situation to the manager. We received two free pizzas an hour later.

I visited Dr. Jessup ten days after the procedure. He didn't touch my face as he took the bandages off. Trying to gauge his thoughts, I watched his eyes as he moved the hanging light in every direction. It felt as if he were trying to look through my skin. Finally, he let out a slight sigh and sat back in his chair.

"Well," he said, "I think you should have the procedure repeated. It is still healing, but we didn't quite get the results I was hoping for."

I could hardly breathe, afraid the surgery had done nothing for me, and it had cost me half my savings. Finally, sounding like an adolescent boy, I garnered enough courage to see my face. In a high-pitched tone, I asked for a mirror. My entire body shook as I took the mirror from Dr. Jessup but didn't look. The doctor gently took my hand and raised the mirror to eye level. I wanted to see a miracle but did not expect one.

"Oh my God!" I could see my face was not perfect, but it was much smoother. I said, "Thank you!" so many times that Dr. Jessup blushed from embarrassment. It was a miracle.

CHAPTER 56

SHALL WE DANCE?

Two months after the cosmetic procedure, I decided to show Mama my improved face. So after dropping my children off with my ex-husband's aunt Autry, I headed toward Whitsett, a small town outside Greensboro.

"They've been at it all morning, and I've just about had all I can take," Mama said as soon as I stepped out of my car. She dropped her half-smoked cigarette onto the ground and stomped it out as though killing an insect. The frown lines on her face were now permanent, making her look hard and mean.

"I'm glad to see you," Mama added as she walked closer to her mobile home, "but don't step on my flowers." She pointed to a sizable bed of mixed daylilies and other plants I could not name. I followed closely behind.

Mama leaned into me and whispered, "They need to stop it. It just don't make sense. I have to listen to that every day."

As we neared the front door, I heard my younger brother Levi and his wife, Maxine, arguing with each other.

As we walked by them, Mama glared. Once we reached her bedroom, where it was quiet, she closed the door and turned to face me.

"Marilyn, I'm 'bout to lose my mind. Why do they come here to argue? Somebody better do something, or I'm gonna do it."

Mama pulled up a chair near her window and slapped the edge of the bed for me to sit. She stared me in the face without speaking. I thought she wanted me to say something.

"I don't know why they argue so much in your presence. Just ask them to stop."

"Shit," Mama said, "I ain't got time for them, when I got to keep an eye out for Little Tony and Vincent. Don't you listen to the news and read the papers?"

I shrugged. "Mama, just clue me in. I don't know what you're talking about."

Mama reached into her apron pocket and lifted out her .38-caliber pistol. "I tell you one thing. He can come around here if he wants to. Just let the bastard try to take Little Tony or Vincent. I'll blow his ass away." She closed the curtains and looked out the window.

"Mama, what are you talking about?" I wanted to know what she was looking at, so I peeped out the window. I saw nothing but young children playing.

Mama placed the pistol back in her apron pocket and said, "My neighbor is killing all them young black boys in Atlanta. He leaves here every Sunday night and is gone all week, and 'fore he gets back, another black boy is found dead. So it ain't nobody but my neighbor."

I looked at the grimace on Mama's face as she sat sideways, peeping out the window.

I started to laugh but stopped when I saw Mama straining her neck to see farther down from her window. She believed the Atlanta serial killer was her neighbor!

I said, "Lots of people work out of town, Mama. What made you suspicious of your neighbor?"

"'Cause he's stout, he's white, and he don't ever have a woman over there. And I ain't never heard of a black man killing up a bunch of people for no reason." She moistened her lips with her tongue. "Every serial killer I ever heard of is white. You ever heard of a black one?" she asked while peeping over her glasses.

"Well, me neither," I said, "but the man who is killing those boys probably lives in Atlanta, near the boys, not next door to you."

I turned the right side of my face toward Mama. I placed my forefinger near the smoother pink flesh of my cheek before asking her if she saw any difference in my appearance.

Mama said, "I sure do wish you wouldn't talk 'bout yo' face and would accept yo'self the way God made you. If God didn't want you to have scars, then you wouldn't have any. That's the way he wanted you to be." She glanced at me and then started to peer out her bedroom window again, watching her grandsons play.

I knelt right in front of her and said, "Mama, look at me. I had a plastic surgeon in Chapel Hill do some work on my face. He made most of the scars go away, but a few are still there."

Mama took another look at my face. She examined it closely. "Oh yeah, it is better." She smiled, turning my head this way and that. "But you need to leave your face alone, and that doctor in Chapel Hill left a pretty big spot right here in the front." She poked the pox hole with her forefinger a couple of times.

I cringed at her insensitivity.

As my brother and sister-in-law's argument got louder, Mama turned her ear toward the living room, frowning and shaking a finger at the door. I felt she wanted me to intervene.

I called Maxine into the bedroom with Mama and me. I asked her if she wanted to go to a disco club with me. I had heard enough of their conversation to know she was angry that Levi wanted to go out without her.

"I would like for you to go—that is, if Levi doesn't mind." I tilted my head to one side and cut my eyes toward Mama, waiting for Maxine's response.

Maxine took the hook. "If Levi doesn't mind?" she bellowed. "I don't care if he minds or not. He goes out without me; I can go out without him. What time are we leaving?"

"Ten o'clock."

Maxine told Levi she didn't mind if he went out without her, and the arguing ceased.

"Be quiet," Mama whispered, and she turned her ear toward the window. "I hear my neighbor leaving." She placed her hand in her apron pocket and clutched her pistol.

Maxine and I pulled into the Forest Lake Disco Club entrance at ten thirty. Unbeknownst to me, a bikers' rally was there, and we had to park maybe fifty yards away.

"Man, there goes a brick house," someone said as Maxine and I walked toward the entrance.

I knew they were not talking about me, and so did Maxine, who had an hourglass figure and had donned skintight black pants and a blouse that left little to the imagination.

"How do I look?" she asked as she twirled around a couple of times, swaying her ample butt under the overhead string lighting.

"You look great, Maxine," I said. "You'd better be glad you're married, because the men are going to try you tonight."

She fluttered her eyes and spoke softly. "Do you really think so?"

As soon as we stepped inside the club, I wanted to go home. I was underdressed and felt unattractive in my simple black polyester pants and beige-and-brown top. My flats made me look as if I should have been in a supermarket instead of a disco club. I gazed at the other women in the club. Most were dressed in sexy attire and were looking sporty and sophisticated. I asked Maxine if she wanted to go back home since bikers filled the club.

"No, no, no," she said just as some man grabbed her hand and pulled her onto the dance floor.

I found a seat and sat down. Men kept asking Maxine to dance, and she obliged. The DJ played every hit, one after another. Finally, I sat at the table alone and nursed a glass of Pepsi.

Feeling too warm and out of sorts, I headed for the foyer several feet away from the dance floor, where it was quieter and more relaxed. A tall, slender man with butterscotch coloring and a thin mustache gently took my hand as I walked across the floor. He had on a blue suit and black boots. He lifted his glasses and said, "Shall we dance?"

I looked up and instantly fell in love.

CHAPTER 57

TWELVE PAST MIDNIGHT

It was twelve minutes past midnight on July 7, 1979, and I was panicking. I had allowed Steven, the man I had met at the disco club, to spend the night with me, and it was our first date.

The girls were spending the weekend with their father, so I invited Steven to Raleigh. We had planned to go to a nightclub after dinner, but instead, we returned to my mobile home and listened to music until the sun came up Sunday morning.

"I never meant to have a one-night stand," I said.

Steven grinned. "This is not a one-night stand. I think this is the beginning of a beautiful relationship. I want to see you next weekend and the next and the next, but there is one thing I must tell you."

"What is that?"

"I'm married with two children"—he threw up a hand before I could say anything—"but I'm separated."

We continued to date, and the second week in December, Steven began to talk about Christmas. I told him I didn't do Christmas. I didn't tell him that I couldn't afford Christmas because I was saving $400 a month to buy a house one day.

Then, one Friday, when I came home from work, Steven's brown Mustang was in the driveway. I got Paris out of the backseat and headed to the front door. Steven opened the door, took Paris out of my arms, and kissed me.

"How do you like it?" he asked.

"I love it."

He blushed. "I know that," he said, "but I was talking about the Christmas tree." He carried Paris over to the giant, decorated fir.

I was speechless. Steven had placed a few gifts under the tree, which made me think of my childhood, when I'd gotten only fruit and two pieces of hard candy.

"Oh, Mama, it's so pretty," Sherondalyn said excitedly.

I didn't know if I should take it down or not. I had no presents to go under the tree and had not put up a tree in three years. Finally, I told Steven the tree was beautiful and thanked him for his thoughtfulness.

Sherondalyn went to Steven and hugged him. She then said to me, "Mama, I want Steven to be my daddy. Can we keep him? We can lock him in the closet, so he will never leave us. Lock him up!"

I explained that we could not keep anyone locked up and make the person unhappy. She looked downward, her eyes teared up, and her bottom lip drooped like a wet towel hanging over a railing. Then Sherondalyn said, "We didn't lock up Daddy, and he left us."

My heart broke again, knowing she felt abandoned by her father.

I looked over at Steven. His earlier happy countenance was now one of sadness, and I wondered if he was thinking of his own two children.

I sat down on the black armchair and pulled Sherondalyn closer while Paris climbed into my lap. Steven sat beside me with his arm across my shoulders.

I said, "Parents sometimes make mistakes. But when they realize it's a mistake, they try to correct it if they can. That is what happened with your father." Steven squeezed my hand, and I felt as though he approved of my explanation to her. I kissed her forehead. "Your father loves you and Paris very much."

Steven went out to his car and returned with a big armful of Christmas presents. He carefully placed them under the blinking tree and handed an unwrapped box of Christmas bulbs to me.

"Here," he said. "I thought you might like to help me finish decorating, starting our tradition."

CHAPTER 58

MEIMEI

After ten years of no contact, I received a letter from my former African boyfriend, Meimei. I held the unopened letter in my hands for several minutes, deciding whether or not I should read it and wondering how he'd found my address. A lot had happened in my life, and things had changed quite a bit since high school. Finally, I ripped the letter open, and I learned that he would be in Raleigh within a week. Meimei gave me a telephone number and asked that I call. I didn't make the call. Instead, I called Steven, told him about Meimei, and said Meimei wanted to visit while in town.

"Sure, he can visit you if you're not going to be alone with him," Steven said calmly.

"He will be at his hotel the whole time," I said.

Steven said, "You can't meet him at his hotel."

I found it interesting that Steven was bordering on being jealous. I said, "It's 1980, Steven. I have not seen this man in ten years. We will spend our time in the hotel's lobby and have dinner in the restaurant."

"No hotel, Marilyn. Period," Steven said firmly, and he told me to keep him posted.

That evening, after my conversation with Steven, I called Meimei and told him I would like to see him as well. So we set up a dinner date for the upcoming Friday.

I overcleaned the house, thinking Meimei might come over during the week, and I would prepare dinner for him. I stocked the refrigerator with beef, fish, and chicken, which I knew Meimei would eat. Being Muslim, he avoided pork.

The following Friday afternoon, soon after I got home from work, my doorbell rang.

"I had some unused vacation time and thought this was a good time to use it," Steven said in one breath as he stepped inside my mobile home.

He set his overnight bag in the hall closet and jimmied the metal door to get it to close. "I'm going to fix that door for you tomorrow," he said.

"This is not your week to come down," I said. "I'm supposed to have dinner with Meimei tonight. We talked about it. You said you were OK with it as long as it was not at his hotel."

"Oh, it's OK to have dinner with him." Steven grinned, took off his black-rimmed glasses, and briefly rubbed his eyes. "The kids should be included, and I would love to meet Mr. Africa myself." He picked up the telephone receiver. "Call and let him know that dinner will be here tonight. Not at a restaurant in his hotel."

As Steven suggested, I prepared a simple dinner: spaghetti with meatballs, a Caesar salad, garlic bread, and apple pie for dessert. Finally, I made a big pitcher of lemonade and set the table for six.

At exactly 6:00 p.m., I got into my car to pick up Meimei since he had no transportation. However, my car would not make a sound. It would not turn over. I began to panic and hurried inside, where Steven watched television with my nephew and Paris.

I asked to borrow Steven's car so I could pick up Meimei, because my car wouldn't start.

"Maybe fate is trying to tell you something," Steven said, laughing about my car not starting. Eventually, he checked under the hood for me. "I think you just need a battery. Don't worry about your car; I'll have you riding by Monday."

I said, "Riding by Monday? What about Meimei? He's waiting for me to pick him up." I threw up my hands in frustration. "Will you please go pick him up for me?"

Steven walked back into the house, poured himself a glass of lemonade, and took a sip. "Let me recap what you just asked me to do. First, I want to be clear on what you expect of me." He spoke deliberately slowly. "You want me to go pick up another man for you—to entertain." He took off his glasses, looked upward, and frowned. "What man in his right mind would do that?"

Once he said that to me, it did sound silly, but I didn't want to dishonor my word. So I poured another cup of sugar into the lemonade and said, "A man who is confident and knows his lady loves him would do it."

A Head of Cabbage

Steven chuckled. "I ain't going to pick up another man for my woman. Not in a million years."

"Steven, I don't love this man," I said, "but I want to honor my word that we will have dinner together. Please go pick him up for me." I hugged Steven's neck and began to kiss him teasingly.

"Marilyn, you can use my car," he said, relenting, "but you have to take Sherondalyn with you."

I picked up Meimei at his hotel near Crabtree Valley Mall. He lifted his head, and I lowered mine. He attempted to kiss me on my lips, but I turned my head, and the kiss landed on my cheek.

"You are as beautiful as ever with your Sophia Loren eyes," Meimei said with a lasting smile.

"Thank you. And you're more handsome than I remember," I said, but before we reached Buffaloe Road off Highway 1, about fifteen miles from the hotel, Meimei's smile was history.

"So," he said, "your boyfriend is having dinner with us at your place?"

Meimei shook his head and made unpleasant sounds with his tongue and teeth as I finished telling him how I expected the evening to go. I had heard him make the same awful sounds years ago when he was displeased about something.

As I neared my driveway, I saw my girlfriend Jannie's car in the driveway, which puzzled me a bit. My best friend, Jannie, and her boyfriend, Ray, were visiting. The four of us were supposed to go out together on Saturday night. I surmised they'd gotten the dates mixed up.

Steven was standing at the door with a glass of lemonade in his hand as we entered.

"I asked Ray and Jannie to come on over," he said, and he raised his glass of lemonade to Ray. "I think it's going to be an interesting evening."

Jannie stood at the kitchen table with her arms folded. She was quiet as she looked from Steven to me. Her eyes sparkled with anticipation of pending drama.

Jannie whispered, "Marilyn, they spiked your lemonade with vodka. You might want to be careful with the children."

I nodded and then introduced Meimei to everyone. "Meimei, these are my friends Steven, Ray, and Jannie. Everyone, this is Meimei," I said, and I turned to face the men.

Ray began to laugh so hard that no sound came from his mouth. He caught his breath after a gut-busting "Oh man, oh man." Then he shook Meimei's hand.

Ray said, "I ain't ever heard of a man giving his car to his woman so she could pick up her old boyfriend." He patted Steven on the shoulder. "Steven, you are more man than me."

Jannie looked over at Ray. Then, unable to mute her laughter, she doubled over, holding her sides, laughing at Ray's comments.

"Nice to meet all of you," Meimei said sarcastically.

"How about a nice cool drink?" Steven asked, and he poured Meimei a large glass of lemonade.

"That's fine if it's not alcoholic. I'm Muslim and do not drink," Meimei said, accepting the drink from Steven.

I started to tell Meimei that it contained alcohol, but I didn't want to be disloyal to Steven and said nothing.

Steven looked at Ray. "Oh, you don't drink alcohol? Then this drink is just what you need."

Ray lifted his drink and said, "It's just what a man needs."

Meimei took several swallows of the spiked lemonade and then complimented Steven on the taste. "The drink tastes fine."

Steven winked at Ray and said, "Let me refill it for you." Steven grabbed the vodka from the cabinet. Then, with his back turned to Meimei, Steven poured more vodka into Meimei's glass.

A few minutes later, Meimei passed out on the sofa.

Steven said, "Marilyn told me this joker can have up to four wives. Can you believe that?" He refilled his and Ray's glasses. "Look at him—he can have four wives but can't handle a little vodka."

Ray said, "He probably handles his four wives about as well as he handles this vodka." He pointed at Meimei slumped over on the sofa.

Meimei woke up about fifty minutes later and apologized for dozing. He appeared embarrassed and asked me to take him back to the hotel to get more sleep, saying he had jetlag.

"Marilyn, I think it's a good idea for you to take your guest back to his hotel, so he can get some rest," Steven said, and he began to help Meimei off the sofa.

Steven and I took Meimei back to the hotel. I went into the hotel's lobby with Meimei while Steven waited in the car.

Inside the hotel, Meimei took my hand and kissed it, and he seemed to be sober. He said, "Marilyn, this Steven guy is not the man for you. He will never marry you. Trust me—he will not."

I asked, "How do you know that?"

Meimei kissed my hand again and said, "If he wanted you to be his wife, he would have already married you."

Meimei called me the next day to say goodbye.

CHAPTER 59

WE ARE FAMILY

Ernest, my nephew, who had come to live with me in 1976 after his father murdered his mother, was now fifteen. He had lived with me for five years and had grown into a tall, lean, and handsome young man. I felt we had a bond and was glad my brothers had not opted to raise Ernest as their son.

On the weekends, Ernest always wanted to visit his sister Eve, who lived in Burlington, North Carolina. Often, I didn't want him to go. I was afraid he would get sidetracked and lose focus on what I deemed most important: his education. Of course, I had no proof that any of my fears would materialize. But I did know that his sister and her husband were both young, which concerned me. How could I interfere with his seeing his sister? That wouldn't have been right, and I didn't want any of my family to think I considered myself better than them because I had graduated from college.

Whenever we had family gatherings, I would encourage the younger children to finish high school and college. I believed we didn't have to remain in poverty, especially the younger ones, who had more opportunities than my parents and grandparents had had.

A niece or nephew often rebuffed me, and sometimes an adult would say there were a lot of educated fools around, or some adult male would encourage athletics instead of academics.

Once, I asked Ernest's younger brother, Anthony, who lived with his older sister Claudia, about school and if he had thought about going to college.

He looked up at me with an evil grimace. His brown eyes were wide and blinking fast. ."Aunt Marilyn," he said, "I hate to see you coming. That's all you talk about—education. Give me a break."

My feelings were hurt, and while I tried to calm my spirit, I thought of Daddy, who did not value education, and wondered if he had passed that belief down to the rest of the family. I didn't say anything else to Anthony. I began to feel sorry for my family because only a few seemed passionate about education. Nevertheless, I was determined to help Ernest graduate high school and college. I began to pay even more attention to his class assignments and started to talk even more about going to college.

But it was not to be. When Ernest returned from visiting his sister two months later, he seemed unusually quiet and appeared unhappy when I picked him up from the bus station. He changed the radio station and increased the volume several times on the drive home.

As soon as he walked into the mobile home, Ernest demanded his money. He went to the end of the bar and grabbed a handful of bills hanging in a mail bin. Then he threw all the correspondence onto the floor because he didn't see the Social Security check.

"I want my damn money, Aunt Marilyn," he repeated.

I had never seen him so angry. I had seen him upset when I insisted he wash the dishes, take out the garbage, clean his room, or study, but this was different. There appeared to be hate in his voice and eyes. I felt a tinge of fear.

"What money, Ernest?" I asked, taken aback by his behavior.

Ernest yelled, "That check from Social Security belongs to me!"

I said, "That Social Security check comes in my name for you. I am supposed to provide clothing, food, and shelter and take care of your educational and medical needs with it. I have done that and much more. That check from Social Security is not even enough to feed you."

I grew nervous as Ernest started opening and slamming cabinet drawers while cursing and looking for the check.

"What happened when you visited your sister this past weekend?" I asked.

"Don't you worry about that," he said. "You just give me my damn money."

I sighed. I made sure my nephew had lunch money every school day. He wore well-fitting clothes to school, and I'd purchased a bicycle, skateboard, jukebox, and basketball for him, trying to ease his loss of a parent. We no longer had to make a meal out of a quarter head of cabbage. Instead, we had two vegetables and a meat every night. Ernest ate like a hardworking man, piling his plate high with food and wrapping his arm

A Head of Cabbage

around the plate as though he were afraid someone would take something off. I had spent more money on him than on both Sherondalyn and Paris. Yet the Social Security check he demanded was only $147 per month.

I managed to speak calmly, but I was agitated. My thoughts moved too fast for me to say all I wanted to.

I said, "This is the thanks I get for taking care of you? Really?"

Ernest walked over to where I stood. Tiny beads of sweat had gathered around his flared nose and his temples. He got close to my face and tilted his head downward.

"I know y'all took our inheritance. Now I want my money, and I want to go live with my sister Eve."

I somehow had lost my nephew for sure. I thought he had gotten hold of a mind-altering drug. I shivered a bit at that thought and wondered what I could do if he attacked me.

"What have I not done for you? What has happened to you?" I asked, puzzled but still afraid.

"Y'all stole our inheritance—that's what happened." He began to pace up and down the living room floor. I felt unsafe near him and slowly moved to the other side of the bar.

"What inheritance? And who stole it?" I asked, becoming more enraged by his accusation.

"You're the main one," Ernest said. "You signed Mama's insurance papers."

I thought back to the day after Blanche had died. Knowing Blanche had to be buried, I'd signed her insurance papers to make them valid. I felt pity for Ernest because he was mad at us, his aunts and uncles, instead of his daddy, who had shot his defenseless mother in the head like a coward. I wanted to tell him that we owed Fulton Funeral Home $200 for his mother's funeral but decided against it. After all, he was only fifteen.

Blanche never had signed the document but had paid the monthly premiums. The funeral home director had said it was invalid without a signature. So I'd signed her name, not mine. The policy was only for $1,000, not enough to cover her funeral expenses.

My heart throbbed harder against my chest, and I thought I might have a stroke. The only thing I wanted to do at that point was slap Ernest into realizing that everything I had done had been to help him and the family. But instead of being grateful, my nephew thought of me as a thief. Disappointedly, I stared at him from a distance.

Finally, I said, "You are correct about one thing, Ernest: I did sign your mother's insurance policy so it would pay off to help us get her buried."

I told him that I was saving more than $400 a month to buy a real house one day and that I didn't need the Social Security check to live, but every little bit helped. Not receiving any positive reaction from Ernest, I told him I wanted his mother, my sister, to rest in peace, knowing her children were not scattered around in foster homes.

"I love you, Ernest, and have treated you like my son," I finally said.

"Well"—his lips trembled—"you make me study all the time. Plus, I know for sure y'all stole my inheritance. That must be why y'all are doing so good."

The angry look on his face made me suggest that he call the police if he thought I or anyone else had stolen anything from him or his siblings. He seemed to mull that over as he rolled his tongue against his jaw, pushing it out like a blowfish. I told him I wanted him to study a lot, get good grades, and go to college so he could make enough money to take care of his own family one day.

He was quiet for a few minutes, so I said, "The reason your aunts and uncles are doing pretty good financially is because all of us work every single day. A couple of your uncles are working two jobs."

Ernest snorted. "Well, you only want me here to get my money and babysit your children when you work late or go out on a date."

I could not convince him that I had his best interest in my heart, and then a thought came to me. Every teenager wanted a car, and he would be sixteen before the year was out.

"Ernest, if you stay with me and finish high school, I will buy you a car and pay for your college education. At least one of Blanche's children should go to college, if only to honor her name."

He didn't respond the way I had hoped, but his frightening demeanor eased a bit.

I said, "You're only fifteen and making a man's decision. I think you should stay home."

Ernest took several steps closer to me and bent down near my face. His nose was almost touching my forehead, and he said, "I want to get out of here right now. I can't stand living with you. All you talk about is studying and going to college. All I want is my damn money that I'm entitled to."

Sherondalyn and Paris walked into the room, and when they saw Ernest and heard him talking, they grabbed my skirt and cowered behind me in fear.

I said, "If you leave this home that I have provided for you, I will not allow you to come back, no matter what, and I mean it. I held on to Sherondalyn's and Paris's hands while taking several steps back.

"I want to get out of your sight, and I mean it," Ernest said mockingly.

His words cut me to the quick. I did not want to believe they were coming from my nephew. I said, "We are family. I think I can raise you to become whatever you want to become. There is nowhere on God's green earth where you can live as well as you are living here for one hundred forty-seven dollars, but so be it if you think so."

Ernest grunted loudly and continued to stare me down. Finally, his angry grunts propelled me to call his sister Eve, and she agreed that he could come to stay with her.

The drive to Burlington was short but long enough for me to feel a great sense of loss and failure for not raising my sister's child to at least finish high school. I looked over at Ernest and decided to reason with him once more.

"Ernest, we can turn this car around and go home. I want you to live with us. I know I don't have a man in the house to do manly things with you, but I promise to pay for your education and get you a car. I mean it, Ernest: if you move out, you cannot move back with me again. Please think about that."

When I pulled into Eve's icy driveway, Ernest turned to me and said, "I've got to get out of this car right now." Then he jumped out and slammed the door as soon as I stopped. I popped the trunk and followed him inside the cold two-story farmhouse.

Eve and her husband, June, sat shivering next to a wood-burning stove. I asked June if it was OK for Ernest to come live with them. He said yes and then looked over at his wife, who sat stoically watching television. I saw her glancing at me out of the corner of my eye.

"We'll be glad to keep Ernest here with us," she finally said.

I wanted to puke. I thought Ernest's sister and brother-in-law were much too young to raise a fifteen-year-old, but then again, maybe Ernest needed to be around a man.

We never said goodbye. Ernest took his belongings upstairs and stayed there until I left.

CHAPTER 60

EENY, MEENY, MINY, MOE

A few months after my harrowing work experience at the Raleigh office and after Ernest moved out, I requested to transfer to Southern Bell's office in Greensboro. I thought Greensboro was a more progressive city, and I would have a better working environment.

I moved in with Steven, who lived in Danville, Virginia, about forty-five miles north of Greensboro.

I worked at the Greensboro office for seven weeks before I fully understood the meaning of the old saying about jumping out of the frying pan into the fire.

"Eeny, meeny, miny, moe, catch a nigger by his toe. If he hollers, let him go."

I listened in horror to the derogatory rhyme recited by one of my new white coworkers. I glanced behind me and then to my left, trying to get a reading from the three black female sales representatives. They met my eyes but quickly lowered their faces in humiliation. I slid out of my blue swivel chair and went straight to the office of Minnie Sue Cannady, the assistant manager.

Minnie Sue, a slender, no-nonsense blonde woman, looked surprised when she saw me standing with a scowl on my face, leaning against her doorpost. She stopped reading a document, looked up at me, and said, "Good morning, Marilyn. Can I help you with something?"

"Did you hear Sally say the word *nigger*? Is that the way people in this office talk? It's 1980, for Christ's sake."

Minnie Sue appeared nervous but looked me in the eye and said, "Marilyn, I'm terribly sorry about Sally's choice of words. I apologize for her." Then, after an uncomfortable minute of silence, Minnie Sue said, "Well, Sally is just Sally."

I said, "Sally is just Sally? Is that supposed to mean that I didn't hear what I heard?" I rolled my eyes around her office deliberately, not looking at her for a moment. I remembered the difficulty I'd had in the Raleigh office. I didn't want Minnie Sue to start a fault-finding campaign with everything I did or said, but I had to address the insult. I kept my voice low and asked, "Is the word *nigger* standard usage in this office?"

"Of course not!" Minnie Sue said. "I never say that word, and I'm very sorry you heard it in this office. Again, I apologize."

I could tell she was sincere, and I had no qualm with her directly. "Minnie Sue," I said, "you don't have anything to apologize for. Instead, Sally should apologize to the office for using such an explosive, hateful, and disrespectful word. What point was she trying to make by saying that in front of the office?" I lowered my voice even more and got closer to Minnie Sue's face. "You don't have a clue how black people feel when someone uses that word, filled with hate. It's just a six-letter word, but what it represents when used by white people makes me want to lash out at whoever used it."

Minnie Sue sighed. "No, I don't have a clue. Marilyn, have a seat, please."

She left her office and returned a short while later with Sally. I sat down in front of Minnie Sue's desk with my head tilted slightly toward Sally, who sat down next to me. She crossed her legs and pulled down her expensive-looking beige-and-purple skirt while I did my best to contain my anger.

"Yes?" Sally said with a smile. Her brown eyes stared at Minnie Sue, questioning.

I watched Minnie Sue's eyebrows rise as frown lines etched across her forehead. Finally, she said, "Sally, you know we have to treat our customers and coworkers with respect, don't you?"

Sally's smile disappeared. "What are you talking about, Minnie Sue?" she asked, appearing to be oblivious to me and the scowl on my face.

"Well," Minnie Sue said, forcing herself to speak, "Sally, sometimes you use words that are inappropriate in the office."

"Like what words?" Sally asked, incredulous.

My whole body tensed up, as I knew shit was about to hit the fan. I tried to breathe more deeply and slowly.

Minnie Sue folded her hands on the desk. "Like the word *nig*—"

Minnie Sue appeared unable or unwilling to pronounce the complete word. She looked as if she were about to pass out.

She tried again. "Like the word *nig*—" But she failed. Then she said, "Well, the word you used in that rhyme just a few minutes ago, about catching a nig"—Minnie Sue looked over at me and swallowed—"by his toe."

My heart throbbed faster and faster. I made up my mind not to lose my temper or my job that day, whether Sally apologized or slung more insults.

Sally said flippantly, "That was my way of deciding which customer to call back first. Who would be upset over that harmless rhyme?"

I was so angry that my blood boiled, but for a fleeting moment, I regretted saying anything to Minnie Sue. Maybe I should have pretended I hadn't heard the word and ignored Sally, as the other black employees did.

My mind returned to Mr. Dillard, my former high school principal, who'd told us that it was our responsibility to show our countrymen the error of their ways. To remain silent was acceptance of disrespectful behavior by others. But on the other hand, I didn't want to start trouble for myself or anyone else in the office. I liked my job and tried to keep it, but my throat was beginning to swell.

Although I was terrified that a vengeful campaign would ensue to make my job harder or impossible, I said, "Sally, I thought you were a fine, educated lady. Now I see that you are just another hateful, mean-spirited white person. Maybe you are the nigger in that harmless rhyme."

"Gosh," Sally responded, "I didn't know I was hurting anyone's feelings. It's only a rhyme, and it doesn't really mean anything." Sally uncrossed her legs and looked directly at Minnie Sue with her mouth open. But the twist of her lips showed that she was being sarcastic.

Minnie Sue, who had folded her hands underneath her chin, was frowning and looked at me. I felt I needed to say something, but I felt inadequate in trying to explain my feelings again. But I tried.

"When I hear the word *nigger*, it makes me feel like I'm hated and will be mistreated and exploited. It's intimidating and provoking, because everyone is aware of how colored people have been mistreated for hundreds of years. And now it's like you're bragging about it. It's like you know you can mistreat us and dare us to complain."

I took in a deep breath. I discreetly held in my stomach with my right arm because it was hurting something awful, as it always did when I was nervous or upset. I didn't want Minnie Sue or Sally to see me twitching in mental and physical pain.

"I apologize. I didn't mean to hurt your feelings," Sally said. "I will never say that word again."

Minnie Sue said, "Then it's settled. Sally, I want you to apologize to the whole office. Please." Minnie Sue looked at me and rubbed her forehead.

"No, ma'am, it ain't settled yet," I said, and I remained seated as Sally stood. "Y'all need to know that colored people are not supposed to bow down to y'all and be a slave or a servant to you. We all are human, and there ain't but one race: the human race. I don't care what you've been taught or think. It's only one race, but we all have different features and colors due to natural selection and what part of the world our ancestors came from. People have adapted to their environment over many centuries, and that accounts for the few differences we have. So y'all need to stop thinking that colored people are less than you or deserve less than you."

I walked back to my desk. Sally followed but stopped in front of the office. She looked from one side of the room to the other.

"Everyone," she said, "I'm sorry about the 'catch a nigger by the toe' thing." Then she swished by my desk to her seat.

CHAPTER 61

BAD NEWS

I could tell something was not quite right weeks before Steven told me to come out of my fantasy. I put the girls to bed and kissed each of them good night. They lay next to each other in the small single bed, staring up at the ceiling, as the theme music for *Barney Miller* began to play.

Sherondalyn turned her head toward me and said, "I hate *Barney Miller*." I didn't ask her why, because I already knew. She had volunteered the reason a few nights earlier without any prompting.

"Mama, we have to go to bed every night right after *Barney Miller* goes off. It's only seven o'clock. It's like y'all don't want us around." Sherondalyn's brown eyes pleaded for an extension of their bedtime to eight o'clock.

"Maybe next year, we'll change your bedtime to eight o'clock," I said as I closed the bedroom door.

Steven was washing dishes when I walked into the kitchen. "Did you hear what I said earlier?" He stopped washing dishes, put the towel to dry dishes down on the counter, and turned to face me.

"I heard you, and I'm not trying to live a fantasy," I replied.

"Your kids are too noisy. I think they should go live with their father. Paris cries too much for a six-year-old, and she gets on my nerves. You really need to come out of your fantasy."

I didn't want to believe Steven meant what he'd said, and I wanted our relationship to continue. So finally, I asked him, "How can we make our relationship work?"

Steven said, "Understand that our relationship will only work if you let David keep your children. You can visit them on the weekends."

All I could think of was what Meimei had said just a few months earlier when he told me that Steven would never marry me. I was a fool in love. My mobile home in Raleigh had been sold, and I'd given away the furniture that the new owner didn't want. I had given Steven $2,500 to help pay for three acres of land where we were supposed to build our home. The pain of his words pierced my heart more than when I'd learned David was gay.

Somehow, I found the strength and good sense I needed and said, "I'm not giving away my children. My girls stay with me."

Steven raised his voice. "So what are you going to do?"

I was in a state of shock, and the room suddenly felt deathly cold as I said, "I will leave within a week."

I sat on his dark brown sofa until midnight, trying to figure out what had gone wrong in our relationship. The sex had always been often and satisfying. We didn't have money problems. I couldn't think of anything that should have destroyed our love. Yet something had. Then it dawned on me to recap what he had said earlier in the evening: he did not want to be responsible for some other man's children. At that moment of clarity, I began to cry. There I was again, without a home for my children and me.

The next day, I pretended to go to work as usual but took the day off and found a two-bedroom apartment closer to where I worked in Greensboro. I signed a six-month lease and purchased new furniture delivered the same day. I moved in that afternoon. The apartment was decorated beautifully, but beauty couldn't camouflage my misery.

I stopped cooking and cleaning the apartment. Instead, Sherondalyn took on the mama role for her younger sister, giving baths and preparing soup and sandwiches for their dinner.

The children mainly ate chicken noodle soup and sandwiches every day. I was neglectful, except for their schoolwork. I helped them with homework, gave them additional math problems to solve, and had them read to me for an hour. Then I would go to bed around seven thirty every night.

I was depressed but functional. I got up every morning, sent the girls to school, and went to work. I hated the weekends. Seeing happy people or couples made me sadder and lonelier.

Three weeks after moving out of Steven's house, I called him. He was breathing hard when he answered the phone, as though he had been doing manual labor.

"Hello," he said dryly.

"Steven," I said, "I wanted to give you my new phone number in case I get some mail at your house." He said OK and nothing more. After several uncomfortable seconds of silence, I swallowed the little pride I had left and said, "And to let you know that I'm pregnant."

"Well, well, well," he said, "so you're really calling to give me bad news. I never thought you would try to trap a man. I guess you want child support like my ex-wife."

His words repulsed me. "I'm not trying to trap you," I said. "I thought you should know. Remember how you thought it was funny when your condom burst last month? Now you're accusing me of trying to trap you. You are a small replica of a man and a pathetic soul." I hung up the phone.

I didn't know what to do. I already had two children and was afraid that having another child would lessen their chance of having a promising future, and I was embarrassed that I found myself pregnant and single at thirty-two. I asked myself if God would punish me if I had an abortion. Worse, would my daughters suffer if I didn't?

I had the abortion three weeks later, but I wanted to undo it and cried every day for about two weeks. Finally, I couldn't stand living in the apartment any longer and started to look for a house to buy. I had a little more than $8,000 in the bank, but I had a low credit score. It took my real estate agent two months to find a house where I assumed the loan. It was a cute brick-front bungalow on Bittersweet Court in a modest-income part of town.

Within days of moving into my new home, I asked Steven if I had any mail at his house and gave him my new address. I really wanted to hear his voice and let him know where I was living should he wish to resume our relationship.

He spoke softly, telling me that I did have mail and that he would bring it to me when he found some time. His words were hard to accept. I had to remind myself that I was no longer his sweetheart and had to wait for him to find time for me.

I fell down onto the bed and cried for what seemed like hours. Steven was like a drug, and shamefully, I was addicted.

About three weeks later, I came home from work and found Steven's brown Mustang parked in my driveway. I walked up to his car, tapped on the window, and waved him inside. I had no expectations and tried hard to remain calm. After all, my sister Terri had recently told me she'd seen Steven at Carolina Circle Mall with his new and pregnant girlfriend.

He sat down on my new sofa. I sat at the opposite end. He slid down closer to me and took my hand. "Marilyn, I made a terrible mistake," he said. "You're the one I love."

My heart fluttered, and my mind spun into a dizzy fog. I sat silently, staring at the floor, not trusting what I had just heard. I held my feelings at bay and asked him if his new girlfriend was pregnant. I squeezed the arm of the sofa to prevent myself from screaming and cussing. I wanted to hit and do bodily harm to Steven. I'd had an abortion a few months earlier that I hadn't wanted to have. It took a gargantuan amount of effort to keep myself from unraveling. Finally, he let go of my hand and hung his head.

"Yeah, she's pregnant."

I walked into the kitchen and made a pitcher of Lipton tea. I knew the answer to my next question might kill me. I gave him a glass of tea and remained standing. "Steven, are you going to marry your pregnant girlfriend?" I asked, closing my eyes and turning my head away to wait for his answer.

Steven gulped the tea down and set the glass on the small, glossy coffee table in front of him. He stood up, placed a hand on the left side of my face, and looked into my eyes.

"Marilyn, she is pregnant. I can't ask her to move out." He inhaled deeply and sighed. "But I'm not going to marry her."

He pulled me close to him. I could not resist. I welcomed his firm embrace and his controlled, electrifying kiss. I savored the moment and his touch, thinking it would be our last.

"What I want to know is this." He paused and took his glasses off. "When can I start to see you again?"

"You can't," I blurted out angrily. "Not if you have a live-in girlfriend."

"I'm not going to marry her." He looked down and then up again and said, "Actually, you can help me get her out of my house."

"You brought her in," I said. "You get her out if you don't want her there."

Steven left a short while later. I stood at the door, watching his car disappear down the street. But in my head, I was saying, *You can come to see me anytime you want to. I still love you and want you in my life.*

On August 8, 1983, Steven called late in the evening to tell me that his girlfriend was at the hospital in labor and that he needed to talk with me.

We talked for a few minutes before my stomach began to ache, probably because I was jealous that his girlfriend was having his child and because I realized he had cheated on me before I moved out of his house. I recalled myself in childbirth without David there. My sense of womanhood made me say what I didn't want to say.

"You should go to the hospital, Steven," I said, carefully censoring my words. "Every woman needs her man with her during childbirth."

"OK," he said, but neither one of us hung up the phone.

I heard him breathing hard and felt that he must have been afraid. "Steven, everything will be OK. You can call me later if you like, but you have to go now."

"I know, Marilyn, but I wish …" His voice trailed off, and then he said, "I'll call you soon."

Several weeks passed before I heard from Steven again. He asked if he could stop by for a few minutes that afternoon when he called.

I arranged to work a half day. Steven arrived around three o'clock. I watched from my living room window as he went around to the passenger side of his car and unfastened a baby car seat. I was careful not to pick up the baby. Steven had no idea of my pain at seeing his handsome, healthy little son, whom I wished I had birthed.

"He's a good boy," Steven said proudly, "and he smiles a lot."

"I'm sure he is," I said dryly, wishing I were the baby's mother.

"Well, when are you going to let me start seeing you again?" he asked nervously.

I couldn't answer right then, because a part of me hated Steven, and another part of me still loved him. I yearned for the strong embrace that had once made me feel loved and secure. I wanted that feeling again, but I thought of Mama and remembered her telling me not to become a stray, because some men were like dogs. If a man had a wife, then the other women he saw were strays. I didn't want to be a stray.

CHAPTER 62

CONFEDERATE FLAG

The following Monday, while I was getting ready for work, the phone rang. I hoped it was Steven, but it wasn't.

It was the real estate agent who had sold me my house. He invited me to his annual cookout. I thanked him for the invitation and told him I would like to attend. Then I glanced at the small wall clock and rushed out the door. I didn't want to be late for work.

I headed north on Greenbrier Road, turned right onto Church Street, and increased my speed just as it started to rain. I needed to make up some travel time. Unfortunately, the light at Church Street and Wendover Avenue was long, and it turned red as I approached it. I didn't know why, but I stopped, shifted gears, and took off again, rear-ending a white pickup truck. I was dizzy for a second, and when my head cleared, I noticed the light was still red. I blinked several times to ensure I saw what I thought I saw.

There was a big Confederate flag plastered across the rear window of the truck. Within seconds, a big-bellied man with a load of curly red hair stepped out of his vehicle. I knew I was about to have a bad day, so I started searching for something in my car that I could use to defend myself. I had nothing—no mace, no pencil, and not even a fingernail file. I pulled my insurance card out, thinking the man would not attack me if he knew I could pay to have his truck repaired.

I was scared shitless as I watched the beefy man assess the damage to his truck. He looked at the rear of his vehicle and at the front of my car. Finally, he gestured for me to roll down my window. I cracked the window about two inches. He gave a slight frown and motioned for me to move the window down some more. I did, about four to five inches.

"Little lady," he asked politely, "what happened?"

I was startled by his pleasantness and nonthreatening demeanor, but I was still afraid of him. I had always been told to stay away from white men, especially those with Confederate flags, because they were racist, waiting and looking for a reason to do physical harm to anyone who didn't look or think like them.

Sweat began to drip from my face, and I almost lost my voice, but I said softly, "My foot slipped off the brake pedal."

I lied, thinking that would save me from an attack. I had the insurance card in my hand but forgot to show it.

"Well, it looks like you got a pretty nasty dent on your front end," he said. "My truck got just a scratch, but don't worry about that."

He paused for a moment or two and looked away briefly and then back at me. I knew he saw the fear on my face, but I couldn't hide it.

He said, "I'll tell you what," and then he reached into his back pocket.

I thought I was going to pee all over myself. My first thoughts were of my two girls. Who would love and raise them if this man shot me? I couldn't even speak, but I began to wave the insurance card.

The man said, "Here—take my business card, and have your husband give me a call if he gives you a hard time about that little dent. I'll set him straight for you, so don't worry."

I took his business card through the cracked window and said thank you.

"Now, you drive safe, and remember that the roads are usually slicker when it first begins to rain, so slow it down a bit."

That man gave me a little hope that the world was not all evil.

Paris was eight years old now and doing great in school. Sherondalyn was eleven and blossoming into a well-behaved preteen. I was lucky in that regard. Neither of my girls ever caused trouble at school. They both mainly were straight-A students. I was proud that they were better students than I had been at their age.

I was shocked one evening in September 1983 when I got a call from Mrs. Little, Paris's teacher at Jesse Wharton Elementary School. She put me at ease by telling me there was no problem with Paris, but she needed me to address a problem with the school's administration.

Mrs. Little proceeded to tell me that she had recommended Paris for academic gifted classes because her California Achievement Test results indicated she was a perfect candidate. Still, the classes were limited, and

Paris had not been selected. She suggested I come to the school to talk with the program's coordinator and the principal.

Fear gripped my gut. I didn't want any more confrontations with white people. I felt inadequate when talking with school officials, but I knew I had to go if it was in Paris's best interest. I called my new male friend Mr. Simpson, whom my real estate agent had introduced me to at his annual picnic. Mr. Simpson appeared to be quite intelligent and had an important job at the Greensboro Fire Department. I told him about Mrs. Little and our conversation about Paris. He insisted I call for an appointment with the program's coordinator.

"Just meet with the coordinator, and voice your desire to have your child in the gifted class because you feel she is a great candidate. Don't go over there fussing and cussing and making accusations," he said. "Show them the intelligent, concerned parent you are."

On the day of the meeting, I found myself overwhelmed with fear. *What should I say? Will the meeting cause Paris problems? Am I doing the right thing for my child? Will I be considered a troublemaker at her school? Will she be singled out and treated unfairly?* I couldn't answer my own questions, but I decided to go. I thought about my baby brother, William Winston, and my own parents' unwillingness to meet with school officials on his behalf before he dropped out of school at age fourteen.

I put on my most expensive dress and shoes and applied heavy makeup to boost my confidence.

When the school's secretary showed me where the conference room was, perspiration ran down my back and underarms. I opened the door and saw Mrs. Little, a plump middle-aged black woman, sitting at the table. I began to feel more at ease after she bowed her head and flashed a smile. I did the same and sat opposite her.

Mr. Cross, the program coordinator, said good morning and immediately explained why Paris could not participate in the gifted program: the class was already at capacity.

Mrs. Little spoke up and said that she had taught all the selected students, and they were bright. "But the little Jamison girl is the most brilliant of them all and should be in the program."

Mr. Stubbman, the school's principal, entered the room. He looked around the table at Mrs. Little and me and then sat down near Mr. Cross.

He ran his fingers through his thinning white hair and adjusted his tie. Then he said somewhat harshly, "Mrs. Jamison, we all know your daughter is bright, and she will be considered for gifted classes next year."

"Mr. Stubbman, Paris needs to be in the gifted class at the onset of its inception," Mrs. Little said.

I looked from Mr. Stubbman to Mrs. Little. I said nothing. I thought of Daddy and now understood what he'd meant when he said that white men were determined not to let black people have good lives and would throw up roadblocks every chance they got. I also remembered telling Daddy that I was not afraid of white people. I placed both arms on the table, laced my fingers together, and stared at Mr. Stubbman.

Then Mr. Stubbman said, "Mrs. Little, you are now excused to attend to your class. I believe your students are waiting for you."

Mrs. Little looked at me with disappointed eyes. I believed she thought I would crumble, but she slowly lifted herself from the chair, gathered her folder and purse, and walked out the door.

I was scared stiff and not sure what questions to ask. My palms were sweating, and I began to itch under my arms. I didn't want to scratch, so I squirmed in my seat, which made me appear to have some type of tic.

Finally, I asked, "What type of criteria were used for the selection of students?" I was embarrassed by my speech and wanted to leave because I was stuttering for the first time in my life. But again, I thought of my baby brother, William Winston. When he'd gotten expelled from school, no one had spoken up for him.

"We used the California Achievement Test, the student grades, and the teacher's recommendation," Mr. Cross said, and then he looked toward Mr. Stubbman.

"How did Paris rank on the CAT?" I asked, although I had a copy of her records in my folder.

He looked at a folder of papers in front of him and raised an eyebrow. "I believe she ranked in the ninety-sixth percentile, and she made all As, with one B in conduct. Although she has the highest CAT score, she was the only student with a B—for misconduct." He looked up at me. "That was the determining factor."

I mustered up enough courage to lose my stutter. My fear was replaced with anger. I knew Paris should have been placed in the gifted classes. I didn't know if they were discriminating against her or not, but I thought they were. I remembered my new male friend Mr. Simpson's words just a few nights ago: "Just let them know you are truly concerned about your child, stay calm, and act intelligently."

I got up to leave, feeling that it was useless to persuade them to accept Paris into the gifted program. Just before I walked out, I said, "I'm going to take a day off from work and drive to Raleigh to see what Governor Jim Hunt can do, after I call the superintendent of public schools and the school board."

"Ah, well now, Mrs. Jamison, it's highly unusual, but we will consider exceeding the threshold for the class by one and will let you know our decision by Monday," Mr. Stubbman said, and they walked out of the room behind me.

Later that evening, I called Mrs. Little and told her what had happened.

"Well," she said, "you did great, Mrs. Jamison." Then she giggled before saying, "I know I'll be transferred to another school before this year is out. That B I gave Paris for misconduct should not have been the determining factor."

Within a week, both Paris and Sherondalyn had been selected to be in the gifted program.

CHAPTER 63

GRATITUDE

Sherondalyn was sixteen now and a junior at Northeast High School. I gave her my aging white Mercury Lynx to drive to Eastern Guilford High School, where she took college preparatory classes. She was also responsible for Paris's transportation to and from Northeast Middle School.

One day they were not home when I returned from work. I called Paris's school and was told that she had left with her sister around four o'clock. I drove the usual route but was unable to locate them. I was sick with worry, when they walked into the house around seven o'clock.

"Mama, how am I going to get to my school every day?" Sherondalyn asked, exasperated. She said that a red light had appeared on the dashboard, and after about thirty minutes of driving, the car had begun to make a rattling sound and started emitting bursts of black smoke before it had slowed to a complete stop. They'd started walking, when a nice white man had picked them up and brought them home.

I was about to lose my mind as unkind childhood memories popped into my head. I must have frowned or grimaced, because Paris saw my uneasiness and stepped closer to me.

"Mama, the man didn't molest us or offer us drugs, so you can calm down," she said in one quick breath. I nodded as some of my angst diminished. I was glad she remembered our many conversations about drugs, child molestation, and sex.

After dinner, I called my brother Levi, an auto mechanic, and asked him to get the car into my driveway and repair it as soon as possible. I didn't want my neighbors complaining about an undrivable vehicle parked in the neighborhood, and Sherondalyn needed it for school.

Levi looked the car over a few days later and said, "Repair it? The motor is shot, and it's going to cost at least six hundred dollars to fix it." He gave me the impression that it was not worth repairing. Finally, now I understood why Daddy was drunk on most days. It was hard just to live, and alcohol must have given him a false sense of well-being.

Two months went by, and Levi had not fixed the car. He said he was up to his neck with work, committed to repairing other people's cars. I drove Sherondalyn to school and dropped her off way too early, and she caught a ride home in the afternoon with different classmates. Paris caught the bus, which she hated.

Late one evening, my old boyfriend Steven called and asked me to wish him good luck at a bowling tournament. When he asked how I was doing, I blurted out that Sherondalyn's car was broken down, I couldn't afford to pay the Bob Dunn Ford dealership to repair it, and my brother Levi had put me on the back burner.

"Where is the car now?" he asked.

I told him it was in my driveway.

"Put the keys under the back floor mat, and leave the car unlocked. I'll send a tow truck tomorrow, and I'll fix it for you."

When I got home from work the next day, the car was gone. I called Steven to discuss the cost. He refused payment. An unfamiliar emotion for Steven stirred in my heart that I had not felt before.

Two weeks later, Steven called to say the car was repaired. After dropping Paris off at a classmate's home for a sleepover, Sherondalyn and I headed to Danville, Virginia. Forty-five minutes later, we arrived at Steven's new ranch-style house with my emotions spilling over. I was excited and jealous, but mostly, I was fearful of Steven's live-in girlfriend. His beautiful brick home and yard were stunning, sitting on three acres of land that I once had thought I would be sharing with him.

As soon as we pulled into the crescent-shaped driveway, I saw Sherondalyn's sparkling-clean white Mercury Lynx parked next to Steven's prized brown 1965 Mustang. Steven was outside with an armload of firewood. He dropped the wood when he saw me, walked over, and gave me a long hug. I felt his heart thumping through his heavy wool jacket. I thought mine would explode.

We entered his home through the basement, where I noticed a large black cast-iron wood-burning stove. I looked at the layout around the room and the carpet, couch, chairs, and curtains. Unfortunately, everything was in a dull shade of brown.

A Head of Cabbage

I lowered my voice and said to Sherondalyn, "Oh well. I would have decorated more tastefully." Sherondalyn giggled.

Malcolm, his three-year-old son, sat in a brown rocking chair like a little man with his legs crossed. He was well-mannered and quiet. Looking up at me, he said, "Hello there," with a smile bright enough to melt the snowcaps off Mount Saint Helens.

Sherondalyn started talking to him about his toys and books. I didn't see Benjamin, the six-month-old baby.

Steven took my hand and said, "Come on upstairs, and let me show you the rest of the house." He was noticeably proud of his home and family, and to my chagrin, he looked happy.

As soon as we entered his bedroom, I tensed up at the sound of a slamming car door. His live-in girlfriend had come home. I heard her walking up the basement steps and thought she might see us in the bedroom and become unhinged. Instead, she went into the kitchen, stomping her feet and slamming cabinet doors.

Steven adjusted his glasses and sighed. He glanced toward the door, listening to the unpleasant sounds. Then he said, "Wait right here." He hurried to the kitchen while I waited in the bedroom. Soon everything was quiet.

The tour resumed as if we were the only two people in the house, but I watched and listened for sounds that might put Sherondalyn or me in danger. Steven noticed my uneasiness.

"Don't be concerned about her," he said. "Everything is under control."

"Are you sure?" I asked.

Confidently, he said, "I'm quite sure."

When we entered the kitchen, his live-in girlfriend was standing by the sink, looking like a sister of activist Angela Davis. She looked mean and angry, with an enormous, wild Afro. She was unlike how I had imagined.

Steven said, "Marilyn, this is Cindy. Cindy, this is Marilyn."

She looked down at her baby sleeping in his bassinet stroller and then slowly looked me up and down, and I did the same. Finally, she said, "Hey."

"How are you?" I said.

She was not a beauty queen, but she must have been doing something right. She had the man I loved. I looked toward Steven, imagining him in bed with her. My heart palpitated so hard I thought I might faint. It was too much for me to bear, lest I become unhinged. As I started to leave, my knees began to wobble. Steven grabbed my arm, and Cindy gasped, grunted, and said something indecipherable.

Sherondalyn and I got home around eleven o'clock, and although Sherondalyn was happy to have her car repaired, she was full of angst.

"Mama," she said, "I wish I had the money to pay Steven for fixing my car. It must have cost a lot because you look so unhappy."

I was glad she thought my unhappiness was about money.

Sherondalyn pulled her long, thick, puffy hair back with a rubber band and said, "All I need to get by at school is a dollar and thirty-five cents a day. One dollar for gas and a bag of potato chips for lunch, but you need to give Paris enough money for a full hot lunch."

I looked at Sherondalyn in amazement. My bright, beautiful, and caring child was worried about her sister and me, when she should have been dating and enjoying being a teenager.

I finally told her that Steven had fixed her car because he was kind and hadn't charged me.

Sherondalyn's face lit up. "Mama, you need to thank Steven."

I went to hug her, but the telephone rang. It was Steven.

"How did the car drive?" he asked.

"The car drove like it was brand new," I said, "and thank you again for being so kind and generous to us." Now I could name the unfamiliar emotion I had felt earlier: gratitude.

Steven said, "You're welcome, and if you have any more trouble with the car, just call me."

CHAPTER 64

MAKE THE CALL

Things were going well for the children and me, at least I thought so until I got to work one Friday in early spring 1989.

"Marilyn, don't try to avoid me," the harsh female voice said. "I have a question for you."

Before she uttered the second word, I knew it was too late for me to escape. I smelled Chanel No. 5, Peggy's signature perfume. I always tried to avoid her. I peeked over the gray plexiglass workstation that separated my desk from three other coworkers' desks. Peggy, an intimidating, impeccably dressed, proud woman, was sitting in my coworker's seat.

I didn't like Peggy much. She could get anybody's goat before saying good morning. I had noticed that the sales managers in the office didn't want her on their teams. So expecting a negative comment about a customer from Peggy, I asked, "Is there a problem?"

She stood up. "What universities are Sherondalyn and Paris being prepared for?"

If Peggy's pug nose could have been raised any higher, it would have touched the nine-foot ceiling. I didn't answer her right away, because I didn't think it was her concern. But she lit into me again.

"Don't look surprised," she said. "I don't have children, but if I did, they would be in Greensboro Day School. I've seen your children's names in the papers. They're smart, so do your part. We've got too many black children failing in school and in life because their parents are lackadaisical."

I was caught off guard but wanted Peggy to know that my children were planning to further their educations. "I'm not sure which college they will attend," I said.

Peggy stood up. "Marilyn, you've got to do more than provide a roof and food. You need to make sure they get prepared for college. Private school does a better job than public school, and the teachers can't do it all."

I felt anxious and sighed. "I'm enrolling them in Greensboro Day School next year."

Peggy looked down and shook her head. A little giggle escaped her lips. "Marilyn, you have to apply. Your children must be accepted into private school." She dragged out the word *accepted*. "You don't just enroll them."

Peggy whisked off, holding her head high with an air of superiority. Sharon, my pod buddy, was standing nearby, watching and waiting for her seat. Noticing my countenance, Sharon asked me what Peggy had said to make me so upset.

Private schools had never crossed my mind, and I became upset because I never had considered it an option. I had not heard of Greensboro Day School until now. But after talking with Peggy, I knew I had to act on Peggy's suggestion.

Strangely, over the weekend, I saw an advertisement in the *Greensboro Daily News* that Greensboro Day School was requesting applicants for the upcoming school year.

When I got to work on Monday, I called Greensboro Day School and asked for two applications. Unfortunately, I was told they did not have any more openings for the upcoming year.

Later in the day, I asked Sharon, my white friend, to call for two applications during our second break. Three minutes later, Sharon came to me and said, "Marilyn, the applications are in the mail, and you have an appointment with the admissions director Thursday morning at eleven." Sharon started to walk away but then stopped and gave me a quizzical look. "Marilyn, you're not afraid to talk to people. Why did you ask me to make that call for you?"

I looked up at Sharon's six-foot frame. "I called earlier and was told that they were no longer accepting applications for the upcoming school year."

Sharon pulled back her long blonde hair, bent down closer to me, and whispered, "You've got to be kidding."

"No, I'm not kidding. That's the way it is for some of us." I pushed the up arrow for the elevator and said, "I called earlier, and they told me they were not accepting applications. You called and not only got applications mailed but got a freaking appointment to meet with the admissions director."

A Head of Cabbage

"There must be some misunderstanding," Sharon said as we stepped inside the elevator.

I said, "Maybe because they thought you were white—and you are—they felt warm and fuzzy about the possibility of getting a white applicant. On the other hand, they knew I was black by the sound of my voice and didn't have warm and fuzzy feelings about getting a black applicant. The truth is in the pudding."

Sharon looked embarrassed, and her face turned deep pink. "Marilyn, I don't understand how that kind of thing still happens. That is just stupid. A child is a child. Lord knows I wish my children were as smart as your girls. For crying out loud, this is the eighties."

Sharon pulled me into a corner when we reached the fourth floor and apologized. "Marilyn, I'm sorry some white people are still racists."

I told Sharon, "Racism has existed for centuries and is still around because it is intergenerational, just like wealth and poverty. Whatever our grandparents and parents pass down to us becomes a part of us."

Sharon grabbed my arm just before I sat down and asked, "Do you want me to go to the interview and pretend to be you?"

That Thursday, I arrived at Greensboro Day School with two folders containing all Paris's records from first to eighth grade—and an awful stomachache. Each folder had copies of two teacher recommendations; a copy of Paris's scores on the SAT, which she had taken while in the seventh grade; her community and academic activities; and newspaper clippings of her participation in Greensboro Children's Theatre.

I stood outside the admission director's office door, afraid of how I would be received. I looked at my Timex watch and didn't want to be late. Finally, at precisely 11:00, I gently knocked. The door opened, and an average-height and medium-build man stood there with a silly grin on his face. His brown hair was neatly trimmed, complementing his brown suit and tie. He looked around as though he were looking for someone else.

He sighed with a hint of irritation. "Yes?"

He did not ask me in. I sensed this would not be a good day. I cleared my throat.

"Good morning. I'm Marilyn Jamison. I have an appointment to meet with you today regarding my daughter's application for admission."

He continued to stand in the doorway as if temporarily traumatized by seeing me.

"Oh," he said, "Mrs. Jamison, there must be some mistake. We don't accept children with learning disabilities."

I had felt I might not be received well, but I hadn't expected to be insulted. I took a deep breath and slowly exhaled. I wanted to get this over with before I lost my voice. I handed the admission director the golden folder with Paris's accomplishments while trying to remain composed. I managed to say, "My child does not have a learning disability. She is quite bright, as a matter of fact. She scored in the ninety-sixth percentile on the last CAT."

He began to flip through her folder and then motioned for me to follow him into his office. I sat down across from him on the edge of a stiff burgundy leather chair. By then, my palms were wet, and my stomach was stinging. I waited.

After reviewing the contents in the folder, the admissions director said, "It appears your daughter has done quite well in public school, but independent schools are much more challenging. We have different standards to gauge a student's level of academic performance."

I looked him in the eye and nodded as he talked. I thought of Daddy and remembered that he once had told me that white men were a curse to the world, doing all they could to prevent others from accomplishing anything of worth, so they would seem brighter.

He leaned back in his seat and said, "Our tests are much more rigorous than the CAT, and before I can submit her name to the selection committee, she must take our independent school test."

My throat began to swell, and even though I feared the outcome, I managed to ask, "When can you schedule her test?"

CHAPTER 65

BLACK PEOPLE NEED A PSYCHIATRIST

I'd had a stressful day at work, resolving irate customers' complaints, meeting an aggressive daily sales quota, and having to defend my daughter's intellect with the director of admissions at Greensboro Day School. I had planned to eat dinner and go straight to bed. But Paris met me at the door, crying.

Before I had a chance to tell her that she had been scheduled to take an independent school test on Monday, Paris asked, "How come black people don't like me?"

I was surprised by her question, but I knew I had to give a reasonable answer. I took my shoes off, and we joined Sherondalyn at the kitchen table. She too looked at me, waiting for a reasonable explanation to Paris's question.

"You mean white people, don't you?" I asked.

"No. I really mean black people," Paris said, "and you won't believe what happened in class today."

I sighed. "Tell me what happened."

"The teacher asked a question. I raised my hand, but I gave the wrong answer. Then the black students in the classroom stood up and clapped. They were happy that I got it wrong." Paris wiped her nose, sniffled for several seconds, and then said, "Later, during the boys' basketball practice, we had cheerleading practice, and one of the black boys on the team pointed at me and said there was only one spook on the cheerleading team."

My heart was breaking to see Paris so distraught. I was angry at first, but then I began to pity the young boys and the thousands of other black people who had no pride or respect for people who looked like them.

Part of it, I knew, was because of their own low self-esteem. I placed my arm around my sobbing daughter's shoulders and said, "Sometimes people, especially children, don't know how to behave properly. I think the psychological damage of slavery is still being manifested by a lot of people in society today. We have to give them time to grow into better people."

"Mama, slavery was abolished a long time ago," Paris said, interrupting me and drying her eyes with the back of her hand. "We can't blame slavery every time a person says or does something mean and stupid." Sherondalyn nodded in agreement.

I said, "The psychological damage of slavery has been passed down through the generations by great-grandparents and parents, aunts and uncles—everybody, really. Paris, I imagine those young boys called you a spook because they are not accustomed to seeing black cheerleaders, or they felt there should have been more than one. In either case, I'm going to your school to speak with their coach about it."

Paris jumped up from the table. "Oh no! Mama, please don't go to my school to complain to the coach or my teacher. If you do, those boys will only bully me."

I said, "Those boys should not be using such mean and derogatory language toward you, so I am going to your school, and I am going to talk with the coach and your teacher."

Sherondalyn placed both elbows on the table, cupped her face in her hands, and said, "Mama, Paris is right. The boys will bully her even more. But what I want to know is this: Are the people at *Ebony* magazine suffering from the psychological damage from slavery?" She grabbed a copy off the coffee table and flipped through a few pages, pointing to every model. "Look at this one—or all of them. It's the same. They only use light-skinned models, as if they don't think dark-skinned girls are pretty enough."

I hung my head down for a moment, trying to think of a reasonable explanation. "They just want to sell magazines. It's a business," I said, knowing that my answer was inadequate.

Sherondalyn sighed. "You may think the magazine owners suffer from psychological damage from slavery, but I think you should cancel the subscription."

I said, "It's subtle. If you don't recognize something, you can't acknowledge it, and if you don't acknowledge it, you can't change it. That is why every descendant of slaves, every black person in America, needs a psychiatrist—to help us stop hurting and hating."

Sherondalyn inched her chair closer to me and repeated my words in disbelief. "Mama, do you really believe every black person in America needs a psychiatrist?"

"Yes, I do believe that."

"Wow!" Sherondalyn rolled her eyes and said, "Paris, we need a psychiatrist!" Her sarcasm made Paris smile.

After a few seconds of silence, Sherondalyn said, "The Europeans are the ones responsible for slavery in America. Do they need a psychiatrist?"

"Yep, they do, but for different reasons," I said, and I watched both girls dart their eyes from each other and back to me.

"What reasons, Mama?" both girls asked.

I said, "The white people responsible for slavery are long dead, but they left ugly and evil roots. The abuser needs help just like the abused. Many social and economic evils today sprouted from America's harsh and ugly beginnings. Many European Americans don't admit that wrongs were done to black and Indian people, nor are they able to recognize the wrongs that are still being done to us as I speak."

"Mama," Sherondalyn asked, "how can a psychiatrist help?"

Paris almost jumped into Sherondalyn's lap, waiting for my response.

I said, "I think psychiatrists can help people see reality. Help them recognize errors of their forefathers, the flaws in their beliefs, and the evilness in their greed and fear, so they don't repeat them. But if they can't see or acknowledge the wrongs of the founders of this country and continue to believe that black people are lesser beings, then instead of becoming more human and just, they will continue to justify their mistreatment of us because of a few different physical attributes. Not Christian at all."

Sherondalyn smirked and then asked, "Mama, what are white people fearful of?"

I thought of my many debates in college. Then I said, "They are afraid of social change, erosion of their political power, and sharing of wealth. Blacks and whites marrying each other is their greatest fear. I think they fear realizing that all men are really created equal. They want to believe that they are on a higher intellectual level because of their skin color. This has been taught to them and to us. This is 1989, and many white people still think we are intellectually inferior, never mind the centuries when it was illegal for black people to read or write."

I wanted to tell them that the admission director at Greensboro Day School had thought Paris had a learning disability before even meeting or testing her. But I didn't want to add more stress on Paris, so I said, "America has a lot of ugly roots."

Sherondalyn said, "There is nothing in the history books about ugly roots and black people needing psychiatrists." While Sherondalyn talked, Paris rushed from the table to get a dictionary.

I said, "What I'm trying to say is that most folks don't even understand why the word *race* is just a concept or why humans are divided into groups. There would be no racists if the concept were to become obsolete."

Sherondalyn smirked. "Mama, we study American history. I have never heard of an ugly root before. You're making stuff up."

Paris came back to the table with a copy of *Webster's* dictionary and said, "It's not in the dictionary."

I thought of Daddy's words to me: "Everything ain't in them shit-ass books, gal." I leaned closer to Paris and said, "Everything ain't in the books. History books were written from one point of view. Our experiences are different from those of the professors and writers of history books. You guys are smart enough to know that some things don't have to be sanctioned, studied, or approved by some board or committee for them to have value and to be true."

Paris started waving her hands in the air. "Mama," she said excitedly, "give me an example of an ugly root."

I thought about what I'd had to go through to get an application from Greensboro Day School just a few days ago, but I decided on another example.

"Paris, do you remember the time we went shopping at Kmart in Danville, and a white man was following us around in the store?"

Paris shook her head. "I don't remember that."

I said, "Well, it happened, and I was afraid the man meant us harm, so I went to the cashier and reported that someone was following me around in the store. The cashier said the man was the store's security person."

Paris smirked and rolled her eyes. "Well, some black people do steal, Mama."

"I agree. Some do. But it's an ugly root to assume that I will or that every person of color will."

Paris said, "That would not bother me. You taught us not to steal. So I say let 'em follow you around if they want to."

Sherondalyn grinned and said, "Mama, I'm with Paris on this one. But the ugly root of racism stems from the vestiges of slavery."

I nodded. "That's what I think. It stems from the making of America, and it affects all Americans. It was tough for Europeans to make a new country, and I believe they did what they felt was in their best interest at the time. They were not wise enough to understand that slavery was destructive. They were taking land away from the Indians and using slaves to build their wealth. They called it building a nation. They either didn't know any better or didn't care about being cruel to Indians or black people."

Sherondalyn swallowed a sip of tea. "So white people need a psychiatrist to help them stop being racists, and black people need one to help them deal with the psychological damage from slavery?" She looked at me quizzically. "Is that right?"

"I think so," I said.

The following Monday, Paris took the independent schools test, and three weeks later, I received a congratulatory acceptance letter for Paris from Greensboro Day School. Paris was given a partial academic scholarship. I called David to tell him the good news and asked if he would contribute toward the cost of tuition before I told Paris she had been accepted.

"Marilyn," he said, "I don't appreciate you arranging for Paris to go to a private school. It's a waste of money."

"But, David," I said, "Paris wants to go Ivy League. So I need to prepare her."

David barked, "Don't expect any more child support from me. I've got to live too."

A few months later, Mildred called me early in the morning to inform me that Daddy's ulcers were acting up again, and he had been hospitalized. We agreed to meet at Danville Memorial Hospital in Virginia around eleven o'clock the next morning.

Although Daddy looked pleased to see his daughters Mildred, Inez, and me, he struggled to see if anyone else was with us. Then, with short breaths, he asked, "How's y'all's mama doing?"

"Mama is good," Mildred said, taking Daddy's hand. "She'll probably come visit tomorrow or the next day."

Daddy talked with Inez and Mildred for more than two hours. He told them his diagnosis was no longer inflamed ulcers. It was pancreatic cancer. It was puzzling to see him in a good mood while seriously ill.

"My doctor said they need to operate on me. So I'm gonna crawl up onto that operating table, but I don't know if I'll be able to crawl off," Daddy said with a bit of humor.

I was more solemn and reserved. I sat in an uncomfortable straight-backed chair as far away from my sisters as possible in the small, hot room. I didn't know what to say to Daddy now because I had wanted him to die when I was a child. Now I wanted him to live. I prayed silently for his healing and asked God to forgive me for wanting him dead for many years. As I got up to leave a few hours later, Daddy turned his head toward me and waved. I waved back and exited the room without speaking to him.

Two days later, on June 4, I had a nagging sense of urgency to visit Daddy. So I took the next day off work and drove to the hospital. I wanted to apologize for defying him years ago when I went to school, even after he had threatened to kill me.

Daddy appeared to be asleep when I stepped into his room. He was alone. I pulled up a chair and sat beside his bed but not too close. After a few minutes, he opened his eyes and turned toward me. His breathing was much weaker than it had been a couple of days earlier.

"Daddy, I'm sorry I defied you and went to school that day. Unfortunately, I may be the cause of your stomach problems," I said.

Daddy frowned. The grimace on his face indicated that he was in excruciating pain. I noticed a morphine pump beside his bed and squeezed it several times.

"Naw, gal," he said, "all of that shit-ass whiskey I's been drinking gave me this here problem." He twisted in the bed even more and squeezed the bed railing.

"Daddy, I used to hate you, but I don't anymore," I said. I couldn't bring myself to tell him that I loved him. I wanted to, but the word *love* sounded foreign in my head and wouldn't form on my lips. I supposed it was because neither of my parents had ever told me they loved me.

"Gal, back then," he said, "I don't know what was wrong wit' me. I was a real dummy." Between his painful twists and grimaces, he would try to talk. "Everybody was sending their brood to school, and there I was, keeping my brood in the 'bacco fields to stay dumb."

I knew it took a gargantuan effort for him to talk between bursts of pulsating pain. I wanted to tell him that all was well, and he didn't have to speak, but the more he said, the better I felt.

"I was wrong wit' all of my chillums. Plain wrong. I shouldn't have been like that. Gal, I just didn't have good sense." He stopped talking for a few minutes as his body contorted in pain.

I pushed the button on the morphine pump again, and a few seconds later, he dozed off. I began to pray for Daddy to have peace and be healed if that was God's will.

When he stirred eventually, I looked at my watch. It had only been eleven minutes. Then, finally, he opened and focused his jaundiced eyes on me again. "I'm still here," he said with a sad smile.

"And I'm still here with you," I responded. I wanted Daddy to continue talking, because this was my first conversation with him sober for more than one day. To hear an apology for the way he had raised us was more than I expected. His words were healing, and something ugly inside me began to float away.

"Daddy, how did you lose your farm?" I asked just to keep him awake and talking.

"Didn't I tell y'all how white people treat you? It was a bad year for farmers back then, and the only way the bank would let me keep the land was if I started over at the beginning with the loan." He moaned as a few tears ran down his face. "It would've been like I hadn't paid nothin'. Gal, I wasn't 'bout to do that. So they took my land."

His breathing became more laborious. I heard what sounded like congestion in his chest. I was afraid he was about to take his last breath. I stood to leave his room because I didn't want to see him die. He reached for my hand, but that made me feel uncomfortable. I moved farther away and stood several feet away from his bed. I was thirty-nine years old, and

Daddy had never hugged, kissed, or touched me. Now, when he tried to, I didn't allow it.

Daddy caught his breath and started to talk again. "I had already paid over half of what I owed, and then they wanted me to start all over like I hadn't paid nothin' to 'em," he said without realizing he was repeating himself. "White folks—"

He heaved, and I thought, *This is it*. But he continued after taking a short breath.

"White folks make good thieves. I couldn't do nothin', gal"—he heaved again—"but let it go. It was legal stealing." His voice trailed off.

I remained standing and watched his lips move without uttering a word.

After a short while, as if he had regained strength, Daddy resumed talking. "I ain't no beggar, and don't you be a shit-ass beggar either." He inhaled and exhaled as if he were tired. His eyes were still focused on me. Then, suddenly, they closed. I came closer to the bed to see if he was dead. But I saw his chest moving under the thin white blanket.

"I wish I could have made life better for you and Mama," I said, and he nodded with his eyes still closed. He looked pitiful, thin and unshaven, and his eyes were sunken into their sockets. I was disturbed by his frail body movements, so I moved my chair closer to the window and sat down.

"Tell me about the happiest time of your life," I said.

Daddy turned his head and opened his eyes once more. They appeared to be getting weaker by the minute. I wanted to bring him home with me to take care of him for at least a little while.

"Shit," he said in a weak, raspy voice, "I ain't had a happy day in my life."

I scribbled a few notes in my composition tablet and then tried to hit the morphine pump again, but it said more time needed to elapse before another dose could be administered. Daddy continued to grimace as his body contorted in pain.

"Do you want me to pray for you?" I asked.

"Naw, I don't," he said. "A bunch of 'em already been here trying to pray me into heaven. I ain't worried 'bout no heaven or hell. Just make sure you take care of everything."

"Don't worry, Daddy," I said. "I'm going to find a deep gully and cover you up with a nice pile of leaves, just like you told me." That was my way of reminding him about what he'd said when I tried to get him to buy life insurance.

"Shit, gal," he said, "I didn't have good sense back then."

I felt I had been a little mean, so I told him I had life insurance on him. He nodded, and in a few minutes, he dozed off again. I wrote down many things he told me about his life and even dozed off myself. When I woke up, his eyes were focused on me again.

"Daddy, do you remember the time you gave me some money to keep for you?"

Daddy nodded but didn't try to speak.

"When I told you that I lost it, well, that was a lie. I gave it to Mama to buy groceries. I should have told you, but I didn't want you to fight with Mama."

He nodded again while trying to give himself a shot of morphine. I took it from his hand and pressed the nozzle. "Nora did the best thing with it," he said, and he closed his eyes.

I watched Daddy's chest move up and down. While I was listening to a rattling sound in his throat for a few seconds, his doctor walked in. I introduced myself, and the doctor quietly told me that Daddy had about three months to live. I stopped praying for God to heal him. Instead, I asked God to ease his pain and give him happiness in the next realm of consciousness.

CHAPTER 66

BEEN IN HELL

On June 12, 1990, we were called to the hospital because Daddy's condition had become much worse. Mildred, Inez, and I were in the room as his breathing steadily became more laborious. Once I realized he could no longer talk or open his eyes, I stepped outside his room and began to pray for God to release him from his painful body.

Mildred held Daddy's hand. Inez rubbed his forehead, while I stood just outside his door, intermittently peeping into the room. That took all the strength I had. I didn't want to see Daddy die.

"Marilyn, where are you?" Mildred repeatedly asked. I would amble into the room for a few minutes and then step outside again. Finally, Daddy mumbled something, and Mildred told him that we were all there with him and would not leave him alone.

"I'm right here, Mildred," I said, "but where are our brothers?"

"I don't know where they are, but we're gonna stay right here by Daddy's side. It won't be much longer." Tears slid down Mildred's and Inez's faces.

Daddy heaved a few minutes later, and a brown liquid erupted from his throat and flowed from his mouth. The offensive odor smelled like cigarette smoke. The monitor flatlined. I turned my back to Daddy's bed just as a nurse and doctor rushed into the room. The doctor placed his stethoscope on Daddy's chest for a few seconds. Then he looked at the nurse and pronounced the time of death.

Later that afternoon, we all gathered at Inez's home in Milton to discuss funeral arrangements. Ronald Jr. told everyone that Terri, the youngest child, was in charge because Daddy had said he was leaving everything to his youngest child. I didn't say anything, and to prevent any controversy, I didn't go with them to the funeral home to make final arrangements, but I did go with them to Daddy's old rented farmhouse to gather a memento.

On June 16, 1990, the funeral was held at Hamer Missionary Baptist Church in Blanch, North Carolina.

Just as Reverend Lea, the pastor, got up to give the eulogy, we heard god-awful wailing from a woman in the rear of the church. I tried not to look back, but I did. There was Daddy's girlfriend with a long black veil covering her entire face. Her arms flailed wildly as she stood up screaming and repeatedly saying, "Oh God, he can't be gone." Several ushers rushed to her aid, fanning her and holding her upright.

I whispered in Mildred's ear, "She was Daddy's girlfriend. Do you think I should go back there and shut her up?"

"What do you have in mind?" Mildred asked humorously as she fanned Mama.

I whispered, "Take her ass outside, and give her a good stomping. She wants everyone to see her in that stupid veil."

Mildred said, "Ignore her. Let it go."

Later, during the funeral repast, I sat beside Mama in the cool basement of the church.

"Mama, do you think Daddy is in heaven?" I asked.

Mama swallowed and laid her fork down. She didn't speak right away. Finally, she said, "Of course he's in heaven. He's been in hell all his life, being poor, mistreated, and cheated." She took a drink of unsweetened tea and stared at Daddy's picture on the obituary for several seconds. "There ain't no place for him to go but to heaven."

CHAPTER 67

ASK A BLACK MAN

The day after Daddy's funeral, I returned to work, even though I could have stayed home. Earlier in the week, I had made an appointment to petition Mr. Henry, the director of Southern Bell consumer services, to make a financial contribution to the NAACP ACT-SO program. I was on a committee to raise funds to send several local high school kids to a national science competition in Washington, DC. I thought Southern Bell would donate a few thousand dollars to help us reach our goal of $25,000.

The walk to Mr. Henry's office was not far, but it felt like a mile to me. Mr. Henry sat behind his vast desk, looking more petite than usual. His thinning brown hair was ruffled on the top and appeared stiff with mousse or hair spray. His round pale face was full of raw red blotches and peeling. The rumor was believable: Mr. Henry hadn't fully healed from a chemical peel that was supposed to make him appear younger.

"Marilyn," he said, "I understand that you are soliciting funds for the NAACP to send some children to Washington, DC. Is that correct?" He pointed to a seat for me to sit down.

"Yes, sir, that is correct," I said, feeling more relaxed. "We are trying to encourage, motivate, and support some of the bright young students in the community. They have been chosen by their teachers, who feel they will go on to college and contribute to society one day."

Mr. Henry opened his side desk drawer and took out a sizeable dark green ledger. He picked up his pen as though ready to write a check. Then, without warning, Mr. Henry slammed the ledger shut and laid the pen down. He steepled his hands and looked down at the ledger and then at me. He was silent for a few seconds, and then he said, "Marilyn, tell me something. Why don't black men take care of their children?"

He tapped the desktop with the tip of his ballpoint pen and stared at me. I had never been quick-witted, and now I sat across from my third-level boss with my brain at a loss for words. I was shocked, but it didn't take long to become angry. I didn't want to offend Mr. Henry, because I wanted the financial contribution, and I didn't want him to block my chance of ever getting a promotion.

I could not think clearly enough to tell him about the controversial Daniel P. Moynihan report *The Negro Family: The Case for National Action*, written in 1965, which many people had read. Although many black leaders disagreed with the report, I had gleaned a lot of information from it that I'd used for debate in sociology class at Bennett College.

I knew I should not try to share real-life experiences, but his question so jarred me that I wanted to articulate what I knew about the psychological damage slavery had done to black people, as well as the economic and social strangling corporate America was continuing to do—CEOs, institutions, bankers, and most of American society excluded, discriminated against, and exploited every facet of black people's existence. People like Mr. Henry did so. I didn't want him to think I was stupid or a smart-ass, but I knew I had to say something and, at the same time, be polite.

Words unfit for the workplace were on the cusp of my tongue. I wanted to tell Mr. Henry that every intelligent white man in America knew precisely why black people were in poverty and then tell him to kiss my ass and walk out. But I knew he would fire me if I said such things, so I cleared my throat and contained myself to be as civil as I could.

Finally, I said, "Mr. Henry, all the black men I know take care of their families. Four of my brothers work and take care of their homes, although they are underpaid. My sisters are married to men who work and care for their families as well. Since I don't know all black men—the ones in other states and countries—and because I'm not a man, I can't really answer your question. Why don't you ask the few black men who work for Southern Bell—you know, the telephone installers, repairmen, and linemen?"

Mr. Henry sat back in his chair, folded his arms, and stared at me with a smug smile.

I couldn't look him in the eye, for fear he might see the hate mounting toward him. Instead, I stared at the wall clock just above his head. Mr. Henry opened the ledger, scribbled on one of the checks, tore it out, and laid it facedown on the desk. His face turned crimson.

"There are too many black children not being taken care of by their families," he said, and he placed one hand on top of the check. I tried to force myself to walk out and be spared further humiliation but couldn't because I felt Southern Bell owed the black community for financially exploiting them so mercilessly. So I sat and waited for him to complete his sport of my request.

Eventually, he slid the bank draft over to me and said, "I sure hope black people start to take care of their children."

I took the check and quickly glanced at it before inserting it into my folder. Disappointingly, the bank draft was for $300. I had been expecting at least $5,000. Finally, I forced myself to say thank you and rushed out of Mr. Henry's office, wondering if he had any clue that I would despise him forever.

CHAPTER 68

MADE OF GOLD

Four months after my unpleasant meeting with Mr. Henry, Mae, my supervisor, gestured me toward her office early one Thursday morning. I sauntered over without much enthusiasm. I inhaled and exhaled deeply. I feared I would have to face some challenging situation orchestrated by Mr. Henry.

Mae said, "A customer called me late yesterday after you left. He insisted on speaking with you." She tore a slip from her pink notepad and handed it to me. "Take care of this by noon."

I looked at the handwritten note and breathed a sigh of relief. The stress I felt melted away when I saw the name on the message: Mr. Walter Dumas. He was a friendly customer I had helped the previous day.

On Sunday morning, I told Paris I was having breakfast at Shoney's on High Point Road to meet a gentleman for whom I had solved a problem earlier in the week. Cringing against my bedroom door, Paris said, "Mama, I know you're not going to meet some man you talked to over the telephone. Please don't do that. It's dangerous."

I scribbled Mr. Dumas's telephone number and address on a piece of paper and laid it on my dresser. Then I called Mildred and gave her the same information before heading out the door. Paris followed me to my car, begging me not to go.

I said, "We are meeting in a public place. It will be OK."

After seven weeks of near-perfect dates, Walter asked me to accompany him to Atlantic City, New Jersey, during Thanksgiving week. I knew nothing about New Jersey but agreed to go with him. I called Mildred, with whom Mama now lived, and told her I would not be coming to Thanksgiving dinner that year. I heard Mildred tell Mama, and a few seconds later, Mama was on the phone.

"I heard 'bout this man who's stopping you from coming round. I don't care if he's made of gold. I expect to see y'all this Thanksgiving and Christmas."

"But, Mama," I said, "we've made plans to go out of town."

Mama asked, "Do you know when I'm going to die?"

I said, "No."

"Well then, I expect to see y'all on Thanksgiving and Christmas. You don't know when I'm gonna die. This may be the last holiday you'll have with me."

For as long as I could remember, Mama had threatened us with her possible death to coerce us to do what she wanted. Eventually, I agreed to be with family on Thanksgiving Day.

I was now in a pickle and didn't know what to do. Finally, a couple of days before Thanksgiving, I called Mildred and told her I enjoyed Walter's company. Mildred listened with the patience of Job as I told her about places Walter had taken me, including the restaurants we had dined in and the museums, zoos, and beaches we had visited, all in less than two short months. Then I said, "Every weekend, he plans something for us to do. He might be the One."

Mildred sighed. "All of that is good, but we still expect your lasagna this Thanksgiving. Can't nobody make it like you."

I thought about my family's history of rudeness. Finally, I blurted out, "I won't be there this year."

Mildred gasped as though I had used a cuss word. I explained, "Paris is spending Thanksgiving with David, and Sherondalyn is staying in Boston. So I don't see the need to come this year."

She said, "I understand. You don't want to bring this new man around us. He must be made of gold. I'll let Mama know."

Walter had been calling me every Wednesday night since we met, but that Wednesday, after my call to Mildred, I sat near the phone waiting for his eight-thirty call. It didn't come.

At eight forty-five, my doorbell rang. I opened the door, and Walter stood there with a smile as big as Alaska. My angst floated away in an instant.

I said, "You must have read my mind. I wanted to see you."

Walter thumped his chest with his fist and kissed me lightly on the cheek before walking inside. I knew the time had come to tell him about

A Head of Cabbage

my family. But first, I needed to see if he would bail before I further invested my heart.

"Walter," I said as I closed the door, "I have eight sisters and brothers, and on every holiday, we get together at someone's home to celebrate, but it has never been a pleasant experience for me. Somebody has to be the butt end of a joke or hear some cruel remark, and usually, it's me."

The smile disappeared from Walter's face as he looked into my eyes and took my hands. "Marilyn, your family sounds like a normal family to me. So why don't you tell me what's really on your mind?" I looked away, but he pulled me a little closer to him, his eyes questioning.

"I simply don't want you to be around my family." I paused for a few seconds, feeling ashamed for having such a thought.

"Well, that's just fine," he said. Then, appearing disappointed, he sat down on the sofa.

I didn't want Walter to think of my family as stupid and uneducated, nor did I want to expose him to my brothers' usual rudeness and ungracious behavior. I liked Walter a lot, and I didn't want anyone to cause him to lose interest in me. So I said, "My brothers are verbally brutal. They will find a way to insult you for sure."

Walter grinned and said, "For a moment, I thought you were going to tell me your family turned into mean green cannibals at midnight. Listen, I roll with the best of them, whether they are illiterate or Duke scholars. If they throw a punch or two, so what? I'll take it and throw a punch or two right back. If they act like they have good sense, so will I. Don't be afraid for me. I can handle myself. Are we clear on that?"

I nodded and said, "You have been forewarned."

Walter pulled an envelope from the inner pocket of his brown leather jacket and handed it to me. Inside were two travel advertisements. One was for Hilton Head Island, and the other was for Myrtle Beach, both in South Carolina. The clippings didn't mean anything to me. I inserted them back into the envelope.

He said, "I came up here to surprise you with a choice of where you wish to spend Christmas. I have already planned for Atlantic City during Thanksgiving week. You get to choose for Christmas. Which do you prefer?"

I knew nothing about either place. I hadn't heard anything good about South Carolina.

"It doesn't matter as long as we are together," I said, and I watched Walter's face light up with excitement.

"Ah, girl, a man has to always give a beautiful lady a choice," he said, and the little girl in me beamed with joy.

So I said, "Hilton Head is my choice for Christmas."

The Wednesday before Thanksgiving, while Walter packed my luggage in the boot of his car, I examined my purse and made sure I had my credit card in case of an emergency. When we arrived in Atlantic City, I was in for a shock. I'd thought we would enjoy walking on the beach, feeling the cool ocean breeze on our faces, as we listened and watched seagulls. But it was a casino. Walter was keen to play poker. He insisted I find a slot machine and entertain myself for a while.

I found the casino floor mesmerizing. People of every nationality were everywhere. Some people were in wheelchairs with oxygen tanks attached and still smoking cigarettes. The colorful slot machines were stuffed with coins by dirty fingers of every size, shape, and color. Falling coins, whistles, and flashing lights could be seen and heard everywhere on the multicolored carpeted floor. Scantily dressed women carried trays with drinks. I turned 180 degrees, watching, observing everything, before I let go of Walter's arm.

I said, "Walter, I have never been inside a casino before, and I'm afraid I will lose my five dollars. Can you tell me which one to play?"

Looking surprised, Walter rubbed his forehead and asked, "Did you say you have five dollars to play?"

"Yes."

"That much, huh?" He stifled a laugh, reached into his jacket pocket, pulled out his money clip, and said, "Baby Cakes, go over there and enjoy yourself." He slipped several bills into my hand and pointed to a row of slot machines.

Once he was out of his sight, I counted the money. Ten hundred-dollar bills! I was shocked again. I put the money in my purse and headed for the bathroom. I inserted $700 inside the lining of my jacket and then returned to the casino floor. After three minutes, I had lost $100. I was stunned, stopped playing, and found Walter at the poker table. He picked up a few chips and dropped them into my purse when he saw me.

I said, "That machine just took—"

Walter didn't allow me to finish my sentence. He thought I had lost $800, because I held two hundred-dollar bills in my hand.

"Goddamn, Marilyn Ann," he said, "you only got two hundred dollars left?" He snatched the two bills from my hand and said, "Baby Cakes, we will win together, or we will lose together; don't worry about it."

I said nothing. Walter took my hand, and we walked over to the high-stakes area. We began to play the five-dollar slots, and the buzzer went off within minutes. Walter had won $3,000! We returned to our hotel room, where he counted two piles of $1,500 each. He handed one to me.

"This is your share," he said proudly.

"Are you giving this money to me?" I asked, and I began to hyperventilate. I didn't know what to make of it. No one had ever given me that much money before.

Walter appeared to get a kick out of my amazement. He chuckled. "It's all yours."

I put $500 in my wallet and handed him the remainder. He squinted and asked, "What are you doing?"

I said, "You gave me a thousand dollars. Now I'm giving you a thousand dollars."

He moved away from me, sat on the bed, and said, "I don't sponge off women. I'm a man. Keep your money."

I inserted ten hundred-dollar bills inside his jacket pocket and said, "You're not sponging off me. You are accepting a gift from me like I accepted a gift from you earlier."

Walter took my hands and said, "Baby Cakes, there's not another woman in North Carolina who would do that. I might be wrong, but I believe we are going places together. However, we have a small problem." He paused a little too long, as though he were searching for the right words.

Oh shit. This man is gay, I thought. Finally, I said, "Tell me the small problem." I braced myself.

"You got some mighty long legs, and they worry me. I don't know if they can be tamed."

I exhaled slowly, wondering how to assuage his anxiety at being a bit shorter than I was. I said, "The only thing you need to worry about is where you want these long legs." Then I mimicked one of Blanche's giggles.

Walter blinked slowly and then grabbed me, and when we finally got out of bed, it was noon on Thanksgiving Day.

CHAPTER 69

HELLO, MARILYN

In 1992, I attended a sweat-equity seminar. The information I gleaned from the lecture and the audience's questions helped me realize that my salary from BellSouth, formerly Southern Bell, would enable me to purchase a more substantial house.

I checked with the benefits office at work and learned I could use my 401(k) without a penalty to purchase a new home. I found a beautiful two-story house in the Adams Farm subdivision in Greensboro, a middle-class neighborhood off High Point Road.

The young white real estate agent took my application and, within a few days, called and told me I had nothing to worry about because I had steady employment for fifteen years, and my credit was good. Furthermore, NationsBank would finance the mortgage, and we could close within four months.

The next day, I called Mr. Simpson, a former boyfriend and Realtor. I needed a buyer's agent, someone to help me navigate buying a new home and renting out my current one. Mr. Simpson scared me enough to make both my eyes twitch.

"Marilyn," he said emphatically, "I hate to break the news to you, but NationsBank doesn't mortgage homes for black people. I don't want you to get to the closing and have everything fall apart."

My anxiety rose to panic level, and I hurried Mr. Simpson off the phone. Then I called the loan officer at NationsBank.

"Mrs. Grooms, this is Marilyn," I said as soon as I heard the receiver lift. "I have a concern. I've been informed that NationsBank does not approve mortgages for black people."

Mrs. Grooms sighed. "Marilyn, that is preposterous. This is 1992. NationsBank gives loans to all qualified applicants, and your credit is great. You've been at the same job for over fifteen years, and you're paying twenty percent down, which you don't have to do. You will not have any problems." Mrs. Grooms sounded confident, professional, and patient.

After our conversation, I called Mr. Simpson back and told him what Mrs. Grooms had said.

"Is that loan officer of yours white?" he asked, sounding irritated.

I answered, "Yes, she is, and she is quite certain that I won't have any problems in getting the loan approved."

I heard a heavy sigh. "That might be the case if you were white," Mr. Simpson said, again with assured authority. "Let me help you out. I will submit a loan application with another loan company for you, OK?"

I agreed and paid the fees to process another loan. Even so, I continued to call NationsBank weekly. Mrs. Grooms soon recognized my voice, and when she answered the phone, she would say, "Hello, Marilyn. Everything is fine—smooth sailing all the way. How is your day going?"

We closed on schedule, and the three-bedroom house on 3 Printers Lane in Greensboro belonged to me. I had no problems with NationsBank.

Two years earlier, Paris had returned home complaining after a sleepover at one of her friends' houses.

"Mama, I don't like living here on Bittersweet Court. My friend's bathroom is bigger than our whole house," Paris said after her friend's father dropped her off.

We sat in our small living room, and I explained intergenerational wealth and poverty and how racism played a role. After our long talk, Paris looked at me and exclaimed, "Mama, you are a racist!"

I had no other words to share with her after explaining that most rich people taught their children how to be and stay rich, while many poor people taught their children to remain poor. I pointed out that it wasn't intentional but had to do with a lack of education, lucrative jobs, inheritances, and business ownership.

Paris stood up. "You went to college, and we're still poor."

I did not feel poor and wanted Paris to see that we were no longer in poverty. We just were not wealthy. I owned our tiny house, we had a car, and I had a 401(k) for my retirement, which I told her.

Paris said, "Mama, we are still poor!"

I lost my patience and screamed, "Get your little self in the car! We're going for a ride."

A Head of Cabbage

I took her to the homeless shelter. We walked in, looked around, and talked to a few people for a while.

On our way home, Paris started to tear up. "Mama, I get it. We are not rich, but we are not as poor as some people. We have a home, a car, and food to eat."

"Exactly," I said through clenched teeth. "My dad left me nothing when he died—no money, no land, no house, no stocks or bonds. Mama has nothing to pass down either. But I promise you that we will live in a new house before you graduate school."

I had to forgo going to the hair and nail salon. I bought most of my clothes at consignment and discount shops. I took my lunch to work and put myself on a strict budget. I made sure I didn't get addicted to anything that cost money, such as coffee, cigarettes, or illegal drugs. I gave money to the church, but I never tithed. I saved more than $400 a month, and I believed God was pleased with my decisions and goals.

Two years after that conversation with Paris, I gave her a key to our new home. It was a long, arduous journey, but it was worth the sacrifices to see her beautiful smile and gleaming eyes.

When she first walked into our new home, she teared up and said, "Mama, you did it."

CHAPTER 70

SIT DOWN FOR THE NEWS

I had been dating Walter for more than two years and had experienced more things and gone to more places than I ever had thought possible. I was living in a new house in a middle-class neighborhood. Life was good, and I was happier than I had ever been.

When I went to work about a week after the closing, I walked into the office with my friend Sharon. Just before we sat down, we saw a big deputy sheriff walking up to the front of the office. I looked at Sharon.

She asked, "Who do you think he's looking for?"

I said, "I don't know, but somebody is getting ready to have a bad day."

We both giggled and started taking incoming sales calls, when Mae, my supervisor, walked over and laid a note on my desk, asking me to come to her office. I finished the customer's request, and just before I reached her office, I saw the big deputy sheriff standing outside Mae's office with his hat and a manila envelope in his hand.

The deputy stepped forward and asked, "Are you Marilyn Jamison?"

I said, "Yes," and then looked around the room as people stared at me.

"This is for you." The deputy handed me the envelope and then left.

As if I were a criminal, Mae and everyone watched me suspiciously as I strolled back to my desk. I was scared and embarrassed and wondered what my coworkers thought about me.

"Sharon," I said, "I don't know what this is. I'm afraid to open this envelope. I've never had any problems with the law."

Sharon snatched the envelope out of my hand, opened it, and quickly scanned it. She said it was just a summons to go to court—my ex-husband had petitioned the court for a reduction in child support. She dropped the subpoena onto my desk over the plexiglass divider as though it were nothing of concern.

After work that evening, I called David and asked him to withdraw his request.

David said, "Marilyn, I have to live too. Sherondalyn is eighteen now, and my child support payments should be reduced by half."

I was still angry and bitter toward David. I hated to hear his or Salmon's name, and if I did, my stomach ached. My depression would last for several days after I saw either of them.

I said, "David, Paris is in private school, and Sherondalyn is at MIT. I need that money to help with their tuitions. It's to help your children, for Christ's sake."

David would not relent. I knew from firsthand experience that he could be stubborn. Finally, he said, "I didn't tell you to put Paris in private school. We will go to court so that I can get a reduction. I have bills to pay just like everyone else."

I had worked full-time and two part-time jobs and stayed on a strict budget to move into the middle class, so I suggested the same to David. "Why don't you get a part-time job? That's what most men do to help their families."

"Well, I ain't most men. I need my time to live my life," David said in such a harsh tone that I decided to hang up.

Just before I slammed the phone down, I said, "I will see you in court."

We went to family court in Greensboro on a Friday. I got there just before nine o'clock and found an aisle seat near another young mother.

"Have you been to court before?" I asked, hoping she would give me enough information to calm me down.

The young mother said, "Plenty of times. It's nothing to worry about." Then she slipped a stick of chewing gum into her mouth and offered me a piece. I accepted and dropped the gum into my mouth to calm my nerves.

I asked, "How does it go? This is my first time in court."

The young mother gave me a quick overview of what to expect and then popped her gum in quick succession and pointed a finger. "Look at that man over there. I know he ain't nobody's daddy. He's a fag if there ever was one." She started to giggle. I felt ashamed.

My gut told me it was David. I sat in silence, hoping her case got called before mine. It didn't.

Judge McCorkle, who taught karate part-time at the community center, was the sitting judge. Sherondalyn and Paris were his former students.

The bailiff called David and then me up front. I walked up and stood on the opposite side.

"Mr. Jamison, you petitioned the court to reduce child support payments. Is that right?" Judge McCorkle's voice was crisp and deep.

"Yes, sir," David said nervously, staring straight ahead at the judge.

Judge McCorkle looked down at David from the bench and said, "Mr. Jamison, you don't want to reduce your child support payments, do you?"

"Yes, sir. I do," David said.

Judge McCorkle shifted through several documents I had provided before speaking again. "I see one daughter is at MIT, the other daughter is at Greensboro Day School, and both are doing well. The mother is evidently not wasting money in the streets. She's providing a good home for the children, raising them properly. Do you really want to reduce the child support, Mr. Jamison?" Judge McCorkle shook his head slightly, and I surmised he disagreed with a reduction.

David said, "Yes, sir, I really do, Your Honor."

Judge McCorkle looked at his bailiff and said to David, "Do you have a pay stub on you, Mr. Jamison?" The bailiff grinned but stared straight ahead.

"Yes, sir, I believe I do." David took a pay stub out of his wallet and handed it to the bailiff, who gave it to Judge McCorkle.

Judge McCorkle said, "Mr. Jamison, in the great state of North Carolina, a child is entitled to seventeen percent of the parent's income. Therefore, I order an increase in your child support in the amount of fifty dollars per month."

The gavel sounded, and the bailiff motioned for us to leave as he gave the pay stub back to David.

That evening, as I reveled in my court victory, my best friend, Jannie, called me from Raleigh. Walter sat quietly on my new gold-and-green sofa, watching golf on TV.

Jannie said, "Girl, you need to sit down because I've got some news for you."

Jannie and I continued our friendship even though it had been more than ten years since I'd moved from Raleigh. I asked, "What news?"

She said, "Steven got married earlier today."

I wanted to scream at the top of my lungs. But Walter was sitting in the den, oblivious to my deepening heartache. My entire body ached with a slow, nagging pain, as if I had come down with an unknown ailment. My chest tightened, and chills spread down my spine. My mind raced with tangled thoughts of Steven.

I finally repeated Jannie's words. "Steven got married!" I felt like dying.

Jannie exhaled and said, "I hope it doesn't bother you after all these years. I called to tell you because I thought you would like to know."

After the call, I excused myself, ran upstairs, and called Steven.

I said, "Hello. I heard you got married today. I just wanted to congratulate you. I wish you nothing but happiness." I tried to sound happy for him, and I hoped he could not tell that I was crying—and lying.

Steven cleared his throat and said, "That means a lot to me coming from you. Thanks for calling."

I felt guilty and disloyal to Walter, but I couldn't help myself. From the moment I had laid eyes on Steven thirteen years earlier, I'd loved him and wanted him in my life.

Walter came to the bottom of the stairs and asked me to join him on the sofa. "Baby Cakes, I'm going to take another trip to Atlantic City in two weeks with a couple of friends. Would you like to go?"

I came downstairs, but I could not look Walter in the eye. I just said, "Yes."

CHAPTER 71

IT FEELS LIKE LOVE

Seven months after Steven's wedding, he called me. He wanted to visit to talk about his daughter's college aspirations. I was fond of his daughter and consented.

I called Walter and told him that Steven had asked me to assist him with his teenage daughter's college application.

Walter sounded befuddled. "Damn, Marilyn Ann, just what are you saying?"

"Walter, trust me," I said unconvincingly. "I'm going to help him with some paperwork for his daughter."

"Didn't you once tell me he was your old boyfriend?"

I said, "Yes, but he's married now."

Suspiciously, Walter said, "A married man has no business in a single woman's home."

I knew that and resigned myself not to see Steven unless Walter consented. "Don't be jealous," I said. "You have nothing to worry about."

"I don't mind you helping his kid," Walter said, "but call me as soon as he leaves."

The following day, my heart raced as though I were running a marathon until I saw Steven pull into the driveway. He appeared more handsome than I remembered: flawless brown complexion, naturally chiseled chin, and a few gray sprigs in his thin mustache. Steven's black boots made him appear taller than his six-foot-two frame. Dark green glasses complemented his green pullover and tight-fitting jeans.

We fixed breakfast together and sat down to eat, when Steven unexpectedly said, "Marilyn, I'm quite unhappy, and I'm thinking about divorcing my wife."

I saw his pain, and I felt both guilty and happy that his marriage was disintegrating. My imagination ran wild with possibilities.

Steven said, "My wife is frigid. She wraps herself up in a sheet like a mummy to prevent our flesh from touching."

I started to laugh, and Steven did too. For a moment, it felt like old times together. Unfortunately, we never got around to talking about his daughter.

Around eleven o'clock that night, Steven stood and gave me a lingering hug at the door. I felt his heartbeat and the hardness of his body against mine. Then Steven buried his face in my neck and tightened his arms around my waist. Finally, he let go of me slowly and looked me in the eye. I saw his jaw tighten, and desire flooded his eyes.

Then he said, barely audible, "I'd better go before I stay."

I wanted him to stay. We belonged together. Then I remembered our history: the blissfulness of being together; the lingering, and, later, the overwhelmingly painful reality of breaking up.

Steven left the door open as he walked down the few steps to his car. He looked back and said, "I'll always stay in touch with you."

I called Walter around eleven fifteen. He was livid.

"What took so long to call, Marilyn Ann? I've been lying in bed, wondering what the hell was going on with you," he barked.

I said calmly, "Steven just left a few minutes ago."

"God damn it!" Walter hollered. "What were you two talking about for so damn long? Marilyn Ann, understand that I don't have to be a nice guy."

I felt Walter's disappointment in me. Whenever he used my full name and did not allow me to get a word in, I knew he was mad.

"Walter, I'm sorry I mentioned it to you," I said. "I wanted to be honest."

Walter yelled, "Your ex-boyfriend had no business coming to visit you, and it better not happen again! I'm going to bed now, and I will see you Friday afternoon. Good night." He slammed the phone down.

I sat on the edge of the bed, trying to reconcile my feelings for Walter. He was dependable and caring, had no baggage, and was financially stable and well educated. I trusted him and felt secure and safe when I was with him. He liked my girls and behaved like a father to them. *Whoever coined the saying that you can only love one person at a time must have lived an uncomplicated life and gotten the right person the first time*, I thought. I knew because I loved both Steven and Walter.

At least it felt like love.

I had not sorted out my feelings when Walter visited on Friday. Time seemed to have slowed down. Three days had passed since I had seen Steven and spoken with Walter, but it felt as if it had been only a few hours. I thought Steven's marriage might crumble and possibly give us one last chance to build a lasting relationship together. I pondered whether I should end my relationship with Walter and wait for Steven to get a divorce. Deep down in a small corner of my gut, I knew it was past time to let go of Steven and fantasies that would never materialize, but it didn't seem possible.

"I think marriage is a good institution," Walter said, grabbing his overnight bag from the boot of his car, "but I don't want to get married again. It doesn't work for me." He lowered the trunk of his car and walked past me into the house. His usual kiss was missing. Beads of sweat slid down his temples.

He was miffed with me for allowing Steven to visit.

I said, "I would like to get married someday because I think it's the best way to live."

I closed the door behind us and attempted to kiss him on the lips, but he turned his head. I wasn't surprised but felt he wanted to even the score.

I had already cooked dinner and was about to set the table, when Walter walked over. He took the two plates from my hand and set them down. "Did you hear what I said?"

I tried to conceal my disappointment and looked away. "Of course I heard you. I'm not deaf."

Walter lifted his eyebrows as if waiting for a different response. "I just told you that I'm not getting married again."

Keeping my composure, I leaned a little closer to him and said in a low voice, "I didn't say anything about marrying you. I said I wanted to get married again someday."

CHAPTER 72

PLAN A WEDDING

Late Sunday night, just as Walter got up to leave for Charlotte, the telephone rang. I didn't answer but glanced at it.

Walter sat back down on the sofa and said, "So you definitely want to get married again."

I was embarrassed to admit it to him again, knowing how he felt. I nodded and said, "Yes, I want to get married again. Do I have to find someone else, or will you marry me? We have dated for three years. You should know whether or not you want me in your life." After saying those words, I felt a burden had been lifted. But part of me hoped Walter would stick to his guns and say to find someone else, so I might have another chance with Steven. Yet another part of me wanted to make a life with Walter, closing my heart forever from Steven.

Walter said, "OK, Marilyn. We will get married. I want to marry you, but I don't want a long engagement, and you have to relocate to Charlotte." He leaned back on the sofa, placed his feet on the coffee table, and started to tell me what our lives would be like together. After he finished sharing the details of his dream home and how I would invest my entire salary, with us living on his, he cupped my chin with his hands and said, "You will forget about that Steven. He must have a low IQ anyway to let a woman like you get away."

I gasped. "That's not a nice thing to say about anyone."

Finally, he stood up and said, "We've got to plan a wedding. Do you like white gold?"

I was excited, even though he did not get on one bended knee and propose. A little voice in my gut said, *Trust Walter, and build a happy life with him.* I didn't know anything about gold, but I said it was my favorite.

Walter grinned as he walked to the door. "March is a fine month to get married in. A spring wedding it will be."

I requested a transfer to Charlotte, and the request was granted in

November. I put my house on the market and moved in with Walter on December 4. I was elated for two short days. Then, on the third day, Walter developed a fever, chills, and shortness of breath. He could not walk up four steps without stopping to rest. I thought something was seriously wrong with his heart, but he was physically fit and walked three miles on most days. I was worried.

When I insisted he go to the hospital, Walter insisted I learn how to use the semiautomatic pistol he had purchased for me.

Walter said, "This baby is for you. It shoots fourteen times nonstop. If you need to turn someone around, praying and begging won't cut it, but this fellow"—he blew on the barrel—"will put a man down."

I told him I didn't want a gun, because guns killed people daily. Walter gave the classic response: "Guns don't kill; people do."

I shot back an equally stupid reply: "Yeah, people shoot people without guns, since guns don't kill."

Walter sat down on a barstool beside me. He handed the gun to me. "Go on—take it. The safety is on. I need you to get a feel for this pistol. It is not dangerous if you know how to use it. Understand that unfortunately, Charlotte is much more urban than Greensboro, and we have more criminals."

I took the pistol and tried to get a feel for it. Daddy had shotguns and rifles that he allowed me to handle occasionally but not a handgun. The gun felt light in comparison. I laid it down on the bar.

Walter said, "It's better to have a gun and not use it than to be without one." Then he took a deep breath. "Marilyn, I think I do need to go to the doctor. I feel like I can't get enough air."

Walter talked much slower on our way to see his doctor, gasping for air between every word.

"Once we get married," he said, "you will not have to cook or wash dishes, just keep me company." He tried to smile as I sped down Park Road toward Abbey Place, to his doctor's office. Then he said, "I don't want to go to bed with one woman and wake up with another one. Sometimes it's hard for me to believe that you are as sweet of a lady as you are."

"I only know how to be me," I said solemnly as I waited for the light to change.

By the time he finished telling me that he expected me to keep my same personality, I had turned into the parking lot. I ran into the doctor's office and asked for a wheelchair. Walter made his way toward the entrance step by step but was out of breath and bent over when I came back to assist him. Walter straightened up when he saw me. Then, struggling to breathe, he said, "You are acting like a wife. I like that."

The doctor saw him right away. I stood several feet back as the nurse drew his blood. It was not red, more like orange. I observed the doctor and nurse exchanging worrisome glances with each other.

By three o'clock, Walter had been admitted to Presbyterian Hospital in downtown Charlotte, where he was immediately given several pints of whole blood. Several doctors came into his room, asking him a multitude of questions. Walter tried his best to answer. I answered for him whenever I could. Finally, one doctor said they needed to do a bone marrow test, and they had already called in an oncologist. Walter looked scared and asked me to leave the room. I headed for the waiting room, but it was crowded, so I ended up in the janitor's closet to cry and pray. I didn't know how long I was in that closet, but Walter was alone when I returned.

"There is nothing wrong with my heart," Walter said, sounding much stronger. "I have some form of blood cancer. The doctors are trying to determine what kind, so they can devise a treatment plan."

CHAPTER 73

CANCER

The word *cancer* shook the core of my dreams and expectations. I felt my future with Walter was slipping out of my hand like a bar of wet soap.

My daddy and a sister-in-law had been taken away by cancer just a few years earlier, but I believed in miracles. I also trusted medical science.

Several days after Walter's diagnosis, I called the National Institute of Health. I was told that Duke Hospital in Durham, North Carolina, was one of the best in the Southeast for cancer treatment. I suggested a transfer there, but Walter did not want to leave Charlotte Presbyterian and believed it was just as good as Duke.

After work every night, I went to Presbyterian and spent the night in Walter's room. He talked about plans to build our dream home and all the places we would visit. I sat holding his hand, listening, and praying for his healing. I was desperate for him to live.

Late one night, Walter said, "Marilyn, I have only one fear, and it's not cancer." He paused and looked at me. I was curled up in a chair next to his bed.

"What is your fear?" I asked, caressing his hand.

He closed his eyes and took a deep breath. He said, "I'm not afraid of death. It will come in about five years or so. I'm afraid that you will go back to Greensboro and leave me alone."

I stood up and started to fluff the pillows on his bed. I didn't want him to see the tears that had begun to flow down my face. I needed a minute to think and pray before giving him words of comfort. I turned my head away and wiped my eyes with the back of my hand. Then I pulled the sheet up closer to his neck, leaned down to kiss him, and said, "Walter, I will never leave you, no matter what happens."

Walter smiled. "Your word is good enough for me. We can go ahead with our plans to marry in March if you still want me."

On December 24, 1993, Walter returned home from the hospital to the welcoming smiles and arms of three women: Sherondalyn, Paris, and me. He was weak and had lost an alarming twenty-seven pounds in less than a month but insisted on making a run without me. While he made his run, I read some books I had gotten from the library about cancer, vitamins, and a macrobiotic diet.

When Walter returned, he gave me a small package. I thought it might be an engagement ring. I didn't want to open it until Christmas Day. Walter insisted I open it immediately, so I did. A debit card was inside.

Walter said, "This card has a ten-thousand-dollar limit. Go buy yourself a mink coat." The smile he gave was not his usual. It looked weak and worried.

I took the card and laid it on his dresser.

In a frightfully soft and whispery voice, Walter said, "I really would like to see your long legs stroll across a room in a full-length mink. Every eye will be on you."

Since I could not share my health with him, I wanted to encourage him, so I said, "I would love to have a mink, but I will wait until we can walk in and out of the store together."

On December 25, 1993, Walter gave me a solitaire engagement ring. I broke down and sobbed. Walter saw the tears and said, "Marilyn, I'm sorry I don't have a lot of years to share with you. I probably have about five years to live, but they will be extraordinary years."

With each word, his strength appeared to be evaporating before my eyes. I said nothing. I sat beside him on the bed and prayed silently.

"I will leave everything I own to you and the girls. I know you love me." His voice cracked like that of an adolescent boy, but he strained to continue. "I know I can depend on you." His Adam's apple moved up and down, but no other words came forth as tears began to run down his face. Finally, Walter lay back on the bed and curled up in the fetal position.

I didn't say anything, because I couldn't. Instead, I lay down behind Walter with my arms around his waist. We lay there, letting our silent tears have their way. After a while, he turned over and wiped my tears, and I dabbed his in silence.

Sherondalyn and Paris returned later after visiting their father in Yanceyville. They came into the room where Walter and I were. Sherondalyn said, "Mama, you and Walter need to be careful. We don't want any little half brothers and sisters running around the house." The comment made Walter smile. After that, the four of us enjoyed dinner together before I returned Walter to the hospital for more treatments.

The doctor said Walter looked good, and he didn't know why because Walter was a seriously ill man. I told the doctor it was the green vegetables, macrobiotic diet, and vitamins I gave him. The doctor told me to stop giving him vitamins, and I did.

On January 3, 1994, Sherondalyn and Paris boarded a Continental Airlines flight to return to Boston. Paris was now a freshman at Harvard, and Sherondalyn was a junior at MIT.

CHAPTER 74

MAN OF GOD

Monday morning, I took my blue Mazda to get an oil change at a little no-name car garage on Beatties Ford Road. I walked carefully on the greasy, uneven pavement toward the entrance. A short, stocky man with a full beard came outside to greet me.

He wiped his hands on a dirty shop rag and asked, "How can I help such a sad-looking lady today?"

"I need an oil change," I said, and I handed him my car keys.

He pulled my car into his garage, hoisted it onto a rack, and started to drain the oil. I went into the small waiting area. While looking for a magazine to read, I spotted a stack of small pink cloths with an inscription of the Lord's Prayer. I picked up one.

The man said, "I'm a man of God too, and I sell prayer cloths for twenty dollars. Are you in need of a miracle?"

I thought about Walter getting weaker and weaker. I told the man that my fiancé was in dire need of a miracle because he was fighting cancer. I laid the prayer cloth back on top of the stack.

"I'm a praying man," he said. Then, with his head bowed, he prayed for a long time. After the prayer, the man walked over to the table, got one of the pink prayer clothes, and handed it to me. "That will be thirty-six dollars, please."

I paid in cash and headed for the hospital to see Walter. When I arrived, I felt like a fool for buying a prayer cloth like some backwoods religious idiot, so I kept the fabric hidden in my purse.

"Hey, Baby Cakes," Walter said as I stepped inside the room. A nurse was taking his vitals. After she left, Walter told me that the doctors wanted to do a bone marrow transplant, but they couldn't find a donor.

I asked if his brothers or sisters could be a donor.

Walter looked sadder than I had ever seen him with his sunken eyes.

He frowned. "Marilyn, unfortunately, I'm of illegitimate birth. I don't have any full brothers or sisters, which means they can't donate."

I was stunned and at a loss for words. I slipped the prayer cloth under Walter's pillow before leaving for work.

Walter's eyes were bloodshot when I returned that evening to spend the night with him in the hospital. He looked alarmingly weaker, but he was eager to talk. I found the prayer cloth where I had left it. I knew it was not helping, but I left it in place.

Walter said, "Marilyn, I probably won't live five years, but as soon as I set foot on solid ground, I'm going to put everything I own in your name. You are the only person who truly loves me. I want you to use the insurance money for the girls' education and buy yourself a Jaguar. I love seeing a long-legged woman stepping out of a Jag. I'll call NationsBank tomorrow to have them give you survivorship rights to everything, OK?"

I nodded but wanted to know what he had not told me. How many years would we have together? I stayed the night, tossing and turning in the lounge chair, but didn't ask him for the number of years the doctor was giving him to live.

The next day, I left for work before the doctor arrived, and I again prayed all the way to work, asking God to take five years off my life and give them to Walter so we would have a few more years together. As I'd lived a life full of hardship and heartache, my nonstop prayer was for Walter to live. I promised God I would not bother him again and would only do good deeds until I died. I wanted to believe that Walter would be healed, even though I saw him getting sicker each day.

I insisted on having Walter transferred to Duke Hospital in Durham on the first of February, even though I knew I could not be with him every day. However, several coworkers were kind and agreed to give up their vacation days for me.

I was nauseated, and gloomy shivers ran down my spine as I drove Walter to Duke Hospital. First, I had a feeling of imminent doom, and then I heard an inner voice that said, *If he goes to Durham, he will not come back.*

After three weeks at Duke Hospital, Walter's doctor was pleased with his progress. Walter and I walked the halls of Duke Hospital holding hands and making plans for his homecoming. It appeared his cancer was going into remission. The doctor said Walter could come home for a few days after another chemotherapy treatment.

"Baby Cakes," Walter said, "as soon as my feet touch solid ground, I will make changes to my will. You will be my sole beneficiary."

I stopped walking and said, "You know that I'm not marrying you for stuff, right?"

Walter leaned against the wall and said, "I know, but a man has to take care of his woman, and I don't know how long this cancer will remain in remission. So I want to make sure the girls get a good start in life. Education is only part of it."

I was happy that he was coming home. I looked forward to the day when we would build our dream house, travel to multiple destinations, and cruise the Seven Seas. But most of all, I just wanted to be his wife.

CHAPTER 75

YOU'RE GOING TO BE HOMELESS

The good news boosted my energy. When I returned to Charlotte, I thoroughly cleaned Walter's house to make it spotless for his homecoming. Then, after grocery shopping for fresh organic vegetables and fruits, I lay down on his navy-blue leather sofa in the den to catch a nap before going to work. Again, I was grateful for the doctor's prognosis. Finally, Walter was coming home!

The telephone rang just as I dozed off. The hospital was calling to tell me that Walter had unexpectedly gone into complete kidney failure and a coma. The nurse asked me to return to the hospital as soon as possible.

I could not drive back to Durham. I was tired and paralyzed with fear. I called one of Walter's friends and asked him and his wife to take me to Durham. We all stayed at the hospital all night, waiting for word about Walter's condition.

The following day, we returned to Charlotte. Walter remained in a coma with a ventilator. I called my siblings to give them an update about Walter's condition.

Ronald Jr. said, "I hope you know that you ain't in la-la land no more. I need to bring my truck to Charlotte so you can pick out a few things you're gonna need, like bedroom and dining room furniture. I know you gave your stuff away."

I was surprised by Ronald Jr.'s suggestion and said, "You've got to be kidding. Why would I take his furniture out of his house?"

Ronald Jr. said, "Marilyn, listen really good to me. If he messes around and keeps his eyes closed for good, you'll be like a lost ball in a thicket of thorns. Shit. Death brings out the worst in people. They will change the locks on the doors before you can get your clothes packed up. People become ugly and vicious when somebody dies." He paused and then said, "You gonna be homeless in Charlotte."

I was surprised at Ronald Jr.'s suggestions.

Ronald Jr. raised his voice. "Shit, Marilyn, if he lives, we can bring his stuff back. It's time to look out for yourself."

Early the next day, a nurse at Duke Hospital called and said, "I'm afraid Mr. Dumas's vital signs are weakening. He will not last the day."

I let out a wail. "Please tell Walter I'm on my way."

Without anyone around to see or hear me, I cried like I wanted to—loudly—and then I called Mildred and asked her to accompany me to the hospital. I could not face Walter's death alone.

I drove ninety miles per hour up I-85 North toward Greensboro, listening to Mahalia Jackson's "Precious Lord." Then, just inside the Salisbury city limits, I heard sirens over the music and saw blue lights in the side-view mirror. I pulled over and looked for my driver's license and car registration.

A broad-shouldered highway patrolman walked up. I already had the window rolled down, letting in the frigid air.

"Good morning, madam," he said politely. "This is a fifty-five-mile-per-hour zone. Do you know how fast you were driving?"

Without answering the officer, I started to cry. The officer looked concerned about my tears. Then he took a step backward.

"I need to see your driver's license and registration."

I handed them over.

He asked, "Why are you in such a hurry, and why are you crying?"

"I need to get to Duke Hospital before my fiancé dies. The hospital called an hour ago and said that he will not be here much longer. He's dying of cancer, and you've got me sitting here on the side of the road." My voice sounded angry, but I was just upset.

The officer handed back my driver's license and registration. He glanced around the car and saw a plastic urinal lying in the front passenger seat, along with several books on cancer that I had not returned to the library.

The officer said, "Miss, I'm not going to give you a ticket, and I'll let you be on your way, but you must slow down and drive the speed limit. I'm sorry about your fiancé."

A Head of Cabbage

A little more than an hour later, I picked up Mildred at her home in Greensboro, and we headed to Duke Hospital.

When we reached the hospital, I rushed to Walter's room and took his hand. I held it to my chest and controlled my voice enough to be able to speak. I wanted to give him my blessing to leave me and enjoy his new beginning. Mildred placed her arm around me, and Garnett, Walter's half brother, who was already in the room, wrapped his arms around both of us. I lowered my face closer to Walter.

"I think you're ready to walk with God. You are going to do more traveling, and you will see your mother. You will see some of the most beautiful sights imaginable. And you will never have any more pain or problems. You will enter God's kingdom happy. You have nothing to be afraid of, because you are one of the best people on earth, and God knows that. I am stronger and a better person because of you. It is OK for you to leave me."

My knees almost buckled, but Walter's brother held me up. I didn't want to see Walter die, but I couldn't bear to leave his room or let go of his hand. I wanted to give him all the comfort I could as my last act of love.

Holding his swollen hand to my cheek, I asked, "Walter, do you want to go now?"

Walter nodded, and after a few seconds, I saw a fluttering in his chest, and his lips quivered just a little, as if trying to smile. Then the machine flatlined. Standing on the opposite side of his bed, the nurse called the doctor, who came and pronounced him dead.

The drive back to Greensboro was slow, painful, and quiet. After I pulled into Mildred's driveway, she turned to me.

"What are you going to do? Are you moving back to Greensboro?" She opened the car door and grabbed our purses.

I wiped my eyes. "I don't know what to do." I had called my real estate agent earlier in the day and explained my circumstances. She'd told me I could take my house off the market, but I would have to pay a commission because she had found a buyer who was ready to close. We had done a verbal power of attorney over the phone, so she could close without my presence.

Mama cried when I told her about Walter's death and then started to wail when she learned that my house in Greensboro had sold and that I wasn't moving back.

Mama prayed, "Lord, my child done been through enough, and I don't know how to help her. She needs some spiritual help." Mama grabbed her Bible and searched the scriptures for words of comfort. It was unnerving for me to see Mama so distraught.

Mama pranced up and down Mildred's hallway for several minutes before she took a seat in front of me. "I done prayed and prayed for you to have a husband, Marilyn. Just when I thought you had a good man, he up and dies. What is you gonna do?"

I knew Mama felt all women should be married, and she had wanted me to marry Walter. I felt as if I had let her down somehow. Finally, I said, "Mama, I will be OK. I will do what I must do. Take care of myself." But I had no idea what to do. I didn't know how to feel or what to think. I was emotionally paralyzed. *Should I try to transfer back to my old job? Buy another house in Greensboro?*

I went to lie down in Mildred's guest room, but before I could go to sleep, I felt an overpowering urge to return to Walter's house in Charlotte. Against Mildred's and Mama's pleading, I left Greensboro a few minutes before ten thirty that night for the ninety-mile drive to Charlotte.

The house was dark when I arrived a little before midnight. I unlocked the front door and then found my way upstairs and showered. As I pulled the covers up around my neck, the bathroom lights I had left on as a night-light became bright and began to flicker. I cussed to myself because I didn't know where the spare bulbs were. I started to cry, when suddenly, a calmness came over me. I had a nonvisible visitor, and I heard Walter's telepathic voice.

Marilyn, I'm OK. I'm happy now, and I want you to stop crying and be happy again.

I didn't feel frightened or weird in any way. I knew it was Walter's essence.

I said, "Walter, I know it's you. I will be all right, and thank you for coming to let me know that you are all right." Although I felt the presence of other beings or spirits with him, no one spoke to me but Walter. The bathroom light lost its brilliance a few seconds later and returned to normal. I sensed Walter's essence descending away from me. I lay there for a few minutes, feeling an indescribable sense of peace.

Walter was buried in High Point, North Carolina, four days later. It was the saddest day of my life.

CHAPTER 76

FORGIVENESS

My life had changed, and my dreams had wilted in just three short, cold months. Sherondalyn insisted on leaving school for a semester to come stay with me. She called a few days after Walter's funeral and said, "Mama, Paris and I have been talking, and we decided that one of us has to come home for a few months. I'm the oldest, so I'm coming home to be with you during this time."

I started to argue. "No, do not take a semester off."

Sherondalyn said, "Mama, the decision has already been made. I'm calling to give you my flight information."

That made me anxious, but it forced me to find an apartment within a week of Walter's death. I wished I had taken my brother's advice.

Sherondalyn returned to college in the fall. Steven and I reconnected as he was getting a divorce. I felt that time had stood still, and I resolved to make my second chance with him a lasting one. But my vision of a happy future with Steven was soon squashed. It happened so fast and unexpectedly that I almost lost my mind.

About three months after we reestablished our relationship, I called Steven late one Friday evening, and a female answered the phone. I heard her gasp and say, "You need to handle this."

Steven took the phone to explain the situation to me. "Look," he said, "I'm sorry, but I've met someone I really care about."

I blurted out, "Yes, you are sorry but not as sorry as you're gonna be when I blow your motherfucking head off!"

Steven said, "I really didn't mean to hurt you again. Marilyn, it just happened. Besides, you need someone better than me."

"I'm coming to see you. You won't be breaking anyone else's heart. I promise you that. See you soon." I hung up the phone.

I got the automatic pistol from the closet and set it on the nightstand. I began to plot Steven's murder. The next day, I called my girlfriend Jannie, my alibi. She refused to go along with me and insisted I call BellSouth's employee assistance program for help, or she would call my brother Ronald Jr. to intervene.

Not wanting my brother to be in my business or have any idea what I was planning, I contacted the administrator for the assistance program. That was how I started to see Dr. Alex, the psychiatrist.

By spring 1995, I completed my therapy sessions, but I would sometimes sit in the dark of my bedroom and think about my life. I'd learned from my psychiatrist that I needed to talk about things that bothered me, learn from my experiences, and decide what I wanted my future to look like. I had to think better thoughts and not dwell on the past. The main thing I'd learned was to forgive myself and others so I would not become mean, irrational, and bitter. I realized that everyone made mistakes—people hurt and damaged others, sometimes without intent. I had done it, and it had been done to me.

During the Fourth of July celebration at my sister Inez's home in Milton, North Carolina, someone spied David, my ex-husband, walking toward the large covered porch where family and friends were gathered. Everyone was in a festive mood, eating, talking, and playing cards. David politely asked if he could sit at the same table where I was. Everyone was surprised to see David at the gathering. They stopped talking and eating. All eyes were on me as David looked around from person to person.

I sat there examining my feelings. I thought of my therapy sessions with Dr. Alex and everything we had talked about. It was as if an old black-and-white film were rolling out my life experiences in front of me.

I remembered the first time I had been molested by my brother-in-law Slim when I was five years old. Then memories of Mr. William Lea and his son Frank popped into my head—each had molested me when I was a preteen.

Then visions of schoolmates calling me Frankenstein's bride made me shudder in sadness, although they hadn't known any better. I could almost hear Mrs. Mattie's shrill voice telling me I was the ugly one of the Abbott children. Daddy's face came into sight and stuck in front of me. I heard his voice, loud and cruel, tell me that I was not worth the salt I ate and that somebody had to be dumb and ugly. I closed my eyes for a second or two. I had to brace myself for the next scene that appeared.

A Head of Cabbage

Pure horror returned as I saw Daddy standing in front of me, telling me he would blow my head off if I tried to go to school to take final exams, because education wasn't shit for black people. I wanted to reach out and slap the image to make it disappear faster, but it remained. Daddy's face grew sad, and as his image faded, I heard his voice saying that he was sorry for the way he had raised us. Finally, I watched myself walk up to receive my high school diploma without any family member present, and no one there clapped for me. Still, in the shadows of my memories, I saw my old African friend Meimei smiling and giving me a *V* sign for victory.

The film kept rolling until an image of David and me getting married appeared. I was happy for what seemed like the blink of an eye. Then I saw him being pulled away from me, into the arms of his gay lover. I felt humiliation and fear and wanted to strike the image, but I couldn't. Then, a split second later, a picture of Sherondalyn as a little girl, screaming for her father, came into focus. She was comforted only by holding on to one of his shoes. Perspiration began to run down my back as I saw another image of Sherondalyn. She was carrying a head of cabbage, asking if that was all we had to eat. I felt proud for a moment, knowing I had never gone on welfare or accepted any food stamps.

My heart fluttered, and I lowered my head. The film continued to roll, flashing pictures of me driving my old three-toned car while looking for a job in eight-degree weather. One painful image stuck in my mind for a second or two, showing me taking a typing test at Gilbarco while the white manager sat on the desk, rattling his newspaper, until the typing test was over. Then a pain jabbed me in the chest as I saw the images of several white people, some bosses and some not bosses, stop in front of me as if they were still images on a slide. I didn't want to look at all those white faces that had caused me so much angst over the years, but the pictures would not fade until I looked at each one. Some had tried to find ways to not hire, sabotage, or fire me.

It seemed as if minutes passed before an image of Steven came into focus. His words flooded my ears, telling me he did not want to marry a woman with two small children. Then, slowly, I lifted my head as the film slowed down, and Walter appeared with a broad smile. My heart raced with joy as I remembered how I'd felt when I was with him. Then, just a few seconds later, he closed his eyes and faded out of sight. It was the last image I saw before a flock of birds flew over, and I looked up at the clear blue sky and understood.

I needed to confront my past and forgive those who had harmed me, so I could rise above it all and be free to live my best life. I told the little girl inside me that she no longer needed to weep over the past; we would be OK as we forged forward into the future.

Eventually, Paris touched my arm and said, "Mama, I invited Daddy to attend."

I looked at Paris, who sat quietly among her family, wanting her father to be accepted and respected regardless of our divorce and his sexual orientation.

Ronald Jr. stared intently at me but did not make any cruel or contemptuous jokes, as he had done over the past twenty years.

Finally, I said, "David, you are welcome to sit here with us." I gave him a hug.

A broad smile crept over David's face as he sat down. "Thank you, Marilyn" was all he said, which was enough.

Then Ronald Jr. walked over to David and shook his hand. Afterward, Ronald Jr. looked around at everyone and said, "Forgiveness is hell of a thing."

ACKNOWLEDGMENTS

Many thanks to my daughters for their unconditional love and for allowing me to remember, cry, and write. Thanks to my siblings, cousins and friends for holding my hand and helping me during the unbearable times.

I am eternally grateful to the North Carolina Writer's Network, the many fellow writers at Charlotte Writers Club who kept me engaged in writing, and especially to Sally, Ruth, Alisha, Tandy, Marquerite, Clara, Jane, Vaughn, Edith, Connie, and Tom.

A priceless blessing to Gilda M. Syverson for her instruction, encouragement, and for sharing her talent with me.

I give my husband, George, all my love for his gentle patience and understanding.

Many thanks to everyone who have helped me to share my life story.

Lastly, Thanks to God who allowed me to visit and stay here for a while.

Printed in the United States
by Baker & Taylor Publisher Services